Writing from deeper within

Published on the twenty-fifth anniversary of my original life-story writing book, *Writing from Within*, this work, *Writing from Deeper Within*, started as advanced classes for writers who were already familiar with and using the original *Writing from Within* program. The techniques in it are for somewhat advanced writers: those who have taken a college course in creative writing and want to develop a more personal basis for their voice; those who have written life stories and want to try their hand at writing fiction; or perhaps the experienced journalist who has written many stories filled with description, dialogue, and narrative, and now wants to explore writing inner thoughts and feelings in novels, short stories, and screenplays.

For those not familiar with my *Writing from Within* program, the techniques and approaches I have developed and taught over the last twenty-five years are summarized in Appendix A of this book. However, the complete twenty-fifth anniversary edition called *Writing from Within: The Next Generation* contains both the foundation *Writing from Within* course, for writers who are just starting to record their life stories, and all the more-sophisticated techniques and approaches described and explored in this book.

A third component of the program, the *Writing from Within Workbook*, is also available now. It provides comprehensive lessons and step-by-step exercises on how to add narrative, inner thoughts and feelings, dialogue, character sketches, and climaxes to life-story writing.

Whether you are a sophisticated writer or a novice, the techniques, approaches, and advice in these books will, hopefully, launch you into the world of the creative writer—a world in which you get to play God and create something out of nothing. Nothing, that is, *but your fertile imagination....*

To Jeff, Will, and Gail
The kindest and most loving children
and former wife possible

Also by Bernard Selling

Henry, Boy of Barrio (film)
First Year, A.D. (film)
Three Miraculous Soldiers (film)
The Flying Machine (film)
Writing from Within
Writing from Within Workbook
The Art of Seeing
Character Consciousness
The Duke's Musician (novel)
Predators (novel)
The da Vinci Intrusion (novel)

Writing from deeper within

Advanced Steps in Writing Fiction and Life Stories

Bernard Selling

Hunter House PUBLISHERS

Hunter House Inc., Publishers

An imprint of Turner Publishing Company

Nashville, Tennessee

www.turnerpublishing.com

Library of Congress Cataloging-in-Publication Data
Selling, Bernard.
Writing from deeper within : advanced steps in writing fiction and life stories /
Bernard Selling. — 1st ed.
p. cm.
Includes index.
ISBN 978-0-89793-647-7 (pb)
ISBN 978-0-89793-629-3 (ebook)
1. Autobiography — Authorship — Handbooks, manuals, etc. 2. Creative writing — Handbooks, manuals, etc. 3. Authorship — Handbooks, manuals, etc.

4. Self-consciousness (Awareness) I. Title.
CT25.S449 2012
920 — dc23   2012019230

Project Credits

Cover Design: Brian Dittmar Design, Inc.	Acquisitions Assistant: Elana Fiske
Book Production: John McKercher	Special Sales Manager: Judy Hardin
Developmental Editors: Jude Berman	Rights Coordinator: Candace Groskreutz
and Jack Duffy	Customer Service Manager: Christina Sverdrup
Copy Editor: Heather Wilcox	Order Fulfillment: Washul Lakdhon
Proofreader: Lori Cavanaugh	Administrator: Theresa Nelson
Managing Editor: Alexandra Mummery	Computer Support: Peter Eichelberger
Publisher: Kiran S. Rana	

Manufactured in the United States of America

9 8 7 6 5 4 3 2   12 13 14 15 16

Contents

Acknowledgments ix

Introduction 1
The Evolving Story: Creating a Work of Art 1
Exploring Inner Thoughts and Feelings in Your Writing 2
Your Writing Process 4
The Path 4
The Plan — Your Personal Mantra for Writing 5
Emotional Obstacles 6
Self-Examination 7

Unit I: Advanced Perspectives in Writing Creatively 9

1. Using Short Sentences, the "Objective Correlative,"
   and the "Hitchcockian Recap" 11
   Using Short Sentences 13
   The "Objective Correlative" 14
   The "Hitchcockian Recap" 15

2. Developing Character Qualities, Backstory, and Denouement . . 17
   Are Character Qualities Evident in the Story? 17
   Creating Backstory to Inform 18
   The Denouement 20

3. Creating Visual Motifs, Minor Characters, and Form 22
   Creating Visual Motifs 22
   Creating Three-Dimensional Minor Characters 24
   Creating a Sense of Form 24

4. Employing the Principles of Art, Subtext,
   and the "Story Within a Story" 26
   Employing the Principles of Art 26
   Developing the Subtext of a Story 27
   Creating a "Story Within a Story" 30

5. Amplifying the Basic Steps in *Writing From Within*:
   Narrative, Dialogue, and Inner Thoughts and Feelings 32
   Narrative 33
   Dialogue 36
   Inner Thoughts and Feelings 40

6. Separating the Writer's Voice from the Central Character's Voice . . 43
   Distinguishing Between the Narrator's Voice and
   the Central Character's Voice 43

Unit II: Chipping Down to Character Through Rewriting . . . 46
   Developing Confidence in Your Rewrites 47

7. Revealing Character: Rewriting Inner Thoughts and Feelings . . . 48
   Self-Assessments: Gaining Access to Self-Knowledge
   and the Inner Life 52

8. Unraveling Character: Rewriting Action and Details 53

Unit III: Leaping into Longer Work 57

9. Turning Life Stories into Novels 59

10. Writing Creative Stories 67

11. Creating Screenplays from Short Stories 73
    Adapting Ernest Hemingway to the Screen 74
    Adapting "The Short Happy Life of Francis Macomber" to the Screen . 77
    Hollywood's Bizarre Recreation of the Hemingway Story 82

12. Front Page to Hard Cover: Bill Rempel's Story
    of *At the Devil's Table* 86

13. Writing Family History 99
    Researching the Past 102

Unit IV: Other Benefits of Life-Story Writing 105

14. How *Writing from Within* Can Help People 106

15. *Writing from Within* and the Human Potential Movement 110
    Conclusion: Bernard's Message 115

Unit V: Stories 117
    Liz Kelly — Tank Top 117
    Sam Glenn — The Board 121
    Sam Glenn — The Circus 122
    Sam Glenn — Epiphany 124
    Sam Glenn — The Ring 125
    Karl Grey — The Garage 129
    Dale Crum — Smoke Rings 132
    Dale Crum — My Sister's Shadow 135
    Paula Moore Diggs — The Turkish Ambassador 138

Paula Diggs — New Shooter: Chapter One: "Just Listen to Me" . . . 140

Marilyn Wirth — The Story of Little Rickey 143

Gail Field — Information I Don't Want to Know 147

Gail Field — A Normal Life? 149

Gail Field — Appearances 152

Gail Field — Goodbye to All That (Summer 1975) 154

Bernard Selling — The Jewish Wife 157

Appendixes 164

Appendix A: Writing Vivid Life Stories:
The Basic Steps of *Writing from Within* 166

Appendix B: Creating a Supportive, Noncritical,
yet Insightful Writing Group 189

Other Books by Bernard Selling 194

Acknowledgments

Writing from Within has been alive and well, and thriving, for more than twenty-five years, its existence due mainly to two men—Joseph Campbell, mythologist and editor of the texts of C.G. Jung, psychologist and philosopher; and Kiran Rana, publisher (Hunter House Publishers) of *Writing from Within* (1988, 1990, 1998).

A personal and professional crisis in the late 1970s led me into a period of self-examination, during which I began attending consciousness-raising workshops. A friend suggested "The Hero's Journey," a workshop by Paul Rebillot in San Francisco, based on Joseph Campbell's work, especially *The Hero with a Thousand Faces*. I began reading Campbell's many works, including his massive *The Masks of God*. I suspected my path to be like that of the hero; I had undergone a spiritual death and was ready to reemerge in a new skin. Soon, I attended Campbell's workshops at the Jung Institute in San Francisco and elsewhere and got to know him personally. We had many things in common, not the least of which was an interest in C.G. Jung and James Joyce…and in playing the baritone sax.

Within a year, an accidental meeting with the principal of an adult school in Los Angeles brought me to a class of older adults whose students wanted to learn about writing life stories. Although I knew next to nothing about teaching creative writing, I soon realized that, in fact, I knew a lot, not because I had a graduate degree in English literature but because of the work I had done with actors as a young director.

I also found that as I saw certain threads of excellence in their stories, threads that I would later turn into *Writing from Within*, I also began to overcome my own difficulties in writing creatively (which had led me to make documentary films for many years instead of writing).

In 1984 Kiran Rana attended a party where he chatted with a student of mine. Her glowing reviews of our life-story-writing class prompted him to get in touch with me. At the time, I had created a thirty-page pamphlet that I sent to him. A year later, a book emerged, a prepublication edition of *Writing from Within*. "We may not sell a lot of copies initially, Bernard," Kiran said in his soft voice, "as we are a small press, and it is not easy for us to get face time on book shelves, competing, as we do, with larger presses." I blanched. But he continued, "However, the book will still be alive twenty-five years from now." Indeed, he was right. Despite having sold no more than ten thousand copies between 1988 and 1998, Kiran authorized a third edition at that time, a much more complete and expanded look at *Writing from Within* and the concerns of life-story writers. His direct sales of this edition, coupled with those of Barnes & Noble, made it a semi-bestseller.

I also would like to express my appreciation to Bill Rempel for contributing the chapter "From Front Page to Hard Cover." I had read his series of articles on Jorge Salcedo in the *L.A. Times* while teaching at a local community college and had let him know how valuable I thought the articles were. Rempel, in turn, volunteered to talk to my students, and I accepted. By the time he came to speak, the class had read every article he had ever written. He was stunned at how well prepared the students were and at the quality of the questions they posed. A high-quality discussion ensued, and we became friends.

I also wish to acknowledge the contributions of the following writers: Liz Kelly, Sam Glenn, Karl Grey, Roy Wilhelm, Dale Crum, Paula Diggs, Mimi Wirth, Gail Field, and Dirk Tousley.

— Bernard Selling
Topanga, CA
February 2012

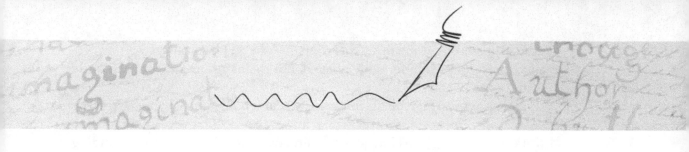

Introduction

Since 1998—the point where I last wrote about the Writing from Within process (*Writing from Within*, 3rd edition (1998)—my writing workshops have taken an interesting turn. As my students have acquired rather quickly the skills suggested in the ten-point checklist of *Writing from Within*, I have had to provide them with more and more sophisticated insights into the art of writing. Since many students are now writing novels, short stories, screenplays, children's stories, as well as life stories, the instruction I have provided them had to apply to these different forms of writing.

As a consequence, the thrust of my work over the past fifteen years has been to delve more deeply into the "art of writing." Much of this involves observing and employing specific techniques such as "Hitchcockian recaps," visual motifs, backstory, denouements, and the like. However, beyond pure technique lay more sophisticated perspectives: understanding and employing the principles of art, creating subtext, developing interesting minor characters, and, most of all, separating the writer's voice from that of the central character.

Having written about these disparate elements of creative writing, I asked myself, "Is there anything that binds all of these techniques and perspectives together—a unifying principle behind this abundance of approaches to writing?" I thought long and hard about this.

Eventually two answers came to mind: First, my concern with helping writers move from writing a "good" story to possibility creating a "great" story—that is, creating a work of art. Second, my concern with undertaking the difficult task of exploring our inner thoughts and feelings in our writing.

The Evolving Story: Creating a Work of Art

Ours is a world energized with a desire to put thoughts and experiences, as well as the fruits of our imaginations, in print. Much of this writing may be interesting, even compelling. Characters may be vivid, narratives well crafted, and literary devices thoroughly planted. But their authors are not necessarily crafting works of art.

What mystical ingredients infuse a work and mold it into a work of art? The answer may not be entirely definable; however, one thing we can say is that a work of art does take us into another dimension in which our understanding of the world becomes richer and our appreciation, even awe, of the power of a human hand to craft such a work, grows. The works of Leonardo, Peter Bruegel, Picasso, Mozart, Ibsen, Strindberg, and Fellini all take us into another universe, one that enriches our understanding of the world in which we function.

Fine writing often provides the reader with interesting, quirky, well-drawn characters around which the reader will find a circle containing a spicy array of obstacles, minor characters, and well-crafted backstories suffused in a taut narrative.

Rising to the level of art are those works that contain a larger concentric circle—of concerns, characters, and obstacles that cause the major characters to do more than solve problems. They must reevaluate the world in which they live while at the same time coming to understand their inner lives, asking and answering fundamental human questions: What is real? What is illusion? What is the nature of man? Is he at heart good…or evil? How do we go about stripping away outer layers of who were/are (and who we appear to be) to get to the deeper layers of who we are?

Since 1998 I have seen certain students explore myriad techniques and perspectives that enable their work to move from "a good story" with interesting characterizations to a higher level that causes us to contemplate our human condition with unending fascination.

Exploring Inner Thoughts
and Feelings in Your Writing

Uncovering inner thoughts and feelings has been a lifelong pursuit of mine—in my personal as well as my creative life. Following my father's early death (when I was barely sixteen), my mother's long bout with manic depression (especially when I was about twelve), and her early death (when I was twenty-two), I found a mass of confused, bewildered, sometimes angry inner thoughts, feelings, perceptions, and ideas exploding inside me.

A friend of mine in college—an art student—often talked at length about her inner thoughts and feelings, especially her fears. Listening to her, I realized that people actually did talk about such concerns, although I was far from sure that I would be able to do so. In fact, I was quite certain that no one would want to hear me babble on about this inner world of mine.

At the same time, I had begun seeking answers to the questions: "Who am I? Where am I going? Where have I come from? Is there a God? If so, what does he/she/it look like? What is love? Is a good relationship possible? Why would a loving God take from me the person I needed most in my life, my father? Why would a loving God create so much misery for a good person, my mother?"

I sought answers in novels, plays, short stories, paintings, films, and music and the answer I got was that the universe holds a multitude of answers, all beneficial to know, if one searches long enough and hard enough.

When I entered the arena of filmmaking—screen—and playwriting and directing, as well as teaching people to articulate their life experiences as stories—I began to see that people's points of view about their experiences were often fascinating to me and my students This was especially true as we delved into our inner thoughts and feelings.

As a teacher and writer, I found that allowing the outer world in which we lived to unfold—the texture of the world around us, including the relationships we enter into—was a rich and challenging experience. But the real challenge lay in getting a hold of the deepest inner thoughts and feelings that all us humans have—but often don't know we have. These issues underlie all the books I have written, the screenplays I have created, and the films I have made.

While writing this book I repeatedly asked myself, "What is this book really about?" I began to see that a part of the techniques and perspectives outlined in the book had one purpose: to make as clear as possible how to express the fabric of our inner lives, the world of our inner thoughts and feelings, in the outer world of pen, paper, and computer. This meant both uncovering our inner thoughts and feelings as well as seeing the almost infinite number of perspectives that we humans have (and can share) about the nature of the world in which we live—especially the nature of the relationships that exist in our worlds.

Throughout my many years of teaching people to write their life stories, this has become my primary goal—to help others give voice to the most fleeting of their inner thoughts and feelings, to help them put into words the things that they barely realize that they know.

This is what you, the reader, can look forward to in this book: how to get the individual inner thoughts and feelings of your characters down on paper, while at the same time finding and creating characters who give voice to your own, personal, inner thoughts and feelings. You will acquire tools that allow you to express your sense of the world in which you and your characters live—good characters intent on surviving in an evil world or a world they never made;

plodding characters, oblivious to their potential for a better, more-examined, more-meaningful life—to name just a couple of scenarios.

Your Writing Process

A great many people who *want* to write have deep concerns about whether they actually *can* write. They wonder, "Will I be able to find an audience, get an agent, solicit a publisher, overcome writing blocks, and perhaps make a living at writing—all in the same lifetime?"

The answer: Who knows? But one thing is certain: Anyone intending to write seriously has to find a way of doing things that feels right and yields results. Everyone wonders whether they have talent. But the larger question is: Do you have what it takes to assume that you have talent and just go do the work? If you can get over that hurdle of doubt (which will return each time you experience a setback), then the next question is: Do you have the discipline and confidence to find your way through the maze of obstacles to create a body of work? Discipline and confidence are important, as is the belief that you have talent.

Five other clear and distinct concerns become visible in the labyrinth that is writing, each worth attending to:

1. Do you believe that a path exists that will get you through the maze of obstacles to completing a work?

2. Do you have a consistent, reliable plan for creating whatever you need to create?

3. Have you foreseen and dealt with the emotional obstacles to completing your work?

4. Are you willing to do the ruthless self-examination that writers must go through to complete their work?

5. Have you truly understood the messages that lie beneath the writing instruction that I will be outlining in subsequent chapters?

The Path

A certain, small percentage of people know their talents at a very young age. The majority knows what it would like to do but seldom knows that the talent for doing so exists within. Discovering what your best qualities are, as outlined in Chapter 2, is a big part of gaining belief in your talents and abilities to write. Writing well in school almost doesn't count, because academic writing is logical and analytical, and rarely creative. If you have an engaging way of presenting this information, that's fine, but it has little to do with becoming a writer.

The writer inside of a person sees the world in a fresh and perhaps different way. This side of a person finds itself fascinated by human relationships, not as described in texts by Sigmund Freud and Alfred Adler, but in the way relationships unfold, as they do in the works of Henrik Ibsen, August Strindberg, Billy Wilder, and Jean Giraudoux. Psychologists want to know *why* things happen concerning human nature. Writers want to know *how* things happen—how people act in certain circumstances.

To make the leap from being an observer of the human condition to becoming a writer about that condition, you must believe a path exists for you to follow, one that will yield a finished work. If you don't have that belief, then you must assume that you will find that path as you go along. And you will. But this path is your path, no one else's.

In his book *The Hero with a Thousand Faces*, Joseph Campbell describes the path of the transcendent hero, be he a person who crossed the face of this earth at some point in time or a philosopher's invention, a writer's creation, or a theologian's supposition. That path looks remarkably similar for all heroes: A naïve young person starts out on a quest, receives a talisman or charm, fails badly in some way, struggles to right themself, fails again, and falls into a pit of despair, loneliness, and confused direction. This pit becomes a spiritual death from which the hero emerges transformed and better armed to meet the challenges ahead. Usually this transformation includes a softening of the self and the ego that drives a young person and accompanies a new way of seeing things—often an ability to see into the hearts of those around him.

Campbell's path of the hero looks very much like that of many artists, musicians, and writers. To bring something into being, one must make mistakes and take false steps. In a labyrinth, a turn unexplored is a turn where light may exist just around an unseen corner. Exploring all ones options takes time.

The Plan—Your Personal Mantra for Writing

The *plan* unfolds as a natural byproduct of, belief in, and willingness to follow the path. The plan is usually simple. The first part is adopting *a workable code or mantra to live by*. Your plan may be, "I will not take at face value anything that I am told." Such a code enabled George Orwell to endure bureaucratic oppression and poverty and see through Fascist, Communist, and Colonialist propaganda. Another code may be, "I will do more than my father." This code drives many people forward. My own code seems quite simple: "Play when others work; work when others play." Your mantra, in whatever form it takes, provides you with ample time and space to work on your craft while making as many mistakes as necessary.

The second part of the plan is *understanding your audience* fully, knowing what it needs and expects and trusting its responses without trusting its reasoning. This means that early in your creative life as a writer, you will need to be willing to make your work visible to the outside world. You do not have to do what your audience tells you to do. It only means that you understand what it needs and expects. It remains your choice whether or not to give it the expected.

It also means you will seek out mentors who can see where your work wants to go, as well as enlist the energies of others who want you to succeed in your artistic endeavors. One of the more effective creative people I have met in my lifetime, jazz great Buddy Colette, used to say, "We are all trying to get to the same place; let's go there together."

The third part of the plan is *articulating your beliefs about the fundamental nature of man and the universe* in your writing. Is man, at heart, good? If so, how do you explain the mistakes he makes, the dilemmas he creates for himself and others? Or is he, at bottom, bad? If this is the case, he must be trained and forced to conform to a moral order. But what happens if he rebels? Is there no hope for him? One aspect of your plan must be to investigate this question as you see it playing out in all the arenas of your experience. The characters you create (and observe) must all have their own take on this issue (and the universe that surrounds them), for this attitude will ultimately drive their quests, their goals, their obsessions, and how they decide to proceed.

Emotional Obstacles

Many obstacles stand in the way of anyone who wants to write (or create) in a serious way. Some are practical concerns—paying the rent, having significant relationships, fulfilling obligations. Often, however, you face less tangible concerns that you hardly know exist—a backstory to your life that may include loss, abuse, neglect, and the like. These concerns may take a toll on your commitment to the craft and art of writing unless you pay attention. Like soldiers going into battle, you must train yourself for the battle ahead, while knowing your strengths and weaknesses and fine-tuning your mechanism for understanding the world around you.

Because obstacles do exist, you can best help yourself by learning early on what character qualities you have and what kinds of talents lie within you. If you function with a clear head, these obstacles, character qualities, and talents may even become a part of what you write about, in one way or the other. Having been a musician all my life, it came as no surprise to me that, in beginning my first novel, I focused on the life of a young musician. My father, a doctor, became this character's father—a fifteenth-century physician.

Often you have to clear away or surmount emotional obstacles before you can write in an energetic way. When my film career stumbled, I spent years getting clear about what I wanted and what was stopping me. Finally, the path became clearer—I had defined myself in a narrow way that had held me back. Once I defined myself not merely as a filmmaker but as a creative person, many opportunities opened up, including my path to writing creatively.

Another obstacle facing many people is the question, "How do I incorporate others into my 'writer's life,' a life that can be quite lonely?" One answer is that at every turn of the road, you will need people to help you, and you will meet people you can help. A writer—in fact people in all walks of life—needs a strong support system which includes family (wife, ex-wife, parents, brothers, sisters, and children) and friends. Creative people function poorly if they try to function in complete isolation. You also need to find people who are doing what you do (write) and find groups in which to exchange feedback about your work. Putting effort into finding people who give quality feedback (insightful but not hurtful) to your work is something you continuously need to do, and you will find it worth all the energy you put into it.

Self-Examination

Many creative people find the work of C. G. Jung, Joseph Campbell, and Abraham Maslow helpful in their various personal quests for identity and support. Why? Unlike Freud and those who followed him, Jung investigated the human condition without a preconceived agenda. That is, he made no assumption about whether man's fundamental nature was evil or good. He saw people as acting and reacting to the world around them in the same way that his contemporaries Ibsen, Strindberg, and Anton Chekhov saw people—as fascinating creatures intent on surviving. Campbell, the editor of much of Jung's work and the author of *The Hero with a Thousand Faces*, saw mankind operating in the same way, although his fascination lay in uncovering common threads in the footprints of stellar individuals through civilizations in a most uncommon way. Maslow saw nothing but enormous possibilities in human beings and believed that everyone needs to do what they can to live up to their potential.

As a creative person, the time you spend pondering the lives and the arcs (the beginning, middle, and ends of their concerns about the human condition) of such individuals gives you strength and determination to see what others do not see, to uncover what others prefer to ignore, and to make visible what others find invisible.

——— • • • ———

This book is divided into six parts, or Units. In Unit I, "Advanced Perspectives in Writing Creatively," we will explore how to reveal character and character qualities through 1) sharing a character's innermost thoughts and feelings and 2) actions and details. Unit II, "Chipping Down to Character Through Rewriting," gives the reader an opportunity to see how these techniques can move a story from sketch (short story or life story) to a full-length novel, screenplay, or play. Units III and IV, "Leaping into Longer Work" and "Other Benefits of Life-Story Writing," give the reader a picture of other uses of the techniques of life-story writing and provide a richer experience of self-examination through writing. In Unit V, the reader will find a number of stories by skilled writers who use these techniques in ways that we might term "works of art."

The reader is also encouraged to observe the ways in which another group of creative people—filmmakers—answers such questions, a discussion that takes place in another of my books, *The Art of Seeing: Motion Pictures as an Art Form and as a Business.*

Advanced Perspectives in Writing Creatively

The advanced perspectives in *Writing from Deeper Within* build on the basic steps in *Writing from Within* and it helps to know those well. Before you start in on the advanced techniques taught in this book, be sure of the following:

- You are familiar with, and quite comfortable in using, the original steps described in *Writing from Within*. If you are a beginning writer and are not familiar with these steps, please take the time to peruse these steps, which are described in Appendix A at the back of the book.

- You are familiar with the feedback process outlined in *Writing from Within* and in Appendix B to this book.

- You understand and embrace the concept of rewriting as many times as you feel are necessary before coming up with a final version.

Note: If you have already had experience as a writer and are looking for additional ways of enhancing your writing, these advanced perspectives may be helpful to you without first absorbing the basic steps of *Writing from Within*.

A good way for you to start building the creative knowledge needed to grasp the material provided in this first section is by learning to recognize how others use these techniques. At a certain point in each chapter, I give you a picture of how I see these methods being used in the stories at the end of the book. I strongly suggest that you go to the end of the book, read these stories, and then look for the uses of the techniques in each story before I talk about them in depth. By reading the stories and noting the use of these techniques in the stories in advance, you will be able to compare your perception of the advanced techniques in the stories to mine. Keep in mind, though, that it isn't necessary that you agree with my perception. It is only necessary that you do the work on your own and have a perception of how and where the techniques are being employed in each story.

By reading the stories over and over, you will come to understand the advanced techniques and perspectives in order to make them your own, like a jazz musician who plays a tune again and again, making changes until the melodic line becomes his own original expression.

For you advanced writers, the following questions will lead you through each technique outlined in the remainder of this book.

Have I, the writer…

1. used short sentences where possible?
2. made the character's "character qualities" evident in the story?
3. used *backstory* appropriately?
4. created *visual motifs* that have a larger meaning for the story?
5. created interesting, three-dimensional minor characters?
6. used the principles of art in creating form?
7. employed a believable denouement to the story?
8. created subtext to amplify the text?
9. used "objective correlatives" in my story?
10. made a distinction between the narrator's voice and the central character's voice?

For the purposes of making these points clear, I refer primarily to the story "Smoke Rings" written by one of my students, Dale Crum, and to "The Garage," by Karl Grey. I urge you to read these stories in their entirety before proceeding (see the "Stories" section starting on page 117).

Note: From time to time I refer to writing techniques that appear later in the book. When I make such references, my intention is not to digress but to give you, the reader, a sense that many of the techniques discussed in this book are deeply intertwined. Likewise, I often mention films and musical and theatrical pieces. On first glance these discussions or mentions may seem to be digressions, but they are not. No matter the medium of expression, the production of creative work is always somewhat similar. As a lifelong musician, photographer, play and film director, screenwriter, and novelist, I have come to see the remarkable similarities that exist so strongly in the many art forms that I have explored.

Using Short Sentences, the "Objective Correlative," and the "Hitchcockian Recap"

"Hi, I'm Dale Crum," grins an amiable, older gentleman as my new adult-school life-writing class gets together in Woodland Hills, California, for the first time. The year is 1998.

For some fifteen years, I had been teaching my life-story writing classes on the west side of Los Angeles, not far from my home in Venice, California. With my kids grown, however, I wanted to live in a cozier, more rural space, so I moved up to Topanga Canyon in the Santa Monica Mountains. Shortly afterward, I began teaching my writing classes in Woodland Hills and Calabasas, California.

From 1998 to 2012 Dale absorbed the original steps of *Writing from Within* without difficulty, integrating them into his stories with ease. The skill with which he did this prompted me to look into and teach more subtle and effective ways of telling a story. At every step along this path, Dale absorbed and integrated the new material with unusual clarity and depth of understanding.

Here is the beginning to Dale's story:

Smoke Rings
by Dale Crum

My cigarette smoke drifts toward Mama's open bathroom window. I smoke two packs of Camels a day and crave nicotine early. Sunshine splashes on the pink shower curtain. Multicolored gold fish fluoresce among its folds.

Reminds me of tame Calicos, orange Orandas, and Bubble Eyes in the Marshall Islands. They swam close to my navy face mask in the coral reefs only three years ago. Wish I were there, now. These rainy Seattle streets depress me.

11

I stand up and look in the mirror. Out-of-focus wallpaper surrounds bloodshot eyes and scruffy whiskers. Eeeyoo, my breath smells rotten. My tongue feels like sandpaper. I hate these cigarettes! Or, rather, I hate myself for liking them.

"Stunt your growth," my dad used to say.

But he said that about playing with myself, too.

Someone rattles the doorknob. Mama calls, "Dale, you in there?"

I yell, "Won't be long" and reach for the Listerine. Oh, didn't think she would get up before seven o'clock. Too cold to go outside and smoke. I pick up the towel stuffed in the crack at the bottom of the door, spray air freshener all around, and unlock the door.

Mama rushes in. She comes out with a sniff. "Thought you quit."

"Yeah, going to college."

"Not what I meant. You got a good job at Boeing."

"Just made up my mind. Talked to Elsie about it."

She frowns, "Oh, her? You like her?"

"She's a college sophomore in California. She'll show me around."

My B-50 flight control rigger's job only pays one dollar and ten cents an hour. That's union swing-shift wages, too. Boeing hired me a year ago for seventy-five cents an hour. Maybe Harry Truman here in the beginning of his first full term can kick-start the peacetime economy.

I sold my 1941 Buick sedan for eleven hundred dollars. Bought a cream puff '37 Chevy sedan for only four hundred. The G.I. bill will pay for my college tuition. With a part-time job, I can have fun in the sun and learn something, too.

This opening to Dale's story incorporates a number of techniques that we will now discuss.

• • •

Having mastered the basic steps of *Writing from Within*, you are able to write a very credible story. The present tense brings the story into sharp focus. Simplifying the language enables the writer to reach the reader's heart and gut. Incorporating feelings glues the story to the reader's heart. Dialogue brings relationships to life. Inner thoughts and feelings bring the reader even closer to the central character. Beginning the story with action or dialogue brings the reader into the story immediately.

Now I want to focus on several other things you can do to give the story even greater impact. For one thing, you can focus on writing short sentences, often dropping the subject and verb in the sentence to add a faster pace to the story without losing clarity. Then, as you begin rewriting, sharpen the characters' character qualities: Every action characters take in pursuit of what they want comes from a quality they have. Finally, in the second paragraph (more or less), you will learn to slow down the action and to give the reader a glimpse of what has gone on before the story opens—what battles, resentments, quirks of fate, and foolish actions have shaped the main character's life.

Using Short Sentences

Where possible, use short sentences, especially in the descriptive passages. This technique moves the story along as fast as possible, allowing the reader to see what is going on rather than being told what is happening.

Here is an example of the effective use of short sentences from Dale's narrative at the beginning of his story "Smoke Rings" (see page 132) The story begins with action, transporting us to another time and place, at least for the moment:

> My cigarette smoke drifts toward Mama's open bathroom window. I smoke two packs of Camels a day and crave nicotine early. Sunshine splashes on the pink shower curtain. Multicolored gold fish fluoresce among its folds.

The second paragraph continues to use short sentences:

> Reminds me of tame Calicos, orange Orandas, and Bubble Eyes in the Marshall Islands. They swam close to my navy face mask in the coral reefs only three years ago. Wish I were there, now. These rainy Seattle streets depress me.

This paragraph, which gives the reader a glimpse of what happened before the story opens, is called *backstory*. The short sentences enable the reader to get a quick, vivid picture of what is going on in the character's mind as well as what takes place around him.

Here is another example of the use of short sentences from the work of Sam Glenn, a musician friend of mine.

The Board

by Sam Glenn

I'm leaving for college tomorrow. Freshman year. Leaving home. Gotta go through my things.

"Sam, I think I'll set up my sewing machine in your room." Mom's voice sounds like she might start crying as she leaves my room and heads to the kitchen.

What to throw away? What to take with me? What to store?

Oh, there's my work board. Should I throw it away? I've had it since I was nine years old. Wow, what a lot of memories. Look at these cut marks — every direction — hundreds, maybe thousands from X-ACTO blades, razor blades, my Boy Scout knife. Crisscrossing the grain of the wood. And my name burned into the corner. Old English–style letters, SAM. Used my woodburning kit. There's a little bit of solder embedded over on this edge. That's from when I built my Heath kit stereo receiver. And all those clamp marks. From the C-clamps I borrowed from my dad's toolbox.

How many model planes did I put together on this board? Those really neat ones with wings made of thin balsa strips, covered with colored rice paper, then dampened, stretched, and glued so it was tight like a drumhead. Rubber-band powered. Sounds simple, but everything had to be just right. They didn't all fly well, but when one did it was heaven. My favorite was a British biplane from World War I. It was blue. Like the kind that fought against Manfred von Richthoven — the Red Baron.

• • •

The short sentences in this opening give a punch and immediacy to the writing. Sam uses incomplete sentences — "Freshman year. Leaving home." — to add more punch and immediacy to the writing. This approach to writing makes the narrator sound youthful and energetic, a no-nonsense person. In this way, the style of writing — short, immediate, sometimes incomplete sentences — conveys a sense of the character's qualities and moves the story forward at a rapid pace.

For more of Sam's work, please go to pages 121–129 in the "Stories" section of the book.

Two other techniques allow writers to add clarity to their stories: the objective correlative and the "Hitchcockian recap." Each one enables the writer to keep the audience on track with the story, avoiding questions that might break the sense of being on a wonderful voyage, which is what the writer hopes is taking place.

The "Objective Correlative"

The "objective correlative" is a rather technical-sounding term coined by T.S. Eliot in the early years of the twentieth century. Eliot was appalled at the excessive emotion that nineteenth-century Romantic writers created in their stories when, in fact, there was no objective reason for all the excitement. (This overabundance of emotion is readily visible in such works as the operas of Verdi and Wagner.) Eliot suggested that if emotion is to be present in a novel, play, opera, or short story, readers or viewers have to be able to see what caused the emotion and to judge for themselves whether the cause warranted the emotionality. He called the actions or circumstances behind the emotion the "objective correlative." It is no accident that the flamboyance of the nineteenth-century romantic novel and opera, as found in Stendhal's *The Red and the Black* and Verdi's *Aida*, gave way to understated but intense realism in drama and film, from Ibsen and Strindberg to Elia Kazan's *On the Waterfront*.

What is the relevance of the objective correlative to your interest in writing effective life stories? Writers sometimes make the mistake of asking the reader to believe there is a reason for a high state of emotion in a character during the concluding section of a story even when the reason for that high state of emotion has not been explained convincingly in the beginning of the story—that is, a *defining motif* (a recurring pattern) in the story is missing. (For a more complete discussion on motifs see Chapter 6.)

A good example of a well-placed motif—an objective correlative—appears in David Lean's classic film *Dr. Zhivago*. Midway through the film, Lara is about to leave Zhivago—for him, a searing departure. The music ("Lara's Theme") swells. Does the audience know why her departure means so much to him? Indeed it does. In the beginning of the film, a young Zhivago stands at the grave site of his mother as her coffin is lowered into the ground. Zhivago's sense of longing and loss are echoed in the music that swells upward ("Lara's Theme") as a panoply of flowers and snow drifts upward along with the spirit of Zhivago's mother. So when the audience witnesses Lara about to leave, sees the sunflower in the corner of the frame, and hears "Lara's Theme," it understands that Zhivago is experiencing profound loss—his mother, as well as Lara—in this scene. In this way, the objective correlative plays a huge part in the audience's experiencing Zhivago's feelings.

In Dale's story "Smoke Rings," he provides numerous examples (objective correlatives) for his suspicions that he shouldn't trust Elsie—she is too naïve. Her smoking is a tipoff that she is young, inexperienced, and hungry for experience. Later, when she throws out the ashes, she reveals herself as "gauche," like Dale at an earlier time. Then when she plows through the mud, the reader sees that she is messy. So, inexperienced, gauche, and messy—not a woman for Dale to trust. Of course, the pleasure of the story—the "aha," the epiphany—is that she reveals herself to be far more calculating and aware than Dale ever expected.

The "Hitchcockian Recap"

Alfred Hitchcock created any number of techniques in his films to keep the viewer glued to their seat. One of the most effective was his use of the "recap"—

that is, retelling what has happened in the film up to the moment when the recap begins. However, this recapping of the events is not mere exposition—in which themes, motifs, and concerns in a story are laid out—but a subtle reviewing of what has been happening mixed in with some distracting action.

In a famous and oft-quoted moment in Hitchcock's *Rear Window*, James Stewart, playing an invalid with a broken leg, has been watching what happens in an apartment building across the courtyard. He sees a salesman, played by Raymond Burr, argue with his bedridden wife, and a little while later the wife disappears. Stewart tells the stunning Grace Kelly—his love interest in the film—that he suspects foul play. She pooh-poohs his observations, trying instead to interest him in her. At the end of the scene, Kelly goes out to run errands. While she is out, a number of significant things happen across the courtyard. When she returns, Stewart recaps what has gone on in her absence. Kelly, who is far more interested in nudging their relationship forward, is all seduction and pouting displeasure. Far more interested in the gorgeous Ms. Kelly, the audience barely pays attention to Stewart's recap.

Nevertheless, Hitchcock accomplishes his goal: reminding the audience of what has happened in the story up to that point in the picture. He uses this technique over and over in his films, always with good results. The audience may not be aware that information is being fed to it, but the recap tells it just what it needs to know to avoid being lost in any way. (This scene from *Rear Window* is also an excellent example of the dialogue/action of one character working at cross-purposes with the dialogue/action of another character.)

This technique is one that you can use in your stories as well. In "My Sister's Shadow," Dale meets up with his friend, Milt, and recaps what has occurred in the story from Dale's point of view. Milt has a totally different take on what Dale has observed. Without the recap from Dale's point of view, the story would not have a great deal of impact. Dale's use of the recap solidifies the reader's grasp of what has happened and, at the same time, leads to an interesting moment when Milt provides Dale with a totally different way of interpreting Dale's sister's actions.

Chapter 2

Developing Character Qualities, Backstory, and Denouement

One of the most important aspects of creating stories is developing interesting characters. In a dramatic film, such as *On the Waterfront* with Marlon Brando, the audience finds itself caring about the characters to the degree that it wants to see them succeed against great odds to attain something they care about. *How* characters go about pursuing their dreams, their comebacks, their goals is what the audience cares about in a story.

Are Character Qualities Evident in the Story?

Every action characters take stems from the *character qualities* they possess, even though the characters may not know they possessed those qualities in the beginning of the story.

Examples of basic character qualities that get people through life are honesty, humor, dedication, adaptability, persistence, ingenuity, passion, and the like.

For example, in *On the Waterfront*, Brando's character has been knocked around the boxing ring for so long, he can't think straight. When his brother, who hangs out with the local mob run by Johnny Friendly, tells him to do something, he does it, no questions asked.

But when he encounters an upstanding woman (Eva Marie Saint) whom he desires, a woman who wants to find her brother's killer, Brando's character finds himself torn between loyalty to his brother and the mob and loyalty to his new love. The character quality that rises to the surface is *emotional honesty*. Brando may not tell his love interest the whole truth in the beginning, but he doesn't lie to her, and he finally admits that he knows who killed her brother… and even that he had a small part in the killing. He risks her rejection in favor of telling the truth about his involvement. Later, he risks his brother's love by going to the government with evidence against the mob.

Note: If you are interested in knowing more about character qualities, a fuller discussion is found in my book *Character Consciousness*.

In writing a life story, in the first draft you need to focus on purely getting the story down on paper, without worrying about such concerns as whether the characters' qualities are visible. However, from the second draft on, sharpening these qualities must become a primary concern. For example, whatever actions a character takes in the development section or the concluding section of your story must be planted, as a motif, in the setup—the introductory section—of your story. Generally speaking, writers get into trouble by having characters take actions late in the story that are not suggested in the setup of the story.

When done well, the incorporation of character qualities gives the reader a sense of knowing a character well, of being able to anticipate how they will handle a situation and whether they will find new inner qualities with which to handle new obstacles. (Please take a look at Bill Rempel's story on page 86 about creating *At the Devil's Table* for a probing look at the character qualities of a very interesting man.)

Creating Backstory to Inform

One of the most effective ways of giving the reader some context to whatever is going on when the story opens, while also giving dimension to certain characters, is to provide some *backstory* to the event that is taking place.

Very often this backstory occurs in the second or third paragraph of the story. The first paragraph is often devoted to an "attention getter" that takes the reader out of their boring, humdrum life and thrusts them into the action of an exciting story of a time long gone.

However, in the second or third paragraph, an effective writer weaves in some history relevant to what's going on into the unfolding narrative. Here is Dale's second-paragraph backstory in "Smoke Rings" (see page 132 for the complete story):

> Reminds me of tame Calicos, orange Orandas, and Bubble Eyes in the Marshall Islands. They swam close to my navy face mask in the coral reefs only three years ago. Wish I were there, now. These rainy Seattle streets depress me.

From this information, the reader learns that the main character is not some rebellious teenager but a veteran of World War II who has likely acquired habits similar to those of others his age, such as a desire to move along in life, to get educated, and to make something of himself.

Effective writers also provide the reader with backstory gradually, as the story progresses, rather than giving it to us all at once.

In Dale's story, a few more sentences of dialogue reveal that Dale is thinking about leaving his parents' home in Seattle and heading for college in Southern California:

> My B-50 flight control rigger's job only pays one dollar and ten cents an hour. That's union swing-shift wages, too. Boeing hired me a year ago for seventy-five cents an hour. Maybe Harry Truman here in the beginning of his first full term can kick-start the peacetime economy.
>
> I sold my 1941 Buick sedan for eleven hundred dollars. Bought a cream puff '37 Chevy sedan for only four hundred. The G.I. bill will pay for my college tuition. With a part-time job I can have fun in the sun and learn something, too.

Another helpful example occurs in the story "In the Beginning…," by Roy Wilhelm:

In the Beginning…

by Roy Wilhelm

The plaque on the wall near the front entrance states this state youth prison was built ten years ago in 1962. How many times have I looked at that plaque in the last half hour as I paced back and forth? This time as I stop to stare at it, a voice interrupts my thoughts, "You sure read slow. You've been studying that plaque the whole time I walked through the parking lot from my car."

I quip, "I have a bachelor and master's degree, but I still read slowly." He laughs. "Actually, I was deep in thought while I wait for my job interview. The receptionist said it will be awhile until they call me. I'm so nervous, I had to take it outside here to get fresh air."

He replies, "Well, it sure is a great place to work. Good luck to you." He walks inside.

Man, I want this job so bad. I'm forty-one years old, and for twelve years I've studied, trained, and had various jobs that would qualify me to be a California state institutional chaplain. Three years ago, they interviewed me, but they hired somebody else. I'm thoroughly frustrated.

My wife and I drove from Phoenix, Arizona, and stayed last night at the home of my friend, Rev. Dan Berth. He told me, "Roy, I visited Ventura School in Camarillo a year ago. It's like a high school campus. I think the Lord made you wait and prepare yourself this long so you'd be well qualified to help those young people." He patted me on the back. "I'm sure you'll get the job."

Notice that the third paragraph describes what has happened in the past, enabling the reader to understand what getting the job means to Roy and how much is riding on getting this job—that is, how high the stakes are.

Most effective stories employ backstory to give a rich sense of where the central character has come from, as well as the minor characters. That is the value of backstory.

The Denouement

Well-developed stories depend on the use of certain artistic principles such as balance, variety, repetition, tension, and release (these are explained in greater detail in Chapters 3 and 4). A skilled writer who understands the need for balance supplies something more after the climax of the story. to make sure the story ends in an emotionally satisfying way. This resolution is called the *denouement*, a French word meaning "falling off"—literally "undoing a knot."

Here is the ending of Dale's story, "Smoke Rings." Pay close attention to the denouement in his story:

> We reach Los Angeles late the next day. I park in back of the women's dorm, shake out the kinks, and open the trunk. I turn with Elsie's bag and bump into a guy. He hugs Elsie and asks her, "Drive nonstop from Seattle?"
> "Nope. Willie, this is Dale," she replies. "Stopped in southern Oregon."
> He persists, "Side of the road?"
> "Nope. Motel."
> She swivels her body away. Willie's face turns color. He slobbers into his red bandana handkerchief. I steel myself for his next question. In the same room?
> He makes choking noises. No words come out. They stand nose to nose. I set her bag down, back out of the lot, and light up a cigarette before he clobbers me.
> I've seen riled up Cajuns in the navy. They hold both hands together in a giant fist and slam down on someone's head. Pole-axed, they call it.
> Four days later I sit near Elsie in the cafeteria. She waves her left hand at me. A large rock sparkles on her ring finger.
> She giggles, "Me and Willie."
> I give her a big epiphany smile of admiration. "Congratulations."
> She outsmarted both her mother and me. Made Willie jealous enough to pop the question. I feel relieved. For once I don't need another cigarette. Any more may drive me crazy, may drive me insane.

from
Deeper
Within

20

The climax occurs when Willie shows his emotions at the thought of Elsie and Dale sleeping together. Perhaps Willie will tee off on Dale. The wonderful twist to the climax is the moment when Elsie shows Dale the ring that Willie has just given her. This is the moment of greatest tension…and release. Dale's realization that his take on Elsie has been wrong—that she has not been trying to hook Dale at all—constitutes a satisfying denouement to the story.

Chapter 3

Creating Visual Motifs,
Minor Characters, and Form

Sophisticated use of visual motifs (strong visual images, often repeated, that underscore certain messages or themes), minor characters, and form abound in the work of fiction writers. However, these techniques are also available to the writer of nonfiction life stories.

This does not mean that as a life-story writer, you invent what is needed, as a fiction writer does. On the contrary, you learn to look at your life and see the things that happen to you as potential parts of your stories. Minor characters throw into high relief the struggles of the central character. Visual motifs underscore the meaning, themes, and plights of the central character. Finally, you want to be sure that any motifs you create—character motifs (actions and the like) or visual motifs—occur in the setup to the story (the first third), unfold in the middle, and pay off at the end of the story. This is what *form* means.

Creating Visual Motifs

One technique that writers and filmmakers use to underscore messages/themes is to employ a strong visual image that resonates in the audience's mind or heart. This visual image or motif is simply a recurring theme of some kind. For example, in John Steinbeck's *The Grapes of Wrath*, the Joad family makes its way to California in a beat-up old truck. In the middle of the road, under a hot, desert sun, a turtle moves across the highway, ever so slowly. The Joad vehicle flips the turtle on its back, leaving it to bake under the hot desert sun, unable to right itself. This image of the turtle is the writer's way of giving a clue as to the fate of the Joad family—a creature struggling to survive, out of its element (the farms of the Midwest dust bowl), helpless under the cruel, hot sun.

As writers of life stories, you can do the same things. All around you, visual images echo the struggles of the central characters. To effectively use these images as motifs in stories they should occur at least three times: you should include them in the setup of your story, again in the development section, and then again in the conclusion.

In Dale Crum's story "Smoke Rings," the cigarette is a visual motif that signifies different things. In the beginning of the story, his cigarette symbolizes his independence from his family, his worldliness and impatience with their way of life. Early on, in the hands of cute little Elsie, it's an expression of innocence seeking worldliness. Later, when Elsie flicks the ashes off her cigarette onto the ground, her casual attitude about her messiness makes Dale wonder if she might also be casual about protecting Dale's well-being. Here is what Dale says about creating motifs in his stories:

> I don't think "motifs" per se when I start a story. But by the time I write the first page, natural motifs, which were there all the time, pop up in my memory—a cloud, a blue sky, a baby's cry. The feel of her hand. Smells of the river. A taste of honey. Then I add them, starting near the top of the story. They work best when scattered throughout.

Visual motifs are a powerful tool for a writer. If the motif is central to the character's actions, the audience will *feel* it through the power of the image. For example, in Shakespeare's *Macbeth* the prophesy—that order will be restored "when Burnham Wood comes to Dunsinane"—connects the motif of the restoration of order and an image of the movement of Burnham Wood in the reader's or viewer's minds early in the play. But the audience thinks little about it until the end, when McDuff's forces emerge from Burnham Wood, concealed beneath brush and trees, as they crawl toward the castle of Dunsinane. When Lady Macbeth sees the prophesy coming true visually, the impact of it makes her—and the audience—gasp.

Often, visual motifs gain significant power from their representation of a moral or God-given order in the universe. The turtle's struggling to right itself or Burnham Wood's coming to Dunsinane suggest a moral order in which the turtle ought to be allowed to right itself and Burnham Wood ought to come to Dunsinane. In an age when the certainty of a moral order is open to question, the presence of powerful visual symbols reassures the audience that a moral order may exist.

It hardly needs to be said that one person's moral order may look like tyranny to another person: Witness the variety of symbols, such as the swastika, that provoke all kinds of emotion in people. So as you search for arresting visual symbols in your stories, you also need to consider the use of false symbols by nonheroic characters in these same stories.

Creating Three-Dimensional Minor Characters

The quality of your storytelling will become substantially better if you allow minor characters to react to circumstances that bedevil the major characters.

Very often, minor characters fall into certain types: the mentor, the playboy, the innocent, the martyr, the trickster, the villain, the mystic, the adventurer, the old wise man, and the like. These "types" often exist in life, and a knowledge of them allows you to recognize them when they cross your path in real life.

In Dale Crum's story "My Sister's Shadow," Dale is uncertain about whether he really ought to be trying to protect his sister. Therefore, he seeks out Milt, a friend who advises him to let well enough alone. But Milt does more than that. He levels a certain amount of criticism at Dale for being naïve. In doing so, the character of Milt reveals himself to be something of a trickster—an impish, mercurial type of person whose unpredictability serves the main character well by saying things to him that others might not be willing to say aloud:

> "Cleo doesn't go with church guys. Claims they're too sissified."
> (Milt) sneers, "Sounds like what my sisters might say about you, Dale."

In the first chapter of J.D. Tousley's *Dangling in the Adios* (see page 60 for the complete text), Mr. Horner is something of this kind of character as well. Seemingly a crotchety old man, he sees through all of Tack's intentions and then reveals he had similar intentions himself when he was young, thus revealing himself to be a man filled with sadness and regret.

The reaction of minor characters is often what governs the actions of major characters. In motion pictures and television shows, such reactions are vital to the progress of the plot.

In the old *Gunsmoke* series, Marshall Dillon inevitably winds up in a gunfight with the bad guys. In and of itself, this might not alarm the viewing audience. However, when the audience sees Chester, Doc, Festus, and Kitty start to react with fear or concern, then the audience begins to do so as well. In film parlance, this is called "coverage"—making sure the director has filmed plenty of reaction shots so the editor can cut away from the main action to another angle.

Creating a Sense of Form

The human mind cannot hold in its memory bank very much of what it receives. Therefore, the artist must create a form that allows the audience to make sense of what it receives and to remember what it understands. The principles of art (which we will talk about next) help in establishing this sense of form.

One of these principles—balance—comes into play by creating a shape to the story, usually a beginning (called "a setup"), a middle (called "development"), and a conclusion (sometimes called "a recap").

At the beginning of a story, or the setup, authors often introduce motifs, which are small, powerful images or sounds that contain the seeds of all the dramatic material to come. Later, in the middle of a story, these motifs are developed into full-blown themes. In the conclusion section, the conflicts related to these motifs/themes are resolved in some way.

Note: In many stories, a motif or motifs may gradually transform into, and predict, a developing theme. A visual motif may not reappear as a motif but in the reader's mind an inner "alarm button" is created which is then set off as the larger theme begins to take shape. The following is an example of a visual motif that morphs into (and predicts) a larger theme to follow.

At the beginning of *The Grapes of Wrath*, Steinbeck introduces a turtle motif. He shows the creature, upended on a highway leading from the dust bowl of the Midwest to California, struggling to survive, roasting under the hot sun, with no way to right itself. Later, in the development section, the members of the Joad family struggle terribly with the poverty into which they have been thrust, with no apparent way of coping with their situation. In the conclusion, they find ways of coping, of righting themselves, and of surviving.

These concepts are explored more fully in the next chapter, "Employing the Principles of Art, Subtext, and the 'Story Within a Story.'"

Chapter 4

Employing the Principles
of Art, Subtext, and the
"Story Within a Story"

For a writer's work to make sense to the audience and for it to remember what the writer is talking about, the writer has to employ certain artistic principles. The writer must compose a story in the same way that a musician or a painter uses "composition" to create the desired impact. Composition, in this context, means manipulating the elements of an artist's craft by using artistic techniques and following certain principles of art—repetition, balance, symmetry, variety, contrast, tension, and release—that are used by all artists at all times.

Some of the most memorable works of art and literature are those that rise above the literal: In other words, what the story *seems* to be about may not be what the story really *is* about. We call this additional meaning subtext.

Employing the Principles of Art

During the Renaissance, artists made every effort to create the illusion of three dimensions by using artistic techniques that create a sense of perspective on the surface. These artists drew lines that converged at a single point, often in the middle of the painting. The viewer's eye is led into the deep distance, as in Leonardo da Vinci's *The Last Supper* or Peter Bruegel's *The Fall of Icarus*. These converging lines create a sense of balance, even as they create an illusion of three dimensions.

By contrast, modern artists often try to arouse emotions by creating strong visual accents on the surface of the painting. Nevertheless, these artists are still governed by the principles of art—repetition, balance, symmetry, variety, contrast, tension, and release. For example, in Matisse's *The Joy of Life*, rounded shapes colored in red, which we interpret as dancing figures, create an illusion of motion and energy through the repetition of the shapes. Colored red, these shapes stand out against (contrast with) the blue of the background.

Dramatists such as Ibsen and Strindberg, filmmakers like Billy Wilder and Orson Welles, as well as composers and arrangers from Beethoven and Monteverdi to John Williams and Quincy Jones use these same principles. In fact, artists at all times and places, working in a variety of mediums, use these same principles of art—repetition, balance, symmetry, variety, contrast, tension, and release—in order to channel the viewers' or audience's perceptions and thoughts.

As life-story writers, you, too, can use these principles of repetition, balance, variety, and the like—but how?

Primarily, you must create a motif (pattern) in the beginning of the story, change and develop it in the middle section of the story, and make its meaning clear as you resolve the story. These principles become clearer via an examination of the subtext of Dale's story in the next section.

Developing the Subtext of a Story

Creating subtext is one of the most difficult yet rewarding tasks that the writer of creative stories undertakes. In a play or a motion-picture screenplay, the writer provides the text—that is, the actions taken by the hero/heroine and minor characters as well as the dialogue.

Interpreting the dialogue so that believable relationships occur is the objective of the director and actors as they work on a screenplay. In a novel or short story, the writer must supply the subtext (the implicit or metaphorical meaning) by supplying dialogue, actions, and inner thoughts and feelings that may conflict. Here is an example: In Dale's story, the subtext emerges little by little. Here are the narrator's lines that provide a picture of what is going on:

> I can't leave my good friend, Vera, a divorcée who works in the blueprint room.... Nor Joanne, the Catholic girl I sometimes go out with. Joanne's parents don't like Protestants. I really like Betty and Rosemary from our church. Mama does, too.

From this description, the reader sees that the narrator likes girls and dates quite a bit.

> She beams, "Mom says I can ride down to L.A. with you."
> Whoa! Her mother is a straight-laced woman from a straight-laced church. Takes two days to get to L.A. Unless you want to switch drivers and speed nonstop on that narrow, winding Highway 99.

Elsie stops in her driveway. Her Mom, Mary, rushes to the car. "Oh, Dale, I'm so glad you decided to go. I trust you with Elsie. I know you will have an enjoyable trip."

I think most mothers want to marry off their daughters by the time they're twenty years old. Wait a minute. Something's going on here.

From what is said, it looks like Elsie wants to go on a trip with Dale, and her mother hopes they get involved so they will wind up married — none of which is to Dale's liking.

"Huh-oh," this time I say under my breath. Takes only a second for the picture to develop in my mind. Mary wants me to take her daughter alone to California. She knows Charlie will find out. Poof! There goes Charlie.

I leer like Groucho Marx, "Long drive with me."

Elsie stares at me for a long time, then takes a cigarette from my package. I hold my Zippo lighter up, and she moves to the flame like a moth to a backyard barbecue. She inhales a little bit, coughs, and waves the smoke away from her face.

Here it appears that Dale sees Willie as no threat, and he makes a "we might have a night in a motel together" kind of a face. She appears to be thinking it over. In taking a cigarette from his packet of cigarettes, Elsie appears to be signaling that she is ready for a new experience.

Soon they arrive at a motel along the way and prepare to spend the night:

The bored clerk looks up from her *True Romances* magazine. She spits out of the side of her mouth, "Six dollars."

"Give me two adjoining rooms."

Her eyes flicker. She looks out the door before she hands me the keys. She makes me feel weird. Why spend the extra six dollars?

I carry the bags and balance on the bricks while Elsie splashes down the middle of the muddy walkway. After I plop down her bag, I move to the door.

She gives me the same quizzical look I saw on the clerk's face.

Now the reader sees that Dale plans to play it safe — no sex with Elsie. He doesn't want to risk winding up with her, just what her mom hopes will happen. No, he's going to outsmart them both.

We reach Los Angeles late the next day. I park in back of the women's dorm, shake out the kinks, and open the trunk. I turn with Elsie's bag and bump into a guy. He hugs Elsie and asks her, "Drive nonstop from Seattle?"

"Nope, Will, this is Dale," she replies. "Stopped in southern Oregon."

He persists, "Side of the road?"

"Nope. Motel."

She swivels her body away. Willie's face turns color. He slobbers into his red bandana handkerchief. I steel myself for his next question. In the same room?

He makes choking noises. No words come out. They stand nose to nose. I set her bag down, back out of the lot, and light up a cigarette before he clobbers me.

Now the reader thinks that Dale feels pretty good about himself. He has outsmarted Elsie and her mom in their desire to lasso Dale into early marriage. And he has not done anything to make Willie mad at him. Good for Dale.

Four days later, I sit near Elsie in the cafeteria. She waves her left hand at me. A large rock sparkles on her ring finger.

She giggles, "Me and Willie."

I give her a big epiphany smile of admiration. "Congratulations."

She outsmarted both her mother and me. Made Willie jealous enough to pop the question. I feel relieved. For once I don't need another cigarette. Any more may drive me crazy, may drive me insane.

Now the reader realizes that Elsie had a whole different take on what was supposed to happen than Dale did, and her take turned out to be the true take. Careful Dale, sure he had outsmarted another calculating woman, realizes he has been too careful: He could have had a good time with Elsie without any consequences, because she was focused on making Willie jealous and getting the ring whether Mama liked it or not.

The *text* of this delightful story is that despite his lusts, Dale avoids the snares of a calculating mother and her lustful, carefree daughter. He may have lust in his heart, but he is too careful, too smart, to fall for mother and daughter's plan to trap him into early marriage. The *subtext* is that women have agendas of their own, and no man is smart enough to figure out all the angles when a woman knows what she wants.

Dale uses the motif of the cigarette throughout the story to underscore its meaning. In the beginning, the cigarette makes him an alien, an unwanted person in his mother's home, something of a fallen angel. In the development section, Elsie takes the cigarette from Dale and coughs, a sign that she is still an angel but is willing to be initiated. Dale, however, is suspicious of her motives (and her mother's), so he does not seduce her and feels elated that he did not. In the conclusion, the reader sees that Elsie is no angel but a temptress. Whether Dale seduced her or she seduced him, she played the seduction card with her fiancé and got what she wanted—the ring. In this way, the repetition of the cigarette motif leads the reader to believe Dale's interpretation of events would be the tune that would be played, but, in fact, her version of what was happening, her tune, was the one that she wound up playing—"Here Comes the Bride."

In this way, the motif of the cigarette builds slowly into a theme (will Dale initiate the uninitiated girl?). However, by the end of the story, we see that this girl has turned everything her way, allowing us to see that subtext of the story: The young girl controlled the situation all along. Motifs developing into themes are very often the route by which subtext unfolds in a story.

Creating a "Story Within a Story"

One of the most effective techniques in storytelling is to have one of the characters tell a story to the narrator. A famous example of this technique is Fyodor Dostoevsky's relating of "The Legend of the Grand Inquisitor" within the pages of *The Brothers Karamazov*. The book, which comes in at some six hundred pages, remains a tough read for most people. However, "The Legend of the Grand Inquisitor" stands alone as a superb piece of history and philosophy.

In these few pages, Christ returns to earth and demands that the Inquisitor give up control of his church—for many reasons, not the least of which is that the Inquisitor and others like him have soiled the pristine beauty of the church, as Christ foresaw it when he went to the cross. In turn, the Grand Inquisitor laughs off Christ's demands, snarling that the church is no longer his, that he abandoned it when he was crucified and then never again returned to earth. It now belongs to those who came after.

Here, the "story within a story" stands alone, outside the novel, but remains a powerful argument in favor of those who embrace the existence of Christ as a spiritual entity but find fault with the church itself.

In a similar way, those who write life stories may find themselves using this "story within a story" technique with wonderful results. Please turn to page 143 and read Mimi Wirth's "The Story of Little Rickey." Here is a short excerpt in which Mimi returns home after an afternoon stroll through the woods near her winter cabin:

> Rickey and Kelly jump on my lap, licking me with a welcoming "glad-you're-home-Mom" greeting. I love my doggies. Petting each one on the top of their heads as they bounce around my knees.
>
> Mom hands me a cup of hot chocolate. "I almost lost Rickey today," she says in a low voice. Mom turns away and settles herself in the easy chair.
>
> "What? Huh?" I say, focusing my attention on the chocolate. I wrap my cold hands around the steaming cup.

Mimi's mother tells her daughter how the dog disappeared and how she just barely got the dog back.

In discussing this story with our writing group after Mimi had read the story, I asked everyone, "What is the meaning behind the story?" Most members of the group believed this was a story about how Mimi selfishly wandered around in the snow, leaving her mother to take care of practicalities like tending to the dogs—that the story was a life lesson in self-centeredness. Even Mimi subscribed to this version of the story.

However, a few other members of the class, including myself, viewed it differently. As the mother told the story, it became clear that the victim in the story was Mama—she worked hard to take care of things that Mimi ignored, with little attention paid to her. As we discussed this take on the story, it became more and more evident that Mama was telling Mimi, "You are ignoring me, and I need and want you to pay attention to and care for me, just as I attend to your needs and take care of you."

This more subtle meaning to the story only emerged as we reviewed the story several times. This interesting take became possible because Mimi carefully observed and listened to her mother's words and tone of voice. As the central character of the story, Mimi felt embarrassed at her lack of concern for her dog and a bit ashamed that she had left the dog's well-being to her mother while she, Mimi, went for walk. As narrator of the story, Mimi allowed her mother to speak for herself, in airing out her complaints. In this way, Mimi, the writer, got out of her own way to allow a more interesting meaning to shine through the story.

In the next chapter, I talk more about this dichotomy between the central character's concerns and the writer's concerns. They are often quite different. In fact, the difference between the two may often be the difference between unfolding a good story and unlocking a great story.

Chapter 5

Amplifying the Basic Steps in *Writing from Within*: Narrative, Dialogue, and Inner Thoughts and Feelings

"Would you help my husband?" asked Jacqui Tousley, an attractive woman in her sixties, after a life-story writing session offered by the University of California at Irvine in the 1990s. "For more than fifty years, he has wanted to be a novelist but got sidetracked." She paused a moment.

Jacqui told me that as a young man, her husband, Dirk, went to Mexico to write, inspired by the life of Ernest Hemingway, but found himself more interested in drinking with the locals than in writing. Finally he returned to the United States with nothing written.

"I believe he can do it. I believe there is a novelist inside him," she continued. "I would be grateful to you if you would help him."

I wondered if Dirk really had the talent or will to write but agreed to start a private workshop in Playa del Rey for a few interested people, among them George Small and his friend Karl Grey.

Dirk's first effort showed little that was remarkable; however, after I suggested he get rid of anything that sounded adult and focus on writing simple narratives with lots of dialogue, details, and inner thoughts and feelings, he returned with a story that demonstrated that Jacqui was right: He had a wonderful writing style, a terrific eye for detail and dialogue, and a strong desire to create.

• • •

Having explored the basic steps of *Writing from Within* and having written and rewritten several of your own stories using several advanced writing techniques, you are now ready to look at your writing these steps in a more sophisticated way — to build on what you have done so far — so your writing becomes even more effective. As I indicated in the Introduction, in doing so, you will learn to better reflect the inner life and feelings of your characters, especially the main character—often you.

In telling a story, every writer has three essential ingredients to work with: *narrative*, *dialogue*, and *inner thoughts and feelings*. The way in which you manipulate these ingredients dictates the style that emerges and the pleasure the audience derives from the story.

Narrative

The word "narrative" is a fancy word for "story"; however, in the world of writing, narrative means telling the facts that move the story forward, sometimes without concern for the characters' particular qualities and the actions that emerge from these qualities.

When is narrative not narrative? For a great many writers and teachers of writing, narrative is interpreted as meaning a series of plot points that move the story from point A to point B to point C. If this is true, a world of writers' concerns such as backstory and character description exists in a kind of never-never land. Here is an example from J.D. Tousley's novel, *Dangling in the Adios*:

> My life as a young pool hustler was about as sweet as life gets. In those days, long before MasterCard, when you could sit down at a nice clean lunch counter and get a bowl of steaming chili for a quarter, a slab of apple pie juicier than Mom made for a dime, and a steaming cup of coffee with free refills for a nickel, I usually carried at least two hundred bucks in my right front pocket and a couple of fifties hidden in my wallet. So I was doing all right.
>
> I'm telling you, business life couldn't have been sweeter, played out day by day on a rectangle of green felt four and one half feet wide by nine feet long. And I knew every inch of it.

In a way, this is good "narrative" (objective fact telling), but it is also *not* narrative. In fact, these two paragraphs are backstory to the story the writer intends to tell. The reader knows it is backstory because he mentions the present: "in those days, long before MasterCard…."

Here is the story after a few more drafts:

> I've had it with stuck-up sorority girls. They act like they're too grand to do it, then when they finally let you in, they own you lock, stock, and barrel. Take Carolyn Forsythe, for instance, safely locked away from us college boys in her panty girdle. After we first met, I rolled around with her in the backseat of my convertible every night for two weeks, trying to pry her

out of that medieval contraption, until late one night I got her to wriggle out of it on her own and start enjoying life. And it's been great. I never had it so steady before. But I'm paying for it with my freedom. Whenever Carolyn crooks her finger, I'm supposed to roll over and bark. You'd think she owned me. Now she's ragging me to quit playing nine ball so we can study together. Hell, I don't need study. That's what brains are for. And I'm not about to give up nine ball. Pool is my life, and besides, it brings in about thirty bucks a week.

How different with Cricket, my appreciative little drugstore clerk. On our second date I slid her skimpy panties down her bare legs and off her feet in a flash, what with no elastic wall, hooks, wires, or buttons to overcome. Panties off, and there it was. When we're not making love, she spends a lot of time in the crook of my arm, looking up at me attentively and asking questions I can answer.

I met Cricket a couple of weeks ago. She clerks at the drugstore around the corner from campus. One day I went in to buy a comb. Five minutes later, I had a new comb and a new girlfriend. Mostly I take her to drive-in movies and an out-of-the-way beer joint called Snookums in south Kansas City where I won't run into anyone Carolyn knows. Carolyn has gone home to St. Louis for a few weeks during summer break, which gives Cricket and me time to get acquainted.

Sex with Cricket is the best ever. Just thinking about her gives me a warm feeling inside I've never had before. Nothing's perfect though. Her father doesn't like me, and he's getting in my way. Just today Cricket reminded me on the phone that tonight is our seventh date. "Daddy raises Cain if I go steady," she said. "We'll have to find another way to meet before he goes berserk."

This excerpt is still narrative—that is, narrative in style, with no dialogue or inner thoughts and feelings. The narrative has transmuted itself into little pieces of action and backstory that do not move the story forward, necessarily, but do give a picture of the circumstances in which the central character finds himself. Already he's in a vise and he's being squeezed. The character qualities of Carolyn and Cricket abound: controlling, possessive, uptight Carolyn; spontaneous, innocent, carefree, adoring Cricket.

As the story progresses, the author brings the characters into greater focus through dialogue and inner thoughts and feelings:

It's nearly dark but still hot and humid as I park my car in front of Cricket's house, get out, and look around. My bright green Mercury convertible is definitely out of place in this working-class neighborhood of fading white frame houses and scrubby lawns. Though World War II has been over four years, some of the houses still display Gold Stars in their front windows.

I'm dressed in a navy blue polo shirt, white duck pants, and cordovan loafers, perfect attire for a summer night date with a cute girl. I'm feeling good and looking good, ready for a Saturday night blast with Cricket.

Looks like I'm in luck. Daddy isn't sitting on the porch steps as usual, and his old tired Studebaker is nowhere in sight. Hot damn! I won't have to face him tonight. But my high spirits are short-lived. As I mount the steps, his gravelly voice coming from inside the screened porch begins the challenge.

"Well, if it ain't Joe College." His cheap cigar smoke hangs in the humid air.

"Evening, Mr. Horner," I muster, unable to see him through the screen. But once I'm inside the porch, I make him out in the dusk, swinging slowly back and forth in his porch swing.

"I brought you a Dutch Master."

"Tryin' to suck in with me, huh?"

I ignore the bastard's remark, hand him the Dutch Master, and ask, "Is Cricket ready yet?"

He rolls the cigar between thumb and forefinger, testing its freshness, before setting it aside on the porch railing. "Why the hell you call her Cricket? Her name's Josephine. If I wanted her to be Cricket, I'd uh named her Cricket."

"Harry, leave that boy alone," comes Mrs. Horner's voice from the darkest side of the porch. "Evenin' to you, Tack."

"Hello, ma'am. I didn't see you," I say, grateful for a second in my corner.

In this brief paragraph, the author gives a picture of the scene as the character sees it: "dark...hot, humid...bright green Mercury...out of place...fading white frame...houses display Gold Stars...." The character is in the present, but Cricket's family and their neighbors all seem locked in the past.

Then the author gives a bit of character assessment through a description of how Tack is dressed: "navy blue polo shirt, white duck pants, cordovan loafers...feeling good and looking good...." He knows he's the wave of the future, and he knows that his cute little date, Cricket, will get that.

He follows this description with some inner thoughts and feelings: "in luck...old tired Studebaker...nowhere...Hot damn! I won't have to face him tonight." These feelings of elation are short-lived. "his gravelly voice... 'Well, if it ain't Joe College....'"

In the short space of five paragraphs, the author has provided a description of the actions, attitudes, and circumstances of the central character, his taste for drama, his love of pool (nine ball), his careful planning of his appearance, his inner thoughts and feelings, and some good dialogue that tells the reader about Tack, Cricket's father, and Cricket's mother. The reader knows Tack plans to try to get away with something, and, sooner or later, he will have to confront both obstacles — Cricket's father and the sorority girl he also dates.

In this setup for the story he intends to tell, the author gives a full picture of the wants, desires, and intentions of this kid and the way he plans to get what he wants, even as the author describes several obstacles that the kid will have to overcome.

In a first draft it doesn't matter whether the narrative is flat or rich. In subsequent rewrites, this narrative becomes richer through the use of dialogue, actions, details, character qualities, setting, and backstory. None of these attributes necessarily moves the story along; however, they make the story infinitely richer and more compelling so as the story does move along, the reader will care more about the characters and the outcome. (For the narrative to move along, something has to happen very soon, and that something is the appearance of Cricket.)

For the purposes of this book, I suggest you consider narrative as anything other than dialogue or inner thoughts and feelings, for the simple reason that backstory, character descriptions, details, and imagery (visual motifs) all do move the story forward, at least indirectly.

Dialogue

In the original *Writing from Within*, I felt it sufficient to point out that moving a story from all narrative to some narrative with spicy dialogue would make the story better, more interesting, and more revealing of the characters who speak.

However, more needs to be said about dialogue. In the nineteenth century, such novels as those of Charles Dickens, William Thackeray, and Herman Melville contained long passages of all narrative. Dialogue was sprinkled in here and there. Theodore Dreiser filled his pages with cumbersome narrative and then punctuated the narrative with pungent, expressive dialogue. By the time F. Scott Fitzgerald emerged in the late 1920s, the characters speak more and more often with less narrative needed to move the story along. Ernest Hemingway and John Steinbeck in the 1930s and 1940s expressed themselves almost completely in dialogue and action.

What is the importance of dialogue? Dialogue is comparable to a two-shot in a motion picture (a shot with two characters in it). It provides a strong sense of relationship between or among characters. Using modern, lightweight cameras, and dollies, deft film directors compose the frames of their films so long shots, medium shorts (two shots), and close-ups occur within single takes. Writers can do the same thing.

The following is a short passage from one of my student's stories. Imagine this opening sequence as a filmed sequence employing establishing shots, two shots, and close-ups:

The Turkish Ambassador

by Paula Moore Diggs

"You know what a Turkish ambassador is, don't you?" Tom Rankin's deep-set blue eyes hold mine as he leans against the wall between the living room and kitchen at the Winders' home. Another English Department party. Our corporate benefactor, Dupont, gave the U of Del a huge endowment to bring big names on campus for a lecture series. The English Department got a chunk to bring famous authors here in hopes of putting Delaware on the cultural map. Sam, our department chair, explained to me that because I'm the youngest at twenty-six and best looking (which isn't saying a lot), I'd be one of the few wives included in the festivities. He didn't mention my cum laude degree…oh well. That invite didn't include lectures, just the parties where old guys run their hands up under my skirt at dinner.

"No, I don't know what a Turkish ambassador is," I tell him. Tom gives me a sly look. He was at the lecture that author James Dickey gave. Dickey's book *Deliverance* was just made into a film. He even played a part in it and strummed his banjo. A very big name. "Dickey told us a Turkish ambassador is sent in when the director thinks he may be losing the audience's interest," Tom tells me. "A guy walks across the scene, everyone says, 'Who's that?' Someone answers, 'the Turkish Ambassador,' music swells, and the audience is hooked, waiting to see what will happen. Dickey talked a lot about filmmaking, then he played his banjo." Tom smiles at me and leans further against the wall.

Next to him on a bookcase rests the Winders' son's fish tank. Fish are at the top gasping for air. The water needs to be changed. One fish floats slowly to the bottom. Gills pumping. Tom's mouth keeps moving faster, but no words come out. He slides noiselessly down the wall and sits, feet splayed out. Finally topples over on his side, mouth still moving. Cigarette smoke and the reek of alcohol rush into my face as this movement of his large six-foot frame disturbs the air. Sloshed.

If this were a film, the challenge would be to create in film terms all the backstory that the author has given. To do so using inner thoughts and feelings seldom works unless it's done very briefly and runs counter to the expressions and actions of the characters. Apart from that, imagine the camera focusing on the two characters in conversation, then recomposing to catch glimpses of other things, such as the fish gulping for air—a parallel to Tom's drifting down the wall, sloshed, dead for all intents and purposes. (For the rest of the story, see page 138 in the "Stories" section.)

Virtually none of this is narrative—that is, virtually none of it moves the story along in terms of plot. The writer provides backstory and, using dialogue, a sense of relationship between the main character and Tom as well as a sense of the pointlessness of the party itself. Taken together, the backstory, dialogue, and description of the texture and atmosphere yield a sense of what the characters want to get away from, which is what happens as the story unfolds.

CREATING VIVID DIALOGUE BY DROPPING SUBJECTS AND VERBS

The most vivid stories that are written or appear on screen as films and television programs often have colorful dialogue. A number of ways to create interesting dialogue exist.

Perhaps the simplest way to create vivid dialogue is to *eliminate the subject and/or the verb from the sentence.*

Here is an example from a story by another student, Dale Crum, in his story "Smoke Rings." Let's look at the first line of dialogue from his story:

"Stunt your growth," my dad used to say.

In this case, Dale dropped both the subject and verb ("It will"). The sentence becomes more effective because a lot of people do talk this way, with just a few words. The next line of dialogue:

Someone rattles the doorknob. Mama calls, "Dale, you in there?"

This time, Dale's mother drops the verb of the sentence ("Dale, [are] you in there?"). Once again, the sentence becomes livelier without the verb in it, because it accurately reflects the way real people talk.

CREATING VIVID DIALOGUE BY HAVING CHARACTERS TALK AT CROSS PURPOSES

A second way of creating lively dialogue is for the people in the scene to talk to each other without entirely hearing or responding to what the other person is saying. This technique is called *talking at cross purposes*. Here is another line from the opening of Dale's story:

I pick up the towel stuffed in the crack at the bottom of the door, spray air freshener all around, and unlock the door.

Mama rushes in. She comes out with a sniff. "Thought you quit."

"Yeah, going to college."

"Not what I meant. You got a good job at Boeing."

In this exchange, Mama nails Dale for smoking in the bathroom. He pretends she is talking about quitting school, deflecting her criticism of him and the smell of cigarette smoke onto a subject of greater importance. She immediately picks up on the new theme—going to college—and tries to argue with him in the sentence, "Not what I meant." In this sentence, the subject and verb have again been dropped ("[That is] not what I meant").

Interesting, huh? Well, this is how people do talk to each other—ideas move quickly from one person to the next without either speaker finishing thoughts or sentences, especially when one person tries to convince another to change their behavior, opinions, or both.

If a writer has a character speak expressively about themselves without talking directly about the thing that matters most to them, this type of dialog is called "off the money." Alternatively, dialogue that says exactly what the character is thinking or feeling is often boring and lacks believability. This style of dialogue is called "on-the-money" writing. It takes a great deal of effort to become skilled at writing "off-the-money" dialogue, but the effort is always worth the trouble.

CREATING VIVID DIALOGUE BY EMPLOYING A "HOOK"

A third approach to dialogue is to employ what might loosely be called a "hook." In this technique, one character says a line of dialogue, and then the character who speaks next repeats that line. For example:

Janine shakes her head. "Tom, you're the most stubborn man I've ever met."

Tom reacts with surprise. "Stubborn, me?"

She laughs and hands him an apple. "Stubborn, me?" She shakes her head. "You seem so innocent."

In this brief exchange, the repetition of the lines of dialogue accomplishes several things. First of all, it is clear that Tom is really listening to Janine. Secondly, her line of dialogue nails a character quality in Tom that he has to deal with. Third, in handing him the apple, it clear that she likes Tom and may give him another chance to change, adjust, or do whatever he must to keep her interested.

As a writer, you may say, "Well, all of this is fine if you are a fiction writer, but I'm just writing life stories." In fact, all the techniques that I discuss are just as relevant to the palette of the nonfiction writer as to the fiction writer. If the life writer is skilled in the use of these techniques, they will begin to notice situations occurring in real life that reflect the techniques just discussed. So in the final analysis, the aim of these techniques is to help the writer fine-tune their ability to listen to and observe life as it passes by.

Inner Thoughts and Feelings

Writing inner thoughts and feelings is a huge challenge for any writer. Writing or recording inner thoughts and feelings came at a late stage in the history of the development of writing. The first stage originated in ancient Mesopotamia, at a small village called Ebla, where clay tablets dating back some five thousand years have been found. These tablets were inscribed with symbols that indicated the recording of food stores and are the oldest-known records of writing.

The second stage occurred some five hundred to one thousand years ago, when storytelling began to be recorded in the epics of Homer's *The Iliad* and *The Odyssey*. These epics are told almost entirely in a narrative style.

The third phase occurred during the Renaissance, especially in England, but to an extent in Italy as well, where Niccolo Machiavelli and William Shakespeare demonstrated that dialogue could point the way toward a fascinating interplay of relationships, with an occasional foray into inner thoughts and feelings.

Over the next several hundred years, the novel in the hands of Richardson, Stendhal, Dostoevsky, and Melville included dynamic adventures (narratives) punctuated by poignant moments of relationship (dialogue). Often, these narratives suggest a godlike point of view, as in Melville and Dostoevsky, in which a transcendent force still operates in the universe, although Dostoevsky looks more closely into the inner thoughts of the central character.

In the intensely masculine writing of Ernest Hemingway, the reader confronts a world in which very little narrative is present, suggesting no organizing force in the universe. Instead, interpersonal forces are in conflict, as reflected in revealing dialogue and occasional glimpses into the characters' inner thoughts. Hemingway's approach to writing inner thoughts and feelings will be discussed more in Chapter 11.

When an author uses the third person to express a character and the character's actions, the author may also use that third person to express intimate thoughts and feelings. If an author chooses to write the central character in the first person, then other choices become available when expressing inner thoughts and feelings. Here is a moment from a story by a student of mine, Karl Grey:

"Please let me in! Please unlock the door." I can hear my mother on the other side laughing at me. I'm pounding on the door, and I'm sure the whole neighborhood can see me in my underwear. They have all come out of their houses and are standing in the dark street watching me like I'm on the screen at a drive-in movie. I can hear them laughing at me and my mother laughing at me and I can't stand the way I feel. I am so filled with panic.

I pound and pound on the door, but all I hear is the echo of laughing from both sides colliding on me. It's like this dream that I have over and over. I am walking on a sidewalk when all of a sudden I'm naked. I want to hide so that the other people on the sidewalk don't see me so I duck around behind the row of trees that is between the street and the sidewalk but the street is full of cars and all of the drivers can see me so I go back around the trees but then the sidewalk people can see me and pretty soon they have all stopped and all of the cars have stopped and they are all laughing and blowing the horns and saying, "Look at the naked fat kid. Does he even have a dick?" The sound gets louder and louder and I can't get away.

CRASH!

The kitchen door flies off the hinges and wood splinters as it hits the stove on the other side of the kitchen. I am in the house before the door hits the ground. My mother screams, and the scotch and water breaks on the floor. My stepfather has his belt undone by now and is pulling it through the loops of his pants.

I am running, into the den, into the cool…and my back stings, again and again, as I drop to the floor and roll myself into a ball and take it on my back. I'm safe now. I'm inside myself, and nobody can see me while he continues to hit me with the doubled-up belt.

"Thank you, ladies and gentlemen, it's been a really big shoooow tonight. Next week on this stage, Elvis Presley"…and the crowd screams and my back stings, but it's cool in here and nobody can see me.

By using the first person, the writer makes the sense of the character's pain all the more acute:

I am running, into the den, into the cool…and my back stings, again and again, as I drop to the floor and roll myself into a ball and take it on my back. I'm safe now. I'm inside myself, and nobody can see me while he continues to hit me with the doubled-up belt.

The reader feels the sting of the belt even as the character has withdrawn into a deep, remote place inside himself:.

> …roll myself into a ball…take it on my back…safe now. I'm inside myself…nobody can see me…he continues to hit me with the doubled-up belt.

Another interesting use of inner thoughts and feelings occurs when dialogue among two or more people is infused with the inner thoughts and feelings of the main character. The following is a simple example that illustrates this point:

> Woman A: "Oh, darling, I love your hair. Where did you go to have it done?"
> Woman B: "Thank you, dear, it's such a mess, but I'm glad you like it. Well, see you at bridge on Friday."

This sounds like typical, mundane, throwaway dialogue, yes? Now let's look at what happens when we add inner thoughts and feelings.

> Woman A: "Oh, darling, I love your hair. Where did you go to have it done?"
> Woman B: "Thank you, dear, it's such a mess, but I'm glad you like it." *Love my hair?! Love my hair?! I saw you at lunch yesterday with my husband—making eyes at him, you slut. You conniving slut. So he and I had an argument. So what! And you're going to lunch with him? I'll make life miserable for you. Oh, yes, I will.* "Well, see you at bridge on Friday."

Here the inner world and the outer world are at odds with one another. We, the readers, have a chance to see that woman B is perfectly content to hide her feelings from the outer world—Woman A—which is what many of us do, in fact must do, in life, in order to survive.

Note: You will have noticed that I have italicized the inner thoughts and feelings. Some books on writing style recommend the use of single quotes or no quotes to set off inner thoughts and feelings. My experience is that the use of single quotes or no quotes creates confusion. The use of italics creates a different feel and, to my eye, gives more of a sense of being "*inner*" than "outer." Use what works best for you.

Chapter 6

Separating the Writer's Voice from the Central Character's Voice

This last perspective on writing perplexes writers more than any other. Writers of life stories find it especially difficult to grasp. Fiction writers know that to create interesting central characters, they must also create interesting contexts (circumstances, settings, obstacles, and minor characters) within which the central characters function. Without these elements, their stories will have little appeal.

On the other hand, the life-story writer often feels that, because they sketch things that have really happened, all they must do is simply record accurately what took place.

The appearance of this task as "simple recording" is an illusion. Everyone knows that the human mind plays tricks all the time. If you have a brother or sister with whom you have grown up, that sibling will rarely recollect shared experiences the same way you remember them. Additionally, many forgotten experiences lie in your subconscious, waiting for you to become ready to deal with them before they emerge.

A writer using their life experiences must create an interesting central character and a context within which the character operates, just as the fiction writer does.

Very often this means that a writer of life stories must look hard for certain characters—that is, minor characters—who cause the central character to act decisively, revealing themselves more fully in the process.

Distinguishing Between the Narrator's Voice and the Central Character's Voice

In Dale's story, Elsie is a fully realized character who has her own agenda in life and fools Dale and her mother. Dale is forced to admit that although he thought he was in charge of the situation, he was wrong; young Elsie was in charge. The laugh was on Dale.

Karl Grey's story "The Garage" gives us a picture of a kid who doesn't have much going for him, a situation made more difficult by an indifferent mother and a brutal stepfather. Any action or movement on Karl's part becomes an opportunity for the insensitive parent to retaliate. So what can Karl do? What will he do? Eventually, he finds a place deep inside himself where no one can reach him, no one can touch him, a place of dignity and safety. At this moment, the reader likes Karl. In his own way, he has triumphed over oppression.

When you write life stories, you know the disposition of the central character—their wants, needs, goals, and hopes and dreams. Readers want to see that character struggle to achieve their goals, not wallow in despair.

Consequently, you must make the minor characters that appear in the story more vivid than you might remember them initially. This does not mean that you should falsify them. But you do have to take a close, hard look at them and get behind their wants and needs, just as you would if you were writing fiction.

Often my students will say, "Well, at the time, my character didn't know these things. Yes, I know them now." (For example, the many types of abuse a woman may have endured.) But the fact is, someone in the picture *did* know about the abuse and probably said something, even though it was ignored, making that person a significant minor character in the story. (So often in life, guides exist who know what is good for us but, at the time, we didn't understand what the person was saying or we chose to ignore what they might have been saying.) All these minor characters must have a voice when you write.

Or in other circumstances, a minor character may be the voice of convention, wanting the central character to behave the way everyone else does. The central character can only define him- or herself by heading off in his or her own direction. Thus in Dale's story, his mother disapproves of Dale's decisions—quitting college, going to Los Angeles, bringing Elsie along, smoking cigarettes. But Dale's independence can only occur if he goes against his mother's wishes for him to lead a conventional life. This arc of his progress is made more difficult for him because he does love and respect his mother. Once again, a minor character helps defines who or what the main character is.

When asked what has helped him become the skilled writer he is, Dale had this to say:

> Sounds mundane, but switching to the computer screen years ago expanded my ability to see what my stories needed on first revisions. Seeing a whole page at once on the bright screen highlights the character/writer concerns, conflicts. Shows a panorama of what's missing, or included. (Some students) amaze me with good writing using pen and paper. As good as

they are, I think they could improve if they applied your "Art of Seeing" and "Character Consciousness" to a computer screen.

To me, after a few paper cross-outs and marginal notes, needed things get lost in the fuzziness. (Also, you have mentioned the better use of left/right brains in two-handed writing.)

Your instruction to get behind the protagonist/antagonists' feelings with their dialogue/actions has helped me the most. My self-centered inner thoughts and feelings [and] narration limited a story's appeal.

Another way of expressing this concept would be to observe that, on the one hand, a central character has a series of concerns (problems) that they want solved. In most stories, they either fail or succeed. On the other hand, the writer's concerns may be something quite different. They may very well be concerned with making a statement about the way the universe works and not so much about the success or failure of the central character who may or may not be an heroic figure. James Joyce's *Ulysses* demonstrates the distinction between the central character's concerns and the writer's concerns.

In this novel—a recreation of the Greek myth in which Ulysses, the warrior, returns home to find his wife is entertaining other suitors—we spend most of the novel with Bloom, the eternal wandering Jew. He knows he must stay away from his home because his wife, Molly, is entertaining Blazes Boylan, her lover. Bloom wants his wife to be his and to have a true identity. Molly, on the other hand, luxuriates in the knowledge that she has the best of both worlds—Bloom's devotion and Boylan's complete, if momentary, affections—all available because of the power of her sexuality. What goes on in Bloom's head is only one aspect of the novel. Joyce, in fact, has a much larger concern—the fate and condition of his beloved Ireland: compromised by its history, its identity uncertain, its future torn among competing factions.

*Separating
the Writer's
Voice from
the Central
Character's
Voice*

Chipping Down to
Character Through Rewriting

Like Michelangelo who spent countless hours chipping away pieces of marble in order to reveal the image he had in his mind, we writers must chip away at the countless words in our mind in order to find the ones that properly create a story. This chipping-away process is what we call rewriting. Some of the pictures in our mind are clichés that we have heard and seen somewhere else. We have to chip away such clichés. Some of the pictures in our mind lack detail, so we must chip until the details emerge. Sometimes our characters' actions do not seem to be rooted in any similar past behavior, so we must create the character's past (backstory), finding similar behavior in that past.

Writers often talk about the importance of rewriting to produce the best possible finished product. However, to beginning writers the concept of rewriting may seem bewildering. For those of us who are a bit long in the tooth, rewriting in school often meant finding spelling and grammar errors in our written work. If I remember correctly, that's how I approached my academic papers, even in college—not much actual rewriting but a lot of proofreading.

For creative writers, the rewriting process is both murky and essential. Of course, no two creative writers rewrite in the same way. Writers like myself create bland structures in the first draft, hardly more than sketches. In fact, I used to criticize myself severely for the inefficacy of my first drafts. Over time, I realized it didn't matter what the first draft looked like, so long as I continued to rewrite with a sense that it would all work out. Writers like my student Dale Crum will go through as many as eight to ten drafts before the final draft is realized. Other writers, like my friend Karl Grey, may not rewrite at all. Karl continuously adds layers and details to the version of the story he has in his head so when he sits down to write, what comes out the first time is well crafted.

Wonderful writing has four main characteristics:

1. The writing style is so rich that the reader can practically taste its quality and deliciousness. The reader feels elevated just savoring how the writer strings words together.

2. The writer's characters are so complete and multifaceted that the reader feels as if they know them well and may share some qualities with them.

3. The storyline grabs its readers forcefully and takes them into another world.

4. The writing gives the reader a sense of the shape of the world—perhaps even the universe—the character lives in. Sometimes it may show the character's life as if the reader is watching events from a great distance.

This unit discusses how to develop an intimate sense of character through the elaboration of inner thoughts and feelings and the delineation of a character's actions and reactions.

Developing Confidence in Your Rewrites

How do you develop confidence that your rewrites are on the right track? Perhaps the most effective way is to work with a writing group that has been trained in how to give helpful, positive feedback. In fact, it is a virtual "must" for every writer to do this. Professional writers, such as Bill Rempel (see page 86), may rely on editors and friends who are writers for feedback. Too often, however, feedback in writing groups is either simplistic ("My, that was nice") or too critical ("Frankly, I was bored by that opening"). I have experienced both extremes as a young writer, and the overabundance of "helpful criticism" I received at UCLA's film school set me back decades in my efforts to write. What each of us needs is insightful, nonjudgmental feedback that focuses on the reader's experience of the story; that is, the feelings that they find have been aroused by the story. Guiding the discussion of the writer's use of techniques is best left to the leader of the group, who is hopefully an experienced professional writer. For more about this process, please see Appendix B on page 189.

Chapter 7

Revealing Character:
Rewriting Inner Thoughts and Feelings

Over the course of my life I have met numerous interesting people, one of whom happens to be my former wife, Gail. During our brief marriage, she finished her bachelor's degree, acquired a master's degree, began a career as a teacher, and had two children.

Having her tell stories of her experiences after our marriage ended has been illuminating for me, especially as Gail is quite adept at revealing her inner thoughts and feelings about her experiences as a woman.

The following is an excerpt from her story "A Normal Life?" which appears on page 149. This excerpt illustrates the importance of finding important, perhaps critical, moments in a story and opening them up through exploring inner thoughts and feelings: (Please note: Gail's references to her "husband" have to do with her second husband, whom she met soon after our separation).

A Normal Life?

by Gail Field

My husband stands over me holding my hand while I lie waiting on the gurney just outside the delivery room. "It's a boy," I say. "We'll name him Martin and call him Marty, just like you."

Marty grips my hand even tighter, his long fingers circling my hand. He swallows hard, blinking, not saying anything. For the first time ever, I see tears moisten his face. He swallows again. "Good job." His voice cracks, and he looks away. I have never felt his hand so tight in mine.

The roses that Marty sent me grace the windowsill in my private room overlooking the entrance to the UCLA Hospital maternity wing. Outside on the narrow patch of green along the driveway entrance, a bed of asters swoon and sway, bending their heads in the slight August breeze, inviting me to take a long look. I, too, was born in the fall, and asters have always been my favorite flower. They bloom just when the weather is changing, just when the cool air comes to surprise us with its announcement of fall. The roses in my room are lovely, romantic, beautiful. But the asters signal a change. Something mysterious and yet inviting. I smile as I think of the change that is coming for our family. This moment, this day, this outcome is what my husband has wanted ever since we met and, I would guess, for long before that.

It was my mother who convinced me that having a baby with Marty was the right thing to do. "He hopes it would be a boy," I began. "I am not sure I am ready, since Jeff and Willy are still in preschool."

Outside my hospital window, the sun is setting now, and I fall into the bed, tired from the labor and from the months of waiting for this day. Now, at age twenty-six, I am a new mother for the third time.

So many times I have taken just one step, without resisting, and things have turned out all right. Like the time I didn't push Marty when he told me he wanted to go out every Friday night to be with his gay friends. Perhaps my reluctance to resist has brought my husband closer to me — has helped him see the value of family and of a traditional lifestyle. So different from what he thought he wanted to be, and maybe, just maybe, what the deepest part of him wanted all along.

Members of our writing group gave high marks to Gail for the sensitivity and deeply felt emotion that her story revealed. When they finished, I added my thoughts and observations — that at the critical moment when she reflects back on her mother's words, we need to see and to feel more of her concerns (that is, more of what the issues are that she has to deal with — the interruption of her teaching career to please her new husband, her concern for the well-being of the two children she has already borne, her uncertainty about her new husband's sexuality and fidelity, and how her mother might handle the latter if she knew).

Gail agreed that the story would be better if she worked on these aspects of the story. Here is the story with the inner thoughts and feelings that occurred at the critical point in the story expanded. (The new material appears in **bold italics.**)

A Normal Life?

by Gail Field

A bluish shaft of light from the hospital ceiling illuminates the side of my husband's face — setting off his sparse beard and the almost undetectable quiver in his strong square jaw. My husband stands over me holding my hand while I lie waiting on the gurney just outside the delivery room. "It's a boy," I say. "We'll name him Martin and call him Marty, just like you."

Marty grips my hand even tighter, his long fingers circling my hand. He swallows hard, blinking, not saying anything. For the first time ever, I see tears moisten his face. He swallows again. "Good job." His voice cracks, and he looks away. I have never felt his hand so tight in mine.

The roses that Marty sent me grace the windowsill in my private room overlooking the entrance to the UCLA Hospital maternity wing. Outside on the narrow patch of green along the driveway entrance, a bed of asters swoon and sway, bending their heads in the slight August breeze, inviting me to take a long look. I, too, was born in the fall, and asters have always been my favorite flower. They bloom just when the weather is changing, just when the cool air comes to surprise us with its announcement of fall. The roses in my room are lovely, romantic, beautiful. But the asters signal a change. Something mysterious and yet inviting. I smile as I think of the change that is coming for our family. This moment, this day, this outcome is what my husband has wanted ever since we met, and, I would guess, for long before that.

It was my mother who convinced me that having a baby with Marty was the right thing to do. "He hopes it would be a boy," I began. "I am not sure I am ready, since Jeff and Willy are still in preschool."

My mother leaned forward, her soft eyes settling on the neat and clean kitchen counter, the flowers in the window, the pictures of family in silver frames on the cabinet tops. She must have been surprised at this orderliness compared with the way I kept my room as a girl, clothes piled high on the rocking chair, dolls scattered about the house. She smiled and lowered her voice.

"You know," she said, her tone soft yet strong, "a good wife does what she can to please her husband. And I know how much Jeffrey and Willy mean to you."

I didn't want to hear this. I preferred to make these decisions myself, without input from my mother. She didn't know the whole truth, and there was no way I was going to tell her. Instead, I nodded as if in agreement and said I understood. I felt like a teenager again, half listening to her, not objecting, then making my own decisions in secret silence.

If she knew Marty spent every Friday night out with his gay friends, doing God only knows what, then she would certainly have an opinion. Then I would have to grapple with that, too, as if I were a child trying to please, caught between the desires of Marty, my parents' wishes, and my own sense.

Outside my hospital window, the sun is setting now, and I fall into the bed, tired from the labor and from the months of waiting for this day. Now, at age twenty-six, I am a new mother for the third time.

I am wondering what my mother would say now, thinking of what I would tell her if I were willing. I'd tell her that I am not really sure whether my decision to give up the birth control pills and have this baby was out of wanting to please my husband or whether I thought I could change him, whether I could make him love us more. Whether I wanted to rescue him from a lifestyle I thought would lead to misery for him and for me. Whether I feel I know what's best for him and for me. Feeling that I could make it all right, like it says in the psychiatry books in Marty's office. I wish I could tell her everything and have her understand without judging.

I would tell her that so many times I have taken just one step, without resisting, and things have turned out all right. Like the time I didn't push Marty when he told me he wanted to go out every Friday night to be with his gay friends. Perhaps my reluctance to resist has brought my husband closer to me. Has helped him see the value of family and of a traditional lifestyle. So different from what he thought he wanted be, and maybe, just maybe, what the deepest part of him wanted all along.

As I read Gail's words, I sense the fullness of her uncertainty. I am drawn into this world of her sensitive, aware, twenty-six-year-old efforts to see clearly what the uncertain future holds. All the threads of her dilemma are well sketched out.

During these years, Gail and I were doing battle, sometimes weekly, often daily. But in later years I came to see, to experience, and to benefit from the deep well of love from which all of Gail's actions stem.

Gail began to write these stories for her son Marty III, who has grown up to be a fine, wise, loving young man, as are our two sons. It is a gift to Marty to see what it is like to have a mother who loves everyone and a father whose lifestyle is quite different from that of the average father. It is also a gift to me to be able to see events from a point of view other than my own and to help her get to the expression of her innermost thoughts and feelings, the ones that she seldom puts into words.

As I mentioned in the Introduction to this book, my primary goal in teaching over the past decade has been to help my students give voice to the most fleeting of their inner thoughts and feelings, to help them put into words the things that they barely realize that they know.

What makes this task easier is that each draft of a story has a life of its own. When you finish that draft, it will call to you in a certain way, and a path toward its final realization will begin to open up. When writers allow each draft to speak to them in its own way, then they allow themselves the most growth, the most awareness, the most understanding of the inner world that many of us inhabit and/or struggle to reach.

Self-Assessments: Gaining Access to Self-Knowledge and the Inner Life

Over the past few years, I have become increasingly interested in how to gain access to one's inner life—my own and that of others. What prompts us, enables us, to look inward and to dig around in our innermost feelings? Gail's story "A Normal Life" tells the reader that she has a rich inner life and that she has access to it. Not everyone has an interest in doing so, but for those who do, Gail's story may prove to be an interesting guide.

The unveiling of deeper levels of inner thought and feeling often occurs at a critical point in a story—the beginning of the "development" section. This is the point in a story where all the important issues have been laid out for the reader (which is the purpose of the "exposition'" section of a story). At the beginning of the development section, the central character must often make a difficult decision regarding the direction they will take. Opening these inner thoughts to the reader provides them with an intimate sense of the character at this early point in the story.

From the beginning of *Writing from Within* almost thirty years ago, I have suggested to my students that they add a P.S. at the ends of their stories if they have additional information they wish to convey to the reader. Over time, I became aware that this P.S. could easily become a place of self-assessment, a place where the writer could look into the mirror of the story and gaze upon their strengths and weaknesses.

Exploring the self-assessment phase of a life story became the focus of a subsequent book, *Character Consciousness*. In this book, I explore an almost infinite number of questions that a writer could ask themselves in the self-assessment phase of writing, such as "Who am I in this story?" "What are my strengths and weaknesses?" and "What character qualities show up in the story that I didn't realize I had?"

These self-assessments have been helpful to a number of my readers and students. They provide a reliable look at their inner lives—their concerns, fears, hopes, dreams, and past history—all based on something objective, the story. Through the medium of unfolding self-assessments, I have been able show students a path into the subconscious, a path that requires neither a PhD in psychology nor the help of an expensive therapist to explore. For an example of a self-assessment, see pages 113–115.

Chapter 8

Unraveling Character:
Rewriting Action and Details

In general, writing done by men and women unfolds in quite different ways. Female writers generally provide their readers with a whole host of inner emotions, very much like the story that Gail Field provided in "A Normal Life." The depth of her emotions as she considered various life options gives the reader a glimpse into her character as a woman.

Men, on the other hand, usually provide their readers with telling glimpses into a character's actions that reveal character qualities, often with strong visual elements against which the character's actions may be seen. Just such a scenario occurs in Bill Rempel's story "Front Page to Hard Cover." (See page 86 for the complete story.)

The depth of his story may be seen in several drafts of one moment from his story. This particular moment unfolds as follows:

> Without question, the biggest challenge in the book was capturing the real Jorge Salcedo. He held high rank in the biggest drug syndicate in history, yet he never trafficked in drugs. He was close to the richest crime bosses on the globe, yet he never got rich. He supervised bodyguards and associated with paid assassins, yet he never harmed anyone. After six and a half years in the company of ruthless killers and traffickers, his biggest crime—and prosecutors considered it a felony under U.S. conspiracy laws—was protecting the security of cartel godfathers and the lives of their families.
>
> To the extent that *At the Devil's Table* succeeds in creating a complex portrait of Jorge, all I can say is: Thanks especially to Will Murphy, my editor at Random House, and to Halpern and friends at the Robbins Office in New York. They battered and abused my pages until the character of Jorge finally shone through in all its enigmatic and ultimately heroic glory. Forty years of journalism may have helped. Not because it taught me how to write, so

much as it taught me to embrace prepublication criticism. Good editing is a lifesaver. I crave it.

As I read over this passage, I asked Bill to give me more details about this moment in the story, especially the interaction that must have taken place between himself and his publishers/editors. Here is his second draft of this moment. (New material appears in *bold italics*)

...after six and a half years in the company of ruthless killers and traffickers, his biggest crime—and prosecutors considered it a felony under U.S. conspiracy laws—was protecting the security of cartel godfathers and the lives of their families.

"But he's too good," Will Murphy, my editor at Random House, complained more than once. The brevity of the original newspaper story had allowed only for the most superficial examination of Jorge's character. It did show how he got recruited into the cartel to help kill trafficking rival Pablo Escobar, Colombia's Public Enemy Number One, how the Cali bosses rejected Jorge's resignation after Escobar died, and how orders to kill a colleague finally drove Jorge to contact the DEA and risk his life to quit the cartel. But the book had to go further—using his actions and often-impossible choices—to show Jorge descend deeper and deeper into the criminal organization. He came out of that process still a good man, but a much better character.

My eyes opened wide with interest at this line: "But the book had to go further—using his actions and often-impossible choices—to show Jorge descend deeper and deeper into the criminal organization. He came out of that process still a good man, but a much better character."

I thought Bill was definitely on the right track, but I still wanted more details regarding the "actions and impossible choices," so I asked Bill to provide me with more details of what had taken place. Bill complied:

"But he's too good," Will Murphy, my editor at Random House, complained more than once. The brevity of the original newspaper story had allowed only for the most superficial examination of Jorge's character *and a handful of key moments. He was recruited into the cartel with an appeal to his patriotism, to help the rival traffickers kill Pablo Escobar, Colombia's Public Enemy Number One. The newspaper story also detailed how the Cali bosses rejected Jorge's resignation after Escobar died and how Jorge finally was driven to risk everything and reach out to the DEA after being ordered to help assassinate a potentially damaging cartel witness. Those were important moments, but the book needed much more. I had to show Jorge descending deeper and deeper into the criminal organization, defining him by the ethical and difficult choices he faced.*

Jorge answered all of my questions, and without apparent hesitation. But, remember, I was learning new details about his cartel years with virtually every interview. Specific elements of his character came into focus well after the first draft and after Murphy's early complaints that Jorge was "too good."

Gradually, that changed. In interviews spanning several months, Jorge detailed over and over his duties with the cartel, adding detail as we dug deeper. He had first designed radio communications systems that served the cartel's business and security interests, but did no one any harm. Later, he was involved in more sinister projects: a blackmail scheme to compromise an anti-narcotics military official. He also bugged phones and earned favor when he once sounded an alarm to protect a multimillion-dollar cash shipment from seizure.

And then there were the paid assassins who considered Jorge a friend. They sometimes told him about plots and murders that he could do nothing to stop without risking the lives of his own wife and children, a seemingly impossible choice. A more imperfect Jorge emerged on the pages of my later drafts—bloodied, haunted, and regretful, but still a good man...and a much better character.

To the extent that At the Devil's Table succeeds in creating a complex portrait of Jorge, all I can say is: Thanks especially to Will Murphy, my editor at Random House, and to Halpern and friends at the Robbins Office in New York. They battered and abused my pages until the character of Jorge finally shone through in all its enigmatic and ultimately heroic glory. Forty years of journalism may have helped. Not because it taught me how to write, so much as it taught me to embrace prepublication criticism. Good editing is a lifesaver. I crave it.

Now I understood what a terrifying, morally compromising position Jorge was in. With each step ("he had first designed radio communications...that did no one any harm..."), I could see, feel, taste, and believe each deeper rung of the hell into which Jorge Salcedo descended.

As a skilled, professional writer, Bill provided me with an ever-more-precise and action-filled picture of Jorge Salcedo. In less than half an hour, we moved from first draft to third draft, e-mailing the various drafts back and forth.

In the real world of storytelling—the world of the journalist—character is revealed through action. Bill and I worked this moment back and forth until Jorge Salcedo's actions revealed how "bloodied, haunted, and regretful" the hero had become by the end of Bill's summary of At the Devil's Table.

My editorial comments to Bill ("more detail") reminded me of the film (and novel) The Andromeda Strain by Michael Crichton, in which "something" from outer space turns the blood of residents of a small town into dust. Eventually that "something" is traced to the inside wall of a vehicle from outer space, which remains invisible until the powers of the camera lens are amplified by a series of "diopters" that magnify the "toxin" until it can be seen, probed, analyzed, and understood.

This process is similar to the way in which investigative writers like Bill Rempel probe the world of their characters, looking for clues to the qualities of their characters in the actions the characters take, a process no different than that used by life-story writers probing their past experiences.

Leaping into Longer Work

Writing life stories often has an interesting impact on writers. As they become more sure of themselves, give themselves up to the task of rewriting over several drafts, and grow skillful in observing and putting into words the actions and thoughts of major and minor characters, they want to do more. "What would it be like if I tried a longer work, perhaps a fictional work? How would I go about it?" they ask.

Writing a novel-length story or work of nonfiction or creating a screenplay may appear to be a daunting task. At one time or another, most people who attempt such a project get bogged down, not knowing where to go, and give up. The key to starting and finishing a large project is to start small. When Leonardo da Vinci conceived of his monumental works—*The Adoration of the Magi*, *The Last Supper*, and *The Equestrian Monument of Francesco Sforza*—he started small. A few sketches of characters around the Madonna and Christ. More sketches of horses. He allowed his concepts to unfold from the characters he observed and created.

Most writers, artists, and musicians draw inspiration for their larger works from smaller works they created earlier in their lifetimes. Picasso's *Guernica* is the product of many, many sketches that evolved over time into the concept he wanted to express: the horrors of the Fascist bombing of the town of Guernica in 1936. It took time for his images of distortion to find their full expression.

In the same way, if you intend or hope to write a novel, you will generally find the inspiration you need in characters you have already explored in life writing. The following stories illustrate how two of my students came to write novels based on characters they created, or re-created, during the time they were in my classes.

One of the most interesting and exciting events that occurs in a writing class is the moment when instructor and student realize that they have just been witness to the creation of a truly fascinating character, one that appears to be so interesting that they deserve to be "set in motion," as we say. In other words, what would this character do in other, even-more-challenging circumstances? How would they react to a different set of obstacles?

That is what took place with J. D. Tousley's character of Tack, which eventually resulted in his novel, *Dangling in the Adios*. It is also what happened when in class we first read about Paula Diggs's impossible, nine-year-old heroine, Suzanne, whom Paula was able to use as the main character in her novel *New Shooter*.

Chapter 9

Turning Life Stories into Novels

Most writers find the prospect of writing a lengthy work of fiction, such as a novel or a screenplay, quite daunting. I know I did when I began writing many years ago. In fact, throughout my years as a filmmaker, I found it almost impossible to tackle a project longer than a few pages. My uncertainties and insecurities got the better of me.

Eventually I began to see that it could be done, and I advised some of my students to take their short life stories into the realm of fiction. I found out that all you need is a *good character*.

If such a character can maintain the reader's interest and can overcome substantial obstacles in a short story, that character can do the same in a longer work of fiction. "Give the character more substantial obstacles and see what happens," I said to my students.

Here is one such character, created by Dirk Tousley, a student of mine for a number of years whom I have mentioned previously. Dirk had been something of a rebel as a youth. He went to college on a hope and a dime, keeping himself flush with cash thanks to his local pool hall skills. His first story looked like this:

> This doodling is an UNFINISHED TREATMENT of a short story or maybe a film I couldn't seem to get a hook on several years ago, but the character undoubtedly morphed into Tack in *Dangling in the Adios*. The story is autobiographical only in my dreams.

The Sweet Life
by J. D. Tousley, author of Dangling in the Adios

My life as a young pool hustler was about as sweet as life gets. In those days, long before MasterCard, when you could sit down at a nice clean lunch counter and get a bowl of steaming chili for a quarter, a slab of apple pie juicier than Mom made for a dime, and a steaming cup of coffee with free refills for a nickel, I usually carried at least two hundred bucks in my right front pocket and a couple of fifties hidden in my wallet. So I was doing all right.

I'm telling you, business life couldn't have been sweeter, played out day by day on a rectangle of green felt four and one half feet wide by nine feet long. And I knew every inch of it.

I was strictly my own man, too. No alarm clock kicking me out of bed at six in the morning. No cranky boss to kiss the ass of. No measly paycheck creating resentment. Instead, I played pool for a living and usually came out ahead. Usually, but not always.

That's when my plucky little blonde girlfriend would rise to the occasion. Sugar loved me dearly and I loved her, loved to hold her in my arms, squeeze her, and feel her quiver in a giggle. Most of the time she had some kind of job, maybe waiting tables, maybe clerking at a drug store, maybe pounding a typewriter in some small office, but always showing up Friday nights with a few tens and maybe a twenty hiding out in a little brown pay envelope. Yet as scant as her pay might be, Sugar was always willing to share if need be. It seems what you may have heard about pool hustlers was occasionally true even of me: chicken one day, feathers the next. But I loved that little gal, and on those rare occasions when I tapped her for a loan, I always paid her back in a day or two, you can be sure.

The opening of this first draft is reminiscent of Dirk's earliest stories of his life as a pool hustler while he was in college. Notice that his first draft is all narrative. Interesting narrative to be sure, but narrative all the same.

Eventually, his life experience as a pool hustler morphed into a novel of a young man's experiences:

Dangling in the Adios

by J. D. Tousley

Chapter One

I've had it with stuck-up sorority girls. They act like they're too grand to do it, then when they finally let you in, they own you lock, stock, and barrel. Take Carolyn Forsythe, for instance, safely locked away from us college boys in her panty girdle. After we first met, I rolled around with her in the backseat of my convertible every night for two weeks, trying to pry her out of that medieval contraption, until late one night I got her to wriggle out of it on her own and start enjoying life. And it's been great. I never had it so steady before. But I'm paying for it with my freedom. Whenever Carolyn crooks her finger, I'm supposed to roll over and bark. You'd think she owned me. Now she's ragging me to quit playing nine ball so we can study together. Hell, I don't need study. That's what brains are for. And I'm not about to give up nine ball. Pool is my life, and besides, it brings in about thirty bucks a week.

How different with Cricket, my appreciative little drugstore clerk. On our second date, I slid her skimpy panties down her bare legs and off her feet in a flash, what with no elastic wall, hooks, wires, or buttons to overcome. Panties off, and there it was. When we're not making love, she spends a lot of time in the crook of my arm, looking up at me attentively and asking questions I can answer.

I met Cricket a couple of weeks ago. She clerks at the drugstore around the corner from campus. One day I went in to buy a comb. Five minutes later I had a new comb and a new girlfriend. Mostly I take her to drive-in movies and an out-of-the-way beer joint called Snookums in south Kansas City where I won't run into anyone Carolyn knows. Carolyn has gone home to St. Louis for a few weeks during summer break, which gives Cricket and me time to get acquainted.

Sex with Cricket is the best ever. Just thinking about her gives me a warm feeling inside I've never had before. Nothing's perfect though. Her father doesn't like me, and he's getting in my way. Just today Cricket reminded me on the phone that tonight is our seventh date. "Daddy raises Cain if I go steady," she said. "We'll have to find another way to meet before he goes berserk."

It's nearly dark but still hot and humid as I park my car in front of Cricket's house, get out, and look around. My bright green Mercury convertible is definitely out of place in this working-class neighborhood of fading white frame houses and scrubby lawns. Though World War II has been over four years, some of the houses still display Gold Stars in their front windows.

I'm dressed in a navy blue polo shirt, white duck pants, and cordovan loafers, perfect attire for a summer night date with a cute girl. I'm feeling good and looking good, ready for a Saturday night blast with Cricket.

Looks like I'm in luck. Daddy isn't sitting on the porch steps as usual, and his old tired Studebaker is nowhere in sight. Hot damn! I won't have to face him tonight. But my high spirits are short-lived. As I mount the steps, his gravelly voice coming from inside the screened porch begins the challenge. "Well, if it ain't Joe College." His cheap cigar smoke hangs in the humid air.

"Evening, Mr. Horner," I muster, unable to see him through the screen. But once I'm inside the porch, I make him out in the dusk, swinging slowly back and forth in his porch swing.

"I brought you a Dutch Master."

"Tryin' to suck in with me, huh?"

I ignore the bastard's remark, hand him the Dutch Master, and ask, "Is Cricket ready yet?"

He rolls the cigar between thumb and forefinger, testing its freshness, before setting it aside on the porch railing. "Why the hell you call her Cricket? Her name's Josephine. If I wanted her to be Cricket, I'd uh named her Cricket."

The following provides another example of a short life story turned into a novel. The author portrayed herself as precocious and impossible, always a step ahead of everyone else, but her mother's exasperation was always evident. This created a fascinating, self-centered, but creative and intriguing character. I suggested she turn this character loose in a story, perhaps a mystery, and see what happens. Here is Paula's original story, followed by the beginning of her novel:

Manana Is Good Enough for Me

by Paula Diggs

I don't want to eat tomato soup again on Saturday, but here it is, and I have to clean my bowl. "As the ships go out to sea, I push my spoon away from me," I say to my little sister Kathleen.

"Show off," Kathleen says. She is only three and doesn't know how to eat soup properly. Since I am nine I have good manners, even though sometimes Mother says I show off and that is a bad thing to do.

Miss Hansen ate her tomato soup properly yesterday when I brought her home for lunch. She is my fourth grade teacher, and she is just beautiful. She has two big braids that she winds around her head. Her fiancé was killed in the war we are having overseas with the Germans, so everyone is trying to be extra kind to her. Mother let me bring her home for lunch. We had tomato soup and cottage cheese on Mother's special clear green plates. I got to walk back and forth from school with my teacher. She is wonderful. She told Mother I am very imaginative and talented. She told Mother that I organized a group of girls to put on plays at recess. I like to make up the plays. Mother said she's not surprised, I like to show off. I guess I can't help it, but I try not to. The plays I make up are about a princess who is captured by an ogre and has to escape. I am the princess, and my friend Sarah is the fairy godmother. There are lots of other parts for elves and fairies. My boyfriend, George, gets to play the ogre and the prince because he wants to play with us even though we are a girls' club.

Sarah is my best friend. She has dark curly hair like Mother's and a happy round face. Mother said she would be pretty if she didn't look so Semitic. Mother likes to use big words. Sarah is thin like me, so I guess that is what it means. Mother told me I would be attractive if I weren't so thin.

Lunch was almost over when the phone rang. I listen and Mother says, "I don't know if she can come. I'll have to ask her father. Thank you for calling."

"Who?" Daddy Don says. "Mrs. Stein, Sarah's mother. They are having a birthday party for Sarah. Do you think I should let Miss Big Ears go?"

"That's very nice of them," Daddy Don answers.

"It's nice, but...."

"But what?" says Daddy Don.

"Well they are Jewish and so ostentatious. The party is at suppertime, and there will be games after. We don't do that sort of thing."

"I don't know what you mean," Daddy Don says. "This isn't Kansas, and 1944 isn't the dark ages in this country."

Ostentatious is a word I don't know either, and I read a lot. Sarah's house is beautiful. It is big with lots of rooms. It smells good, like lemons. Maybe that is what it means, something like fancy. Her father has a department store. They have pretty plates with flowers on them and long lace curtains. I went to her house two times. Her brother, Aaron, has good manners for a boy. He is twelve years old and shook my hand when we were introduced. He is nice and quiet and is always reading. When I went to Sarah's, we read our Nancy Drew books and made up plays where we were the detectives and solved mysteries. I love Sarah's house.

Mother said Sarah can't come here because she would be uncomfortable because we are Christians. I am happy that I got to go to Sarah's house. She is my best friend ever. I am always comfortable with her.

Now I am going to get to go to Sarah's birthday party because my little sister Kathleen let her friend Joanie, who is two, take my darling turtle Sweetie out of its bowl and stepped on it and squished it all over the place. When I saw what happened to poor Sweetie, I started screaming until I thought I was going to faint. Mother said I could go to Sarah's birthday party if I would just calm down. So I did.

The afternoon of the party I was so excited. I made a mask to wear in case it is a costume party. I put on my prettiest electric blue dress with big sleeves. Mother braided my hair in French braids and put bright ribbons at the end. Daddy Don drove me to the party. I felt just like a princess. All the girls in my class were there and a few boys who were Aaron's friends. There were lots of relatives too. It was a big party. The food was delicious, and I spilled a little of my Coke, but no one said anything. There was a cake from a bakery with flowers all over. It was just like a dream. Sarah had on a beautiful dress with ruffles and was nice to everyone.

After dinner we played games. Pin the Tail on the Donkey and Telephone. Then Mrs. Stein said the last game will be a talent show. Everyone was very excited. Some girls sang a song, and some did a dance. One boy recited a poem about a ship that sunk. I couldn't think of anything to do. At the very end, I raised my hand and got up and sang this song.

"Manana is good enough for me. The faucet, it is dripping, and the fence is falling down. My pocket needs some money, so I can't go into town. My brother, he ain't working and my sister doesn't care. My car it needs a motor so it won't go anywhere. Manana, manana, manana is soon enough for me."

I knew all the words and got really loud and expressive as I went on, and on the last verse every one sang with me. Then it was over, and the adults decided the prizes. I was amazed. I got the first prize. It was a heart locket. I cried when they gave it to me, I was so happy. I felt like I was full of bursting bubbles.

Then it was time to go home. Mrs. Stein drove me home in their big Buick. The night was dark and full of stars. Mrs. Stein was smiling all the time. She smelled like flowers. She had sort of a face of a fairy godmother. I felt just like a princess with a magic locket. When we got to my house, I surprised myself. I gave Mrs. Stein a kiss on the cheek and thanked her for the best day of my life. She gave me a hug and laughed. Mother waved at her when I came in.

"Did you have a good time?" she asked. "Oh yes," I said, "it was very ostentatious and I had a wonderful time."

"You must be tired, " Mother replied, "go to bed. We have our Love One Another meeting at church early tomorrow...."

In the story, the reader sees that this little girl loves attention, loves to use big words, loves to shade meanings to her advantage, gets into trouble, and pretends not to know why. It is easy to see what a handful she would be to her devoted but exhausted mother, who is not nearly as broad-minded and observant as is this little girl. The reader delights in this character because, even though she is based on Paula's own person, the writer does not shy away from showing the character's many flaws, include her love of showing off and the way it annoys those around her.

At my suggestion, Paula decided to create a fictional story around this child. Because the child in real life liked to play detective, I suggested that she allow this child to become a detective, at age nine. The result is shown in the following section.

New Shooter
A novel by Paula Diggs

Chapter One: Just Listen to Me

A huge slobbering Doberman Pincher clamps his jaws on the little dog's throat. Blood shoots out and splatters all over me. A swarm of bats flies at my eyes. I can't see. Run and climb a tree to get away. Climb higher and higher foot slips and start to fall. Falling and falling down, down, down… Below me a large bug stands on home plate, his bat in position to swing as I fall in front of him. A hand touches my shoulder and grabs me. "Help," I cry, "help, help me, please!"

"Calm down, Suzanne. It's all over. No one's going to hurt you. You're dreaming." Daddy Don and Mother stand by my bed.

"No," I tell them. "Out there on the street. I can hear them."

"It's only crickets, Go back to sleep. You're nine years old, a big girl, stop imagining things. Nothing's going to hurt you now."

Those bad dreams keep bothering me. Things without heads follow me around. They try to make me eat stuff that smells bad. Spam. Poison. It makes me gag. Sometimes I throw up in my bed. Last night was the worst ever.

So when I come down for breakfast the next morning, Mother tells me I look like something the cat dragged in. What does that mean? I couldn't get back to sleep at all. Ideas of dark things jumped around in my head. All night. A claw grabbed me. It held on. I had to stay awake, or they would get me. I was alone. Really alone. All by myself. No one would help me.

"I cried in my sleep all night, Mother. I thought they were coming to get me. I could hear their feet." Mother takes things in and out of the drawer. Over and over. Everything nice and tidy.

(For the rest of the chapter, turn to page 140 in the "Stories" section at the back of the book.)

If a writer has at their fingertips a character who can maintain the interest of the audience, then writing a novel becomes much less of a burden. What makes an interesting character? Every character must have a goal, an objective that they intend to pursue. The more noble the goal, generally the more interesting the character, although this may not always be the case. This is also true for the antagonist and the minor characters.

Writers often talk about "the stakes," as in, "How high are the stakes?" In Hollywood films, the stakes often involve saving a life, or perhaps all of civilization. In more subtle films and novels, the stakes are often matters of identity, self-worth, and unrealized dreams from long ago.

When a character's goal is clearly defined (even though it may change in the course of the novel), the obstacles they face become important. The greater the obstacles, the more interesting the conflict.

With the goal and the obstacles in mind, the writer must create character qualities in the central character and in the minor characters that make overcoming the obstacles possible.

Conflicting qualities often make for an interesting character. In Paula's story, the nine-year-old detective knows a great deal—about a lot of things that don't matter. And she often knows nothing about what's going on around her. Sometimes this disconnect can contribute to a wonderful sense of fun, even absurdity.

Backstory contributes to the audience's understanding of what has happened before the curtain comes up on a story and is essential to most, although not all, novels. In Dirk's novel, *Dangling in the Adios* (see the excerpt on page 60), his second-paragraph backstory gives the reader all the information necessary to understand Tack's predicament.

The main difference between a novel and a short story, such as a life story, is in the arc of the story. A short story generally has only one climactic scene followed by a denouement. In a novel, the writer must create smaller climaxes and denouements that culminate in a final, climactic scene.

Chapter 10

Writing Creative Stories

Writing life stories is to a writer as sketching is to an artist. It is a first step to creating something bigger. Leonardo da Vinci, the great Italian painter, filled up many, many sketchbooks with ideas before he created *The Last Supper*.

Creating sketches from life based on your life stories will help you do other kinds of creative writing. One kind of writing is called "creating personal myths."

In this kind of writing, you choose a legend, folktale, myth, or fable and look for the meaning behind that myth or legend. Then, find a moment in your own life that also illustrates that meaning or message. If you cannot find it in your own life, make up or imagine what is necessary.

Some examples are provided in the following section.

The Tortoise and the Hare
(The Turtle and the Rabbit)

The tortoise and the hare started a race. The hare raced off to a big lead. The tortoise crawled along very slowly. Soon the hare got tired and rested. The tortoise kept crawling along. The hare saw the tortoise coming and bounded off. Soon the hare became tired again. The tortoise kept crawling. This time, the tortoise crawled past the hare. The hare laughed, sprang to his feet, and raced past the tortoise. Again he got tired, rested, and let the tortoise pass him. When at last he started hopping toward the finish line, it was too late. The tortoise had passed the finish line.

MEANING OR MESSAGE

The slow but sure way wins out against the fast and furious.

Personal Myth or Legend

Hector and Jorge are in love with Elena, who likes them both but is not sure whom she wants to marry. Both men decide they will go to the United States to become successful.

Hector is a handsome young singer and trumpet player. He is a big success playing in a band. He makes good money, dates beautiful women, and sends Elena expensive presents.

Jorge works as a box boy, learns English, becomes a citizen, and works his way up to manager of the store. Every week he sends Elena a letter and a rose.

Sometimes Hector doesn't get work, so he doesn't write to Elena. Sometimes she doesn't hear from him for several months. Then she gets an expensive present. But she gets a letter from Jorge every week.

In the end, they each propose marriage to Elena.

Whom does she marry? Well, since the author is illustrating the moral of the tortoise and the hare with a real-life story, we know she chooses Jorge. What would you do?

EXERCISE: MAKING UP A MYTH

Look up one of the following myths:

1. The myth of Daedalus and Icarus

2. The myth of Sisyphus

3. The myth of Oedipus

4. The myth of Orpheus and Eurydice

5. Another myth you know about, not necessarily of Greek origin

Summarize the myth.

What is its meaning or message?

Now make up a personal myth from your life or imagination based on the existing myth's meaning.

Once you have the basic story, add the following elements to it to make it better, based on your life-writing skills:

1. present tense

2. feelings

3. dialogue

4. inner thoughts and feelings

5. thumbnail sketches of the characters

Personal Note: These myths from ancient Greece continue to be of interest because they tell us so much about ourselves. They have formed the backbone for education in the Western world for the past two thousand years.

During the last twenty years, the growing recognition of the great value of other cultures, particularly Latino, African-American, and Native-American cultures in the United States, has awakened interest in the myths, legends, folk tales, and fables of these cultures.

Those of you who come from a non-Anglo/WASP background can bring to your writing group an understanding of some myth, legend, or fairytale that you learned in your family, church, or school. Write down the story now to share with and enrich the group.

If you need more ideas, here are a few:

Interesting Legends

1. The Coyote (The Trickster) — Native American
   Just when you have what you want, the coyote comes along and steals it away.

2. The Phoenix — Egyptian
   The phoenix is a bird that lived five hundred years then made a pile of spices in the Arabian desert, burned itself to ashes, and came forth from the ashes to repeat the cycle.

3. The Hare — African
   The hare tricked all its victims into doing its bidding. When the people of the village set a trap for it, the village chief was the one trapped, and the hare got away.

4. El Dorado — Spanish
   El Dorado was a mythical city located in the desert of the western United States where everything was golden.

5. Fountain of Youth — Spanish
   The fountain of youth was a spring filled with a liquid that enabled the user to remain young forever. People exhausted themselves in pursuit of this mythical spring.

6. Faust — German
   Faust was a man who made a pact with the devil. Satan granted him one wish: to have greater knowledge than anyone else. Then the devil forced him to pay the price.

Can you convert your culture's myth into a story from your life or your imagination? Do it now.

The following is another example of a highly creative story. After writing a few life stories to acquire the skills of using narrative, dialogue, and inner thoughts and feelings, the writer created a series of stories about mammals and wrote each story from the point of view of the baby coming into the world, growing up and learning to fend for itself:

Molloko, the California Condor
by Inés Horovitz

I can hear the wind blowing through the pine trees. It's sunny outside, and I am waiting for my mom or my dad to bring me some food. I live in a cave high up on a cliff. It's a little scary: I almost fell off a few times. I am also a little scared that a golden eagle will find me. My mom told me to watch out for them. I think I can hear my mom or my dad now: There's a hissing sound.

"Hi Molloko, good morning!"

"Hi Mom! I love it when I hear the hissing sound because I know you or Dad are near. How do you make it?"

"It's the wind going through our wing feathers."

I'm really hungry, so I'm very excited to see her! She smells really clean. I can tell she took a bath. I would love to take baths too, but I have to learn to fly first to get to a bathing place.

I flap my wings as hard as I can to let my mom know I can't wait for my food anymore. She stands beside me and opens her bill over my head, so I stick my head in it. Some food comes out of her throat. It's been in her tummy and it's a little digested already. I take the food in my mouth. After I swallow it, more food keeps coming. When we're done, I try to get my head out of her throat but I'm stuck. My mom puts her foot on my neck and pushes me down to the floor of our cave so my head comes out. What a relief! I can breathe now!

"What food was that, Mom?"

"It was a dead weasel I found on a big boulder. It probably fell off the cliff above."

"Have you ever caught any animals, Mom?"

"No, dear. We don't catch animals. We just find dead ones."

"But I like to play I catch things, Mom. I will catch animals when I grow up."

"You like to play that way because a long, long time ago, our great, great, many times great grandparents were different from us, and they hunted for their food. But we condors and vultures have changed over millions of years to just eat carcasses, dear. Our babies still play that way because you are born with the need to learn that skill, but you will lose the need to use it when you grow up. It's okay to play that way, though—it's fun, isn't it?"

A few weeks later I start walking out of our cave onto a narrow ledge, and I wait for my parents from there. I am a little afraid of flying still, but I have been flapping my wings inside our cave to practice and get stronger. If I fell off the ledge, I think I would be okay: I could flap my wings hard enough that I would not hit the rocks below too hard, I hope.

"Have you preened your feathers this morning?"

"Yes, Mama."

"They look shiny! I can tell you've been taking good care of them. Just a few spots need a little preening. I'll feed you, and I'll preen those spots after," says my mom.

I love it when she does that. I feel a little ticklish. Sometimes I preen her feathers, too.

"Molloko, you should start flying off into the canyon. We've had five full moons since you hatched. You are old enough now, and your feathers look great! You should start using them! I'm off to find more food now. See you later!"

I am feeling good now that my mom fed me. They don't feed me that often anymore: Some days they don't feed me at all. I can see some birds flying by from my ledge. It looks like so much fun! Maybe I could try flying off. Maybe I am ready to do it now. My heart is beating so fast, it feels like it's going to take off before I do. Here I go…. One, two, three! Weeeeeee!!!!!!

I'm off, and I flap my wings as hard as I can. They sound loud! At first I am going straight down, but then I manage to fly forward for a short stretch, and then my wings get tired and I start going down again. Mom, Dad!!! Anyone around???? Help!!!! There's a tree coming straight at me!!! "No, no tree, out of my way, move, move!" But it won't move. I crash right into it. OUCH!!!!!

I hold on to a branch for a while until I recover from my emergency landing. I'd love to get back to my nest! But I'll have to do it little by little. I'll try to get to a nearby sequoia tree as my first stop. It's not far. Maybe I can do it! I take off and lose height at first but manage to fly up a little and ahead!

"Here I come, sequoia! Stick out a branch for me!!!!"

But the sequoia won't listen. It just stays still, and I have to find a branch myself. It's hard, though! I can't really aim at anything to land on, I can't fly that well yet. I finally crash against a branch. OUCH!!!!

— • • • —

This unit has explored other ways that writers can profit from writing from deeper within.

Additionally, don't forget that the world of your creative imagination is as fertile a breeding ground for stories as any other part of your life experience. Practicing life-story writing as a regular part of your weekly routine gives you confidence and the momentum to explore fascinating, off-to-the-side, almost-out-of-view dimensions of your imagination. Such people as engineers, doctors, and academics, with a plethora of degrees (indicating their left brains operate well) may be surprised to find that they have active, creative, right brains that can be as fertile with imagination as those of any writer, actor, or painter. It just takes a little patience and openness to a new process to find the wonders of the imagination…and the ability to go ever deeper into mysterious places within yourself.

Chapter II

Creating Screenplays
from Short Stories

(Please note: This section is a chapter from my book *The Art of Seeing: Appreciating Motion Pictures as an Art Form and as a Business*.)

Writing a motion-picture screenplay is a subtle art form and a maddening craft. By their very nature, screenplays are incomplete in the same way that plays are incomplete: They provide only the text with which the actors and director must work. Creating subtext that breathes life into the screenplay and the finished film or play is the job of the actor and director. However, a skilled screenwriter can give strong indications to the actor and director about what the subtext should look like. A good script means nothing until the screenplay gets to the screen, so any indications of subtext may enlist the interest of a producer, director, and/or actors.

As I described earlier in this book, every writer—whether novelist, short-story writer, playwright, or screenwriter—has three basic tools with which to work: narrative, dialogue, and inner thoughts and feelings. The novelist or short-story writer must be skilled at narrative and good with dialogue. Both have the advantage of being able to express inner thoughts and feelings directly. The screenwriter must be skilled at creating narrative that can be communicated through action and dialogue. Their success, however, derives from the way that they handle inner thoughts and feelings that can seldom be expressed directly.

There are, of course, many ways for screenwriters to fail (or succeed) in translating a novel or short story to the screen. Eliminating the author's use of inner thoughts and feelings may be one of those failings. Misunderstanding and changing a character and their qualities is another place where screenwriters go astray. Sometimes a slavish devotion to the external events of an author's work may create a bed of quicksand from which the screenwriter cannot free themselves.

Because many scripts are adaptations of novels, short stories, and plays, let's take a look at a classic American short story to see how it was adapted to the screen. I have in mind Ernest Hemingway's "The Short Happy Life of Francis Macomber." An example of American short fiction at its best, "Macomber" was one of Hemingway's favorites. The short story was also made into a 1947 movie, *The Macomber Affair*, starring Gregory Peck. The story is typical Hemingway: Every moment in the story is a test of a man's manhood.

In the short story "The Short Happy Life of Francis Macomber," a handsome, athletic, very rich, rather naïve man goes on safari in Africa, accompanied by his wife and their guide, Wilson. Let's look at the opening:

The Short Happy Life of Francis Macomber
by Ernest Hemingway

It was now lunch time and they were all sitting under the double green fly of the dining tent pretending that nothing had happened.

"Will you have lime juice or lemon squash?" Macomber asked.

"I'll have a gimlet," Robert Wilson told him.

"I'll have a gimlet, too. I need something," Macomber's wife said.

"I suppose it's the thing to do," Macomber agreed. "Tell him to make three gimlets."

This seems like idle conversation, yes? Except for the phrase "pretending nothing had happened." What does this line mean? Hemingway goes on:

Francis Macomber had, half an hour before, been carried to his tent from the edge of the camp in triumph on the arms and shoulders of the cook, the personal boys, the skinner…he had shaken all their hands, received their congratulations, and then gone into his tent and sat on the bed until his wife came in. She did not speak to him when she came in and he left the tent at once…to sit in the shade.

So the public perception of Macomber is that he has done something to be proud of, but Mrs. Macomber doesn't share that view. Next, Hemingway describes these characters:

Mrs. Macomber looked at Wilson quickly. She was an extremely handsome and well-kept woman of the beauty and social position which had, five years before, commanded five thousand dollars as the price of endorsing, with photographs, a beauty product which she never used. She had been married to Francis Macomber for eleven years.

"He's is good lion, isn't he?" Macomber said. His wife looked at him now. She looked at both men as though she had never seen them before. One, Wilson, the white hunter, she knew she had never truly seen before. He was about middle height with sandy hair, a stubby mustache, a very red face, and extremely cold eyes with faint wrinkles at the corners that grooved merrily when he smiled. He smiled at her now.

Francis Macomber was very tall, very well built if you did not mind that length of bone, dark, his hair cropped like an oarsman, rather thin-lipped, and was considered handsome. He was dressed in the same sort of safari clothes that Wilson wore except that his were new, he was thirty-five years old, kept himself very fit, was good at court games, had a number of big game fishing records, and had just shown himself, very publicly, to be a coward.

Ah, so there it is: Macomber has shown himself to be a coward. What kind? Because this is a safari—probably a wild animal hunt—the reader can suppose that Macomber ran from a lion or a rhino. If so, what will the consequences be?

Early in the paragraph Hemingway damns Macomber with faint praise: "if you didn't mind the length of bone" (gangly), "thin-lipped" (unsensual), "good at court games" (a too-civilized form of mano-a-mano competition).

"Here's to the lion," he [Macomber] said. "I can't thank you enough for what you did."

Margaret, his wife, looked away from him and back to Wilson.

"Let's not talk about the lion," she said.

Wilson looked over at her without smiling and now she smiled at him.

"Hadn't you ought to put your hat on, Mr. Wilson...you have a very red face."

"Drink," said Wilson.

"I don't think so," she said. "Francis drinks a great deal but his face is never red."

"It's red today," Macomber tried to joke.

"No," said Margaret, "It's mine that's red today. But Mr. Wilson's is always red."

From this we see that Macomber has done something to be ashamed of, apparently something cowardly, such as running away from danger. In all likelihood, Wilson saved his life and shot the lion. Macomber tries to joke about his cowardice, as if it's a small thing—and maybe it is to Macomber. But it's a big thing to his wife. She is ashamed. Or is it something else? Perhaps they have a relationship in which each struggles for power and now Mrs. Macomber has the power on her side. It seems that way, from the way she flirts with Wilson.

The two men talk about the natives, Wilson allowing that a good beating every now and then keeps the natives in line. Macomber replies, "We all take a beating every day, you know, one way or the other," a line suggesting that Mrs. Macomber has been indulging herself in exercising her power over her husband quite often. Moments later, Macomber says:

> "I'm awfully sorry about this lion business. It doesn't have to go any further, does it? I mean no one will hear about it, will they?"

So now we see that Macomber is ashamed of his actions and he doesn't want the world to hear about them. Or is he? It is an odd line, so "on the money" (see page 39 for an explanation of this term).

If the reader repeats the line, remembering that Macomber is a very rich man, they get the impression that he is more concerned about the annoyance of having failed at this sport than the shame. He certainly sounds more matter-of-fact than deeply wounded. Wilson is put off:

> "You mean will I tell it at the Mathaiga Club?" Wilson looked him coldly. "No, I'm a professional hunter. We never talk about our clients. Supposed to be bad form to ask us not to talk, though."

Hemingway follows with several lines of Wilson's inner thoughts and feelings:

> He had decided now that to break would be much easier. He would eat by himself and could read a book with his meals. They would eat by themselves. He would see them through the safari on a very formal basis—what was it them French called it? Distinguished consideration—and it would be a damn sight easier than having to go through this emotional trash. He'd insult him and make a good clean break.
>
> "I'm sorry," Macomber said. "I didn't realize that. There are a lot of things I don't know."
>
> So what could he do, Wilson thought. He was all ready to break it off quickly and neatly and here the beggar was apologizing after he had just insulted him. He made one more attempt. "…you know in Africa no woman ever misses her lion and no white man ever bolts."

A moment later, Macomber says, "I bolted like a rabbit." We might expect him to feel humiliated by his lack of courage, but he's strangely forthright—not ashamed, just nonplused. Hemingway reveals more of Wilson's thoughts:

> Now what in hell were you going to do about a man who talked like that, Wilson wondered.
>
> Wilson looked at Macomber…[who]…had a pleasant smile if you did not notice how his eyes showed when he was hurt.

"Maybe I can fix it up on buffalo," he [Macomber] said. "We're after them next, aren't we?"‘

Here, the exposition comes to an end. Macomber has shown he is a coward but not a blustering, silly coward — just a matter-of-fact coward, not a man for whom Wilson can summon any contempt.

Mrs. Macomber, however, enjoys her husband's vulnerability to the fullest, savaging him like a picador teasing the bull before sticking the sword in its shoulders:

"Why not let up on the bitchery just a little Margot," Macomber said.
"I suppose I could," she said, "since you put it so prettily."
So, Robert Wilson thought to himself, she is giving him a ride, isn't she? Or do you suppose that's her idea of putting up a good show. How should a woman act when she discovers her husband is a bloody coward? She's damn cruel but they're all cruel. They govern, of course, and to govern one has to be cruel sometimes. Still, I've seen enough of their damn terrorism.

Before going on to the development of the story, Hemingway takes the reader into a backstory that allows them to experience and to feel every bit of Macomber's cowardice in facing the lion.

Returning to the present, Hemingway begins the development section of the story by having Margot continue Macomber's humiliation by sleeping with Wilson.

Yet Macomber does not go to pieces. Like one of the animals being stalked, he's wounded and hurt, but not crippled. Despite her infidelity — which has taken place many times before — he is alert and ready for the hunt. (For a more complete analysis of this story, please see my book *The Art of Seeing: Appreciating Motion Pictures as an Art Form and as a Business*.)

Adapting "The Short Happy Life of Francis Macomber" to the Screen

How might a writer translate parts of this story into the language of the motion picture? Let's look at the beginning, this time cast by me in motion-picture script format.

The Short Happy Life of Francis Macomber

EXT. AFRICAN DESERT — TENT — DAY

On a vast plain of the Serengeti Desert, several small tents dot an oasis. Two Land Rovers sit behind the tents, as the "beaters" eat their lunch at some remove from two men and a woman who sit beneath the fly of the dining tent.

EXT. UNDER THE TENT FLAP

A tall man leans back in his chair. He is Francis Macomber, rich, wealthy, mid-forties. A sportsman. Next to him sits his wife, Margot, a once-beautiful woman, now a bit lined in the face. Across from them sits the guide, Robert Wilson, middle height, and red-faced from living outdoors all his adult life.

MACOMBER

Will you have lime juice or lemon squash?

WILSON

I'll have a gimlet.

MARGOT MACOMBER

I'll have a gimlet, too. I need something.

MACOMBER

I suppose it's the thing to do. Tell him to make three gimlets.

• • •

This is the scene almost exactly as Hemingway wrote it. The physical descriptions, the dialogue, everything. Except that it means nothing. The most pregnant phrase in the beginning—"they were all sitting under the double green fly of the dining tent pretending that nothing had happened"—has not been dealt with in any way. Consequently, there is no opening.

Ask yourself what each character wants. According to Hemingway, Macomber is there to shoot lions. But in reading the story, the reader learns that he's there for some other reason. His wife taunts him as she has done in the past, so he's looking for a way to get past her taunts. And perhaps her taunts serve a purpose—to goad him into facing what he has never faced: his basic cowardice.

So that's what he wants: to gain his manhood.

And that's what she wants: to remind him of his smallness, his insignificance, his impotence. Is that what she wants, really? No, the author has something else in mind.

What does she really want? To feel powerful.

Having used her beauty all her life to get what she wants, she knows her power lies in her face and her figure. But now that both are fading into middle-aged wrinkles—and knowing that her husband looks a hell of a lot better than she does, she must find some other way to feel powerful. How does she go about it? By reminding Macomber of his impotent insignificance. Thus he will stay close because she's smarter and stronger. Uh-huh, that'll work.

What does Wilson want? The reader knows from the story that he loves the opportunity to match wits with and to test the mettle of wild animals. He also loves bailing these "sporty" fellows out of trouble and bagging their wives, if the occasion warrants, as his bounty for saving their skins. So he wants to feel superior to these rich people. But if a man who has shown himself to be a cowardly sport suddenly turns out to be ready to test his mettle in some earnest way, Wilson will give him all the credit in the world. So his secret desire is to help men become men, as would a top sergeant who brings his infantry troops to the front lines for the first time.

What does he want? To free men of their cowardice.

So if Macomber wants to find his manhood, running away feels bad, feels like a defeat, or perhaps he's trying to overcome some inability to focus when panic surfaces. How would a writer express this in action and dialogue?

— • • • —

EXT. UNDER THE TENT FLAP

Francis Macomber leans back in his chair. Rich, wealthy, mid-forties, a sportsman with a surprising innocence about him. His smooth cheeks and bright eyes suggest a man who has not been out in the sun more than necessary. Next to him sits his wife, a once-beautiful woman, now a bit lined in the face, who has been out in the sun too often. Across from them sits the guide, Robert Wilson, middle height, and red-faced from living outdoors all his adult life, coupled with a pint of whisky at the end of each day.

A servant brings them vodka gimlets, frosted, out here in the desert.

MACOMBER
(raising his glass)

A toast.

MARGOT MACOMBER
(giving him a look)

How you do love your toasts.

WILSON

I'm in.

He lifts his glass, just barely. Macomber clinks his glass against his wife's.

MACOMBER

To Mr. Wilson, a crack shot.

MARGOT MACOMBER

(*eying Wilson*)

Umm, yes. A crack shot. Put it right where he wanted it. I suppose you're always pretty much on target, aren't you, Mr. Wilson?

Macomber's eyes narrow as he gives her a look. Wilson catches their look.

WILSON

Paid to do it, Mrs. Paid to do it.

MARGOT

My husband's a crack shot, aren't you, dear?

Macomber eyes her, holding back something.

MACOMBER

(*shrugging*)

No one's perfect, my dear.

Margot leans toward Wilson.

MARGOT

A perfectly wonderful shot, Mr. Wilson. Yours, I mean. A work of art I should say, you—standing there waiting—until the last moment. Then pow! The crack of the rifle. Down it goes, poor helpless, frightened beast.

She gives Macomber's arm a patronizing pat.

MACOMBER

(*shrugging*)

Helpless, eh?

(*looking up*)

Tomorrow, Mr. Wilson?

He clinks Wilson's gimlet glass. Wilson who has closed his eyes to the two of them, awakens with the slow rattle of a snake uncoiling.

WILSON

Tomorrow, Mr. Macomber? I should have thought you might want to wait a day. Gather yourself.

MARGOT

(*laughing*)

Oh, you know how we Americans are. Fall off a horse, get
right back on. We're taught that from birth.

Wilson, fully awake now, sizes up the two of them. He downs his gimlet.

> WILSON

If you'll excuse me.
> *(getting up)*
Tomorrow, eh?

He gets up, taking his gimlet glass with him, walks over to where the
"beaters" are eating, and tosses the glass to an elderly black man who
washes dishes.

> SERVANT
> *(laughing, showing rotten teeth)*

Americans, boss?

> WILSON
> *(shrugging)*

Americans. They say the women all have one breast—so they
can draw back the bow string a little better.

He motions as if to draw a bow string across his chest and shoot an arrow
then swings around as if to send it into the servant's heart. They laugh.

———— • • • ————

As you evaluate the job done on this section of the story, consider six questions:

Q: Is it faithful to Hemingway's intent?
A: It has established what each character wants: Macomber to test his manhood again; Margot to make him pay for all the ways in which he has failed her,
imagined or not; and Wilson to play a waiting game.

Q: Has it found a way of keeping the inner thoughts and feeling of the characters present through dialogue and action?
A: Wilson's inner thoughts and feelings are difficult to reveal in a story
such as this, so they must be externalized somehow. Thus the moment with the
elderly African-American man—"Americans."

Q: Has it managed to keep the dialogue interesting—that is, does the dialogue avoid being too much "on the money" (obvious)?
A: The excerpt keeps alive the sense that something went wrong and these
people are reacting to it, trying to make everything normal, as happened in the

story, but on the other hand Margot is not going to let an opportunity like this go by unchallenged.

Q: Are the character qualities of the actors faithful to the author's intent, and do these qualities still work to make the story interesting?

A: The excerpt keeps alive Macomber's sense of innocence, his singular focus on getting his manhood back "tomorrow." It keeps Margot's sly bitchiness in sight as well: "Always on target, Mr. Wilson?" Wilson remains slightly contemptuous but open to possibilities—to Margot's in-your-face infidelity as well as to Macomber's intent on righting his ship and proving he's a man.

Q: If changes have been made, do they work on behalf of the original story?

A: The changes made have been in the direction of shortening the dialogue while keeping Hemingway's sense of characters in conflict. A film has a life of its own, so being too faithful to a book or story can be a drawback. But if the script moves too far away, it loses the feel of Hemingway's life experience. The goal is to find a happy medium.

This excerpt is a script from which actors and directors can draw upon their talents to bring the conflict into focus. At the same time, it is visual enough and sufficiently readable that a producer will be satisfied that it will serve their purposes: to raise money and to encourage talent to want to work on the project.

Hollywood's Bizarre Recreation of the Hemingway Story

Now let's look at the 1947 Hollywood version of the story starring Gregory Peck, Joan Bennett, and Robert Preston, and directed by Zoltan Korda. The first frame reveals a wholly different film in which Wilson (Peck) and Margot Macomber (Bennett) have boarded a Ford Trimotor returning to Nairobi, Africa.

The Macomber Affair

INT. AIRPLANE

Wilson, a tall, good-looking American, leans over to Margot Macomber, a trim, attractive brunette, and touches her face with affection.

WILSON

Don't worry, you'll be alright.

EXT. LANDING STRIP

The plane lands. Wilson and Margot debark. Newsmen and police await them.

This scene indicates that Hemingway's surprise ending has been obliterated and a love story inserted. Hemingway's intention—to show a man, Macomber, who finds his manhood and pays the price for it—has been subverted in favor of a Hollywood love story, a triangle, if you will.

A few moments later, Wilson tells the police inspector:

WILSON

He was just unlucky—

INSPECTOR

Gored by a buffalo?

WILSON

No, shot in the back. Accident.

Wilson looks deeply troubled by this report. He appears conflicted. Later, he is given a form to fill out, a questionnaire about the "accident." The screenwriter takes the opportunity to include a flashback that begins with Macomber (Preston) meeting Wilson (Peck) in the lobby of the hotel.

HOW SCREENWRITING AND CASTING CAN BETRAY A WORLD-CLASS SHORT STORY

A film can only as good as the screenplay upon which it is based. For a screenplay to be "good," the character's qualities as discussed earlier in this book must fit the novelist or short-story writer's delineation of the character and then the producer must cast the parts in accordance with these qualities, as laid out by the screenwriter. In this film, the screenwriter got the qualities all wrong and thus the casting was also all wrong. (Note: the demands of the film business being what they are, the availability of a star often requires perfectly good screenplays to be rewritten so that an available star (not necessarily the best one for the part) can play it.

Let's look at the qualities the screenwriter gives to the characters as well as the casting based on these qualities.

Preston is a short, compact, extroverted sort of man—a quick-talking, friendly man. Margot (Bennett) is pleasantly outfitted in feminine garb as if waiting for a garden party to begin.

Peck is tall, soft-spoken, genuine—an American archetype.

Already this interpretation of the story is in trouble. The original story calls for a too-tall sportsman type to play Macomber, someone like Peter Graves, who starred a few years later in *Stalag 17* (1953) and later in the television series *Mission: Impossible*. Graves has deep-set, rather haunted eyes that could communicate the fear that Macomber experiences.

Bennett seems to be miscast as well. The original story suggests that Margot should be played by a great beauty whose gorgeous appearance is fading, leaving her desperate to regain some power. Therefore, the film calls for a woman with transcendent beauty—Rita Hayworth, Ava Gardner, or Lana Turner. All would have been terrific. All could have been sufficiently bitchy, especially Lana Turner. But Ava Gardner would have trumped the other two—a woman whose beauty could drive men crazy. Peck is the most completely miscast of all. When Wilson is called upon to bed Margot Macomber, the turn in the script is completely unbelievable. Peck's most enduring quality is his loyalty and fidelity to a cause or a mission. Recall his performance in *Twelve O'Clock High* or in *To Kill a Mockingbird*.

Wilson is an observer of life, even as he does his job extremely well. He is all man, with contempt for humans generally and Americans in particular, especially American women. He has contempt for unmanly Americans, but he's open to seeing them change their stripes. Thus Wilson needs to be a tough guy, preferably an Englishman, or an English version of Hemingway, whose values are flexible—not a big guy, not a great-looking guy, but certainly a fellow who has been in combat, preferably an Australian or an Englishman.

Why not Richard Burton? Or someone like Burton—perhaps Robert Shaw—who has the depth to convey the inner thoughts that Hemingway writes into his story.

Up to this point, the screenwriters have failed to capture Hemingway's theme—regaining manhood—turning the focus instead onto an implausible love story.

They have failed to catch Wilson's wonderful inner monologues on women, on hunting, on Americans, trying instead to create a story through dialogue that would interest audiences—not Hemingway's audience, mind you, but large audiences who remembered the bitch Joan Bennett played in *Scarlet Street* (1945) with Edward G. Robinson. Sadly it didn't work, but the failure of the film to work underscores my point, which is that screenplays often live or die with the degree to which they can recreate the inner life—the inner thoughts and feelings—of the main characters.

• • •

This chapter has explored some of the problems and solutions facing the writer who adapts a story written in one medium into one written for the screen. The successes are so few that those receiving Oscars for film adaptation usually deserve the award many times over.

Two things make the Hemingway short story a fine piece of writing: (1) the themes that a man can always redeem himself, no matter the circumstances, while a woman can only control a man so long as he is governed by fear and weakness; and (2) the quality of the inner life of these characters—Macomber reveals his inner life in his actions, and Wilson reveals his inner life in a few brief lines of inner thoughts and feelings. The screenplay turns these rich themes into Hollywood fluff—silly romantic conflicts of no consequence—and it cannot figure out how to bring the rich inner life of the characters to the surface.

In creating a screenplay from another medium, the screenwriter must find a way for the characters' inner thoughts and feelings to be visible. Very seldom does it work for a character to say openly what he thinks and feels. Film works by indirection, so characters have to speak "off-the-money" dialogue—speaking at cross purposes to what they feel and think (see explanation on page 39)—and their actions often need to be at cross purposes with what they say, as Dale Crum writes in his stories "Smoke Rings" and "My Sister's Shadow" and J.D. Tousley writes in *Dangling in the Adios*.

For writers of life stories, the lessons of this chapter are many. First and foremost, if you, as a writer, depend on narrative and an interesting narrative style, that way of telling a story must be transmuted into something else—primarily into action and hard-hitting or spirited dialogue. If you depend upon dialogue in your stories, you must find ways of building subtext through characters speaking at cross purposes and actions that tell a producer, director, and actor clues about the subtext. If your story depends on deeply revealing inner thoughts and feelings, as does Gail Field's "A Normal Life," then you will have to give the characters bits of action that work at cross purposes to their dialogue. That is the film way of working: It must be visual.

Chapter 12

Front Page to Hard Cover:
Bill Rempel's Story of *At the Devil's Table*

by William Rempel
Author, *At the Devil's Table*

At the Devil's Table began as a featured article published in the *Los Angeles Times* in February 2007. As a newspaper story, it received extraordinary treatment — front-page display with a photo spread inside along with another one hundred column inches of what writers admire most: beautiful gray type. Still, the story of Jorge Salcedo and his incredible life in the Cali drug cartel had to be drastically abridged to fit even those generous limits. Thankfully, Random House would step forward to provide bounteous book-length space. What I soon discovered, however, was that taking a 3,700-word newspaper account to a 100,000-word book manuscript would require much more than additional nouns and verbs or expanded anecdotes and details. I would also need loads of patience, a marathoner's stamina, an appreciation of criticism, and a healthy dose of ruthlessness to slash good material for the greater good of the big story.

First, some background: This was an unusual project from the start. It took more than eight years of reporting, and waiting, to finally publish those initial 3,700 words. Debriefing Jorge was not a simple matter. He and his family were hiding somewhere in the Federal Witness Protection Program. I had no idea where he was and no phone contact information. Rules of the U.S. Federal Witness Protection Program discouraged such sharing. And because I could not call him, I had to wait — days, weeks, months, and sometimes even years — for Jorge to call me. Contacts occurred entirely at his discretion. He called when he had the time and felt safe. And sometimes, Jorge acknowledged, he had second thoughts about telling his story to the world.

We first met in the fall of 1998 in a Miami federal courtroom. I had been tipped by a news source and flew out to Florida on short notice to attend a morning court hearing. I stepped into the public seating area a few minutes early and realized that I was the only member of the public in the room. No other spectators, no media. Down in front, inside the courtroom railing, as-sorted officials seemed busily engaged preparing for the next hearing while waiting for the judge. Off to one side, near the vacant jury box, two beefy U.S. marshals in dark business suits chatted amiably with a tall, distinguished-looking Latin man. Jorge Salcedo was easy to spot from across the quiet cham-ber. I have no idea what I was expecting, but he didn't look at all like the chief of security for the Cali drug cartel. He didn't look the least bit dangerous. Indeed, he appeared almost professorial, more like a math teacher than an organized-crime operative.

I already had introduced myself on the phone to his lawyer, so Jorge was expecting me.

"I'm so pleased to meet you," he said in perfect English, offering a warm, firm handshake when I introduced myself at the railing. He was instantly like-able. He also had been thinking about telling his story. I happened to be the first journalist he met since stepping into witness protection.

Jorge was in court that day to plead guilty to one felony racketeering count, but the proceedings seemed more like an awards ceremony. In all my years of covering or following high-profile court cases, I had seen nothing like this. The federal prosecutor advised the judge that Jorge had performed courageously. The lead investigator, a Customs service agent, testified that at great personal risk Jorge had saved a number of lives. The prosecution team wasn't piling up accusations; it was blowing kisses — crediting Jorge with helping bring down the biggest crime syndicate in history. Instead of a prison term, U.S. District Judge William Hoeveler thanked Jorge, then imposed an almost meaningless sentence: five years of unsupervised probation. I knew then that my tipster was right. Behind this man had to be a remarkable story.

As the hearing broke up, Jorge's federal bodyguards escorted him toward a side door through which he would disappear back into witness protection. Jorge turned to find me in the otherwise deserted public gallery. We smiled and nodded to each other. Then he was gone. I wouldn't see him again for nearly ten years. But our telephone relationship began within a few days.

◆ ◆ ◆

During his six and a half years in the Cali cartel, Jorge Salcedo had served as a high-ranking security adviser and intelligence analyst. His ability to protect the drug bosses from their rivals and from police authorities ultimately led him into the role of cartel security chief. Later, he would apply those same skills and instincts to protect himself and the security of his family even as he gambled with that security by talking to me — a journalist and a stranger. We could not meet. To this day, I don't know where he lives or what his new family name is in witness protection. Our interviews were held exclusively on a telephone. We connected through the *Los Angeles Times* labyrinth of phone lines, used disposable cell phones with blocked IDs or disguised numbers, and applied various other cloak-and-dagger tricks that concealed his new identity and whereabouts from me and from anyone who might even inadvertently be listening in on our conversations. Some of our interviews lasted three to four hours. But after a few months, the calls became less frequent.

When I learned that the Cali cartel bosses had been extradited and were about to be sentenced in a plea deal with the Department of Justice, I knew I had to write Jorge's story. I called Jorge's defense attorney in Miami and asked that he relay a message through the U.S. Marshal's Service. I hoped that Jorge would call again for one more interview. Nearly two weeks later, he did. I filled more notepads in a series of calls. It was like old times. Again, I tracked down old government sources, and the resulting story ran on February 24, 2007.

I was in New York City shortly after the story appeared, dining with friends on Sixth Avenue. Jorge called on my company cell phone. The restaurant was noisy, so I slipped outside, eager to hear his first reaction to the article. But the street noise was even worse. I pressed the phone to my ear. "Can you call in the morning?" I shouted. But he didn't—not for nearly a year.

The newspaper account had produced a flurry of interest from literary agencies and filmmakers. I was invited to meet the development executives of several prominent production companies. Of course, they all wanted access to Jorge, access I couldn't provide since I didn't even have it myself. As months went by without further word from Jorge, interest waned. All that remained from those meetings with eager Hollywood executives was a collection of business cards in a desk drawer.

One day early in 2008, a call came. "Hi Bill. It's me," Jorge said. We spent the next two hours catching up. There had been a death in his family and some business reversals, a difficult time, but he said he now was ready and willing to help on a book project. I was delighted. "But, Jorge…" I hesitated. "You'll have to call more often than once a year." We laughed. And I went to work.

I had prior experience writing a book, *Delusions of a Dictator*, for Little, Brown and Company in 1993. New York literary agent Robert Ducas, a garrulous and colorful Brit, had represented that project, but we had lost touch. His phone number was disconnected, and he was no longer at his old address on Hudson Street. Sadly, while Googling his name, I did find Robert's obituary.

Author friends immediately recommended other literary agents in New York. I sent two of them copies of the newspaper story and a cover letter. One agent asked that I write up a formal proposal. The other, David Halpern of the Robbins Office, flew out to Los Angeles and bought me a drink. I realized immediately that I was dealing with a potential partner as well as a skilled salesman. I had from the beginning hoped to keep the project secretive until it was written, until Jorge no longer had to be in regular and potentially vulnerable contact with me. But with Halpern, I didn't even have to raise that concern before he said, "I'm worried about Jorge's safety. I think I'd rather take this out to two or three selected publishers, very discretely, with nondisclosure agreements. Let's see if we find some interest without drawing too much attention."

It was not only wise strategy but it was also very effective. I traveled to New York in July of 2008 and met the next day with three different publishers; two of whom bid immediately for the project. Once the terms were settled upon, I agreed to deliver one hundred thousand words to Random House by the following summer.

•••

Journalists tend to be highly respectful of deadlines. Deep down we may loathe them, but we chase them the way beagles chase Frisbees. In this case, the Frisbee was well out of reach. I just didn't know it yet.

Before getting very far into a fresh round of telephone interviews, Jorge insisted that we meet and talk in person. It was a great idea, but it wasn't that easy. He picked what he called a neutral city and said he would meet me there. We each arranged our own separate hotel accommodations. I told him where I would be staying. Jorge kept his hotel a secret. He would show up at my door only after he was satisfied that it was safe. It was mid-morning the day after I arrived when I heard his knock.

Ten years had passed since we last met across the railing in Judge Hoeveler's Miami courtroom. He hadn't changed much—a little grayer, maybe, with a few more lines, and he seemed a bit tired. But he greeted me with the same warm smile, like an old friend. And we were friends, despite decidedly odd circumstances. In our phone conversations over the years, Jorge had come to trust me with his deepest secrets. He had revealed his fears and weaknesses, talked without apparent reservation about mistakes he made and lies he had told himself. He shared harrowing encounters that even his family knew nothing about, making me part investigator, part confessor, and part pal—and all of it over the phone. That morning I reached out to shake his hand in welcome, but Jorge grabbed me in a bear hug.

We spent three days in morning-to-night interview sessions, breaking only for lunches and dinners. Jorge was remarkably relaxed. He used measured tones even as he recited harrowing moments. And through it all, he wore what I came to regard as a mask of serenity, no doubt the same mask that allowed him to survive the real-life role of double agent inside the cartel. As an interviewee, Jorge in person was as prone to understatement as he was during telephone calls. It was part of his charm and his believability. I could sometimes lose track of how dangerous his days had been in the cartel. One afternoon, sitting on a couch in my hotel suite, he described walking into a cartel meeting where he knew the topic of discussion was "who's the snitch?" Many eyes were justifiably on Jorge. He was playing out a bluff, hoping to buy time by acting innocent to minimize those suspicions.

"I sat down and leaned back, just like this," Jorge said, reenacting the way he slouched casually into a chair. "I realized that my hands were shaking, so I put them behind my head like this, trying to look relaxed—then I put them down again. I was afraid I was sweating." Little moments like a fear of sweaty armpits conveyed so much information and insight. And watching him brought that moment to life. It not only gave me a glimpse into Jorge's state of mind and how he handled risk, but it also used a very human response to remind me that no matter how cool he was acting, Jorge had been scared.

Those remain the only extended face-to-face meetings we've had. I'm enormously grateful for that time together, but such limited access proved to be a tremendous handicap to the project. So many important signals and subtle elements of personality, emotion, and credibility come from eye contact and body language, but I had almost none of that. Most of all, I feared missing something important.

One particularly grisly and telling sequence in *At the Devil's Table* occurred, during which Jorge finds himself at the site of a cartel-directed mass murder. The violence is taking place all around him. He is terrified of two prospects: one, that he will be asked to assist in the killings, and the other that he might be killed himself. From a storytelling point of view, this was a great dilemma, rich with opportunity to reveal Jorge's character. It also showcased the cartel's use of murder as a business strategy. I wanted to know everything—how did it look, feel, sound, taste, and smell…who did what, when, and where…what was said and who said it? We must have revisited some aspect of this episode dozens of times. Maybe it was one hundred times. And every time we did, I learned a bit more—a nuance, a small detail, an observation.

Very late in the process, maybe during revisit number eighty or ninety, something in the conversation triggered a recollection, and Jorge remembered another cartel-era murder. To Jorge, it was no big deal. In his violent world, the incident had been relatively trivial and strictly personal—two men, one woman, jealousy, booze, and a gun. But, as Jorge told me the story, its importance grew. The killing had occurred at a public dance that the cartel godfathers had sponsored. Jorge remembered the irate drug lords summoning the killer the next day to explain and plead for mercy—not because he committed murder, but because he had embarrassed them.

This gem of an anecdote gave me such insight into life in the cartel. But it scared me. I had been interviewing Jorge across a span of ten years, and I had never heard about this story. That fact unnerved me for several days—until the other side of my brain made the case that I already had a treasure trove, that I didn't have to know everything, and that I didn't need to worry about a few anecdotes getting away…not even good ones. That reality check helped. But sometimes I still wonder: What did I miss?

• • •

On the research side, I got a big break about eight months into the book project. My negotiations with the U.S. Drug Enforcement Administration led to a promise of cooperation. Agents on the long-closed case were cleared for on-the-record interviews.

Back in the summer of 1995, Jorge had secretly teamed with two young DEA special agents to hunt down the cartel boss of the bosses. A full accounting of their work together had never been told. For the original newspaper article, I had relied on court records and interviews with Miami-based prosecutors and investigators to flesh out and corroborate Jorge's stories. But for the book I needed more.

Of particular importance was learning everything possible about the relationship between Jorge and the American drug agents. I needed to go deep into their shared dangers, their moments of doubt, conflicts, motives, fears, and triumphs. I had to see and sense the tensions they faced taking on the world's most powerful crime boss. The DEA agents—who, more than a decade later, still regarded Jorge's past heroics with awe—not only confirmed their informant's accounts, but they also expanded on them.

The story value of their contributions surfaces soon after they are introduced in the book, beginning with a description of the agents' first meeting with Jorge. That scene opens with Jorge driving to a prearranged rendezvous miles outside of Cali in a remote sugarcane field. If he were seen meeting with the agents, Jorge would be killed. But the agents, too, were wary, unsure if it was safe to trust this cartel figure. As the scene unfolds, readers are with Jorge as he parks a few car-lengths in front of a white Sprint, the DEA agents' unmarked car. Jorge steps out, unarmed and keeping both hands conspicuously in plain sight. To underscore his harmlessness, Jorge carries only an identity card as he starts toward the agents. Then the point of view shifts:

> In the white car, Chris Feistl was seated behind the wheel and David Mitchell was in the backseat, leaning forward to watch Jorge amble toward them.
>
> "You know, that guy reminds me of somebody," Feistl said.
>
> "Yeah, right. It's that actor. He could double for Sean Connery," Mitchell said.

The fun fact is that readers are there at the moment Jorge's DEA codename (Sean) is born. But most important is how much richer a scene becomes when viewed from more than one perspective. The DEA agents opened the way for dual points of view throughout the final third of the book. In another example, after Jorge tells agents where to find his fugitive drug boss, we see the Americans frustrated and unable find him; then we cut to Jorge, sweating out the failed mission.

Through repeated interviews, agents Feistl, Mitchell, and others delivered a mother lode of anecdotes, timelines, and strategies, along with glimpses of high emotion and periods of low morale, insights into the politics of international criminal investigations, and revelations of tragedy and near-disaster—much of it occurring beyond Jorge's view at the time.

For me and the manuscript, it was priceless. The new material was so fresh and so exclusive that even Jorge was going to have to read the book to know what he had missed.

Faced with writing a manuscript, I realized one thing right away: Composing the earlier newspaper story had been a relative breeze. News elements dictated how best to open that first version. In the *Los Angeles Times*, under the headline "The Man Who Took Down Cali," the story had started like this:

> MIAMI—The official end of the notorious Cali cocaine cartel came late last year here with little more commotion than the rap of a judge's gavel.
>
> The Colombian drug lords…entered guilty pleas and were ushered off to federal prison for the next thirty years—no *Miami Vice*–like dramatics, no bodies riddled with gunfire in the manner of Medellin rival Pablo Escobar.
>
> But behind the bloodless fall of the ruthless (Rodriguez Orejuela) brothers and collapse of their $7-billion-a-year empire lies a little-known story of daring and betrayal.

For the book, however, details about the extradition and sentencing of godfathers Miguel and Gilberto Rodriguez Orejuela amounted to little more significance than a footnote. In fact, it is mentioned only in the book's epilogue. The challenge for *At the Devil's Table* was how to introduce Jorge while also quickly setting up the dilemma that would dominate the story's narrative plotline. A screenwriter friend who had read the newspaper account pointed to a paragraph deep in that story. It was a brief summary of Jorge's first failed attempt to offer his help to U.S. authorities by reaching out to the CIA with a long-distance phone call. "That's where I'd start the movie," said my Hollywood friend. "And that's where you should start the book." Agent Halpern shared the opinion.

That's why the book opens in a Cali, Colombia, telephone booth with a nervous man secretly dialing Langley, Virginia, setting up this partial exchange:

"Central Intelligence Agency."

"Yes, hello. Please pardon my English…I'm calling from Colombia. I have some important information about the Cali drug cartel—the head of the cartel, I know his location."

"Yes, sir. And how may I direct your call?"

"Well, your agency has people here. They are trying to find this man. I am offering my assistance."

"Thank you, sir. How may I direct your call?"

And so it continued….

Jorge never did get past the CIA switchboard operator, but the episode introduces the unnamed Jorge Salcedo as a desperate family man who is taking a dangerous step by offering to betray a ruthless organized crime boss. It raises so many questions: Why would he do this? What has driven him to risk everything, even the lives of his family? Right away, the incident conveys a strong sense of menace, promising a story of suspense and an insider's view of the criminal world.

Now, of course, the book had to deliver on that promise.

• • •

In an ideal world, the writer doesn't sit down to write until the reporting and research phases are substantially complete. Clearly, I don't live in that ideal world. Between the difficulties of limited access to Jorge and my promise to provide a first draft by the end of summer 2009, I had no alternative but to write and research at the same time. I don't recommend it.

While I started the book project with enough interview notes from past years to know the major turning points of the story, it wasn't enough. I wanted the story to unfold as if before a camera. It was important to *show* this story, not *tell* it. For that, I needed far more detail—and much greater insight into the man and his world.

I ended up focusing our telephone interviews on portions of Jorge's story that I was writing at the time. For instance, in the first chapter after the opening prologue, I was writing about Jorge's life-altering trip to Cali—a visit during which he was recruited to join the cartel. I knew from prior interviews that the meeting with cartel bosses was arranged by one of Jorge's closest friends and a former commanding officer, Mario del Basto.

As I roughed out that chapter at the keyboard, I repeatedly probed during the interviews for deeper meanings and the kinds of detail that illuminate a scene. It was from that microscopic questioning that I learned more about Jorge's loyalty to Mario and about his initial reluctance to meet the cartel bosses. He described his first impressions of the godfathers, told me his seat assignment on the flight to Cali, and described the hotel where he stayed. Eventually, Jorge shared a wonderful range of detail: the color and style of the bosses' furniture…the flawed security arrangements he noticed inside the compound walls…snippets of dialogue from their midnight meeting. Brought together on the page, it made possible entries that put readers in the scenes—even with small entries like this:

> Jorge Salcedo stowed his carry-on bag in the overhead compartment and dropped into a window seat of the aging Boeing 727. It was an early morning flight out of Bogota to Cali, Colombia, and he was a reluctant traveler.…He had no idea why he was going to Cali.…
>
> "What's the deal, Mario?" Jorge couldn't hide a tone of impatience as he turned to his friend settling into the aisle seat. "What are we doing here?"

As the scene unfolds, readers witness Jorge's surprise and apprehension just as it happened. And as the trip continues, they discover the cartel godfathers just as Jorge did. Readers are there for his first impressions, for his initial doubts, and for the debates raging in his own head. It's the beauty of narrative, made possible by Jorge's patience and willingness to go deep within himself as I plumbed his memory.

Telling Jorge's story in 3,700 words had required plenty of detail. But making the tale read like a 100,000-word novel with detailed scenes and real dialogue, three-dimensional characters, and dramatic pacing required detail on a cosmic scale. I needed Jorge to call me two or three times a week. In between those calls, I worked ten- and twelve-hour days at the keyboard, roughing out the first draft. I often found myself writing scenes that needed more detail than I had in my notes. Typically, I would write a temporary version based on my imagination, making up the missing descriptions pending the next conversation with Jorge.

Once, I was laying out a bribery sequence in which the Cali cartel was about to pay off a Salvadoran colonel to acquire military bombs on the black market. I wrote the scene describing crime boss Miguel handing over the $500,000 to Jorge, his courier, in a black leather briefcase. As usual, on matters small and large, reality turned out to be far superior to my imagination.

In this case, when Jorge called, I learned that the Cali boss had personally gift-wrapped a large shoebox-sized block of wrapped U.S. currency, disguising it as a birthday present. Not only that, but Jorge described the boss as a meticulous artist, neatly folding each corner and finishing off the wrapping project with a handsome bow. I asked the obvious: What color was the paper…and the ribbon? And suddenly a rather ordinary scene came alive in red and gold trim, along with unexpected insights into a quirky mob boss.

Given that it took about eight months to gain access to the DEA agents, it was a good thing that, as characters in my story, they did not show up until the final third of the book. The interview load increased, too, but Random House liked the new material as much as I did—and my impossible summer deadline for a first draft shifted to the end of the year.

● ● ●

Without question, the biggest challenge in the book was capturing the real Jorge Salcedo. He held high rank in the biggest drug syndicate in history, yet he never trafficked in drugs. He was close to the richest crime bosses on the globe, yet he never got rich. He supervised bodyguards and associated with paid assassins, yet he never harmed anyone. After six and a half years in the company of ruthless killers and traffickers, his biggest crime—and prosecutors considered it a felony under U.S. conspiracy laws—was protecting the security of cartel godfathers and the lives of their families.

"But he's too good," Will Murphy, my editor at Random House, complained more than once. The brevity of the original newspaper story had allowed only for the most superficial examination of Jorge's character and a handful of key moments. He was recruited into the cartel with an appeal to his patriotism, to help the rival traffickers kill Pablo Escobar, Colombia's Public Enemy Number One. The newspaper story also detailed how the Cali bosses rejected Jorge's resignation after Escobar died and how Jorge finally was driven to risk everything and reach out to the DEA after being ordered to help assassinate a potentially damaging cartel witness. Those were important moments, but the book needed much more. I had to show Jorge's descent deeper and deeper into the criminal organization, defining him by the ethical and difficult choices he faced.

Jorge answered all of my questions, and without apparent hesitation. But remember, I was learning new details about his cartel years with virtually every interview. Specific elements of his character came into focus well after the first draft and after Murphy's early complaints that Jorge was "too good." Gradually that changed. In interviews spanning several months, Jorge detailed over and over his duties with the cartel, adding detail as we dug deeper. He had first designed radio communications systems that served the cartel's business and security interests but did no one any harm. Later he was involved in more sinister projects: a blackmail scheme to compromise an anti-narcotics military official. He also bugged phones and earned favor when he once sounded an alarm to protect a multimillion-dollar cash shipment from seizure. And then there were the paid assassins who considered Jorge a friend. They sometimes told him about plots and murders that he could do nothing to stop without risking the lives of his own wife and children, a seemingly impossible choice. A more

Front Page
to Hard Cover:
Bill Rempel's
Story of
At the
Devil's Table

95

imperfect Jorge emerged on the pages of my later drafts—bloodied, haunted, and regretful, but still a good man…and a much better character.

To the extent that *At the Devil's Table* succeeds in creating a complex portrait of Jorge, all I can say is: Thanks especially to Will Murphy, my editor at Random House, and to Halpern and friends at the Robbins Office in New York. They battered and abused my pages until the character of Jorge finally shone through in all its enigmatic and ultimately heroic glory. Forty years of journalism may have helped. Not because it taught me how to write, so much as it taught me to embrace prepublication criticism. Good editing is a lifesaver. I crave it.

My first draft came in at 120,000 words and would take nearly one year to revise and rewrite into a final draft. From his first read, Murphy suggested lots of deletions. I quit counting how many times he scribbled "bland…too slow…boring…do we need this?" and assorted other notes that a more fragile writer might regard as devastating insults. One of my favorites: "This sucks—improve!" There is nothing more frustrating than a demanding editor—and nothing more valuable.

If something "sucks" or doesn't make sense to Murphy or Halpern or anyone else, it might not work for Joe Average Reader, either. If the pace seemed to sag for my editor, it very likely sags for others, too. A writer has to be ruthless in defense of his story—but also ruthless with himself. Many a nice turn of phrase never made it between the covers of this book. Of my first 120,000 words, I probably deleted close to 50,000 in the first revision. In one typical edit, a provocative 1,500-word description of a murder that embarrassed the godfathers was cut to barely 200 words—focused only on what it taught Jorge about his bosses.

No story element, regardless of how colorful or telling, is worth preserving if it threatens the dramatic pace. I know. As a schoolboy, I fell asleep whenever Herman Melville put aside the chase for Moby Dick to examine in numbing detail the whale oil business. I don't presume to suggest a Melville rewrite, but as a newspaper editor I've seen too many writers fight to protect favorite lines that are really sure cures for insomniacs. It seems obvious that every writer's first rule should be: Don't put your readers to sleep.

To that end, I cut out page after page—including an entire chapter representing well over three weeks of work. It simply didn't move the story along. The excised chapter came early in the first draft, a colorful, even outrageous, tour of the Colombian jungles with Jorge and a group of British commandos as they secretly plotted an assault on a guerrilla outpost. The Brits were great characters, full of swagger. Unfortunately, their anti-guerrilla mission was never launched. There was no dramatic payoff. The episode took place months before Jorge had anything to do with Cali cartel bosses and revealed more about the British mercenaries than about Jorge, the main character. Most of the original three-thousand-word section vanished in a *click* of my "Delete" key. Yes, I cringed at the time, but I have no regrets. It improved the story, just as a thousand other cuts did.

A colleague and friend of mine for many years at the *Los Angeles Times* was a revered writer and editor, part of an elite team of long-form journalists affectionately known as "The Poets." Words mattered to Rick Meyer—they mattered a lot. But his philosophy of research, writing, and editing could be summed up in a short sentence: "It's all about the story." By that, he meant that all efforts, all motives, and all words—even the poetic ones—must first and foremost serve the greater good of the story. It's that simple—and that demanding.

Of course, the one thing that eases the pressures of deadline and keeps the tedium of cutting and polishing in perspective is having a great tale to tell. For that, you'll have to find your own Jorge Salcedo.

● ● ●

Bill's experience in expanding a news article (which, in this case can be seen as a life story of his experiences with Jorge) into a book holds many valuable lessons for those who write life stories. First, it illustrates the enormous patience it takes to get "deeper" into the story. Without such patience, Bill would never have seen the project through to the end, no matter how much confidence he had in his abilities. After all, finding the truth of things depended on Jorge's willingness to surface, a willingness that Bill could not predict.

Second, it shows that Bill could not have gotten anywhere alone. His network of contacts made it possible for him to hear of Jorge in the first place, and his genial personality and work ethic put him on the good side of a host of people who could help him—DEA agents, FBI personnel, literary agents, editors, and the like. For life-story writers, this means going about your tasks in a similarly professional way—committing yourselves to establishing a regular pattern of writing, getting feedback, and putting your work—sharing your work with others as well as seeking out publication—without being discouraged.

Third, Bill is always looking for "actions that matter"—that is, actions (and obstacles) that reveal the character of Jorge in an ever-more-telling way. The longer he is involved with the cartel, the greater his challenge to retain his soul. These are the heroic qualities of which Joseph Campbell speaks in *The Hero with a Thousand Faces*—descending into the hell of the drug cartel's activities, undoubtedly feeling lost and alone, adrift, ruled by forces larger than himself. Finally, as he devises a plan to bring down the cartel—a plan that works—he is reborn, spiritually.

Fourth, Bill seeks the points of view of minor characters, such as the DEA agents whose voices play a significant part in the drama as well as other "players" on this dramatic stage.

Fifth, the experience offers a glimpse of a "cosmic" view of the world through Bill's and Jorge's eyes: a world of chaos and madness within which a good human can easily become lost and destroyed. However, resilience, patience, and focus eventually provide an opportunity for "good" to have its day. This is also important for the life story writer who, too frequently, sees only the very small world of their own actions as being important. Seeking a sense of how the universe works and recreating it in your stories is an important consequence of going "deeper within" your stories and yourself. This effort reminds me of the arc of *Pan's Labyrinth*, a fine Spanish film in which a woman who experiences a number of wrongs done to her finds the strength to do the "right" thing by first diving deep into her inner life and imagination.

The final chapter of the previous unit, "Separating the Writer's Voice from the Central Character's Voice," demonstrates how to do this in your life stories. It examines the distinct worlds of the writer's voice (the creator of the universe within which all action takes place) and the central character's voice (the smaller world of the protagonist's story, or arc).

In his book *At the Devil's Table*, Bill is the creator of this world of action and events that has behind it a view of the cosmos as beneficent (God exists and works on humanity's behalf) or antipathal (God either does not exist or is furious with humans and works against our well-being). The reader has to decide which view Bill takes in his book. Jorge, of course, speaks for himself, the central character in his own drama of good and evil.

Chapter 13

Writing Family History

Recently, exploring family histories has become much easier as vast quantities of information have been stored and made available on the Internet. And as researching the past becomes easier, the writer is given the corresponding opportunity to expand their historical imagination, which allows them to begin to see the past more clearly and link one area of family history to another. When I think of my mother's ancestors fighting the British during the American Revolution, I am able to imagine my father's ancestors in Germany going about the business of life during the same period of time.

Many writers who set out to write life stories are primarily interested in writing about the struggles and history of their parents and grandparents. Typically this kind of story is a simple narrative retelling of the past:

> My grandfather was born in the Ukraine. When he was sixteen, he was forced to serve in the Czar's army. After a year, he escaped and made his way to America.

While reading this sort of narrative, the reader finds themselves asking a number of questions:

1. How did the narrator hear about his grandfather?
2. Who told him the story?
3. How do I know it is true?
4. How did the people involved (the grandfather and the narrator) feel about these events?

Out of a need to answer these questions, another, more authentic, way of telling family histories has emerged in which the feelings of the storyteller and the writer are evident while the story is unfolding.

When they are working on writing this kind of family history, I tell my students, "Let the reader know how you learned about the story. Were you sitting on Grandma's knee or taking a walk with Grandpa? Let the reader know what you remember Grandpa or Grandma doing or feeling while they were telling you the story. That way we get both the story and your relationship to the storyteller. We will believe it and feel it more fully."

John Strong's "How I Became a Rebel" (excerpt on the next page) is a good example of this kind of writing.

(Note: In this story, the narrator, the teller of the story, happens to be the writer, John Strong, and then the reader experiences a story-within-a-story. This kind of story—a touching, personal experience with a famous or important person in history—might well be passed down within a family from one generation to the next.)

How I Became a Rebel

by John Strong

I am nine years old and in elementary school in Clymer, Pennsylvania. The year is 1922. One day the teacher tells us, "Class, we have a special treat today. We have two visitors…who fought in the War between the States. They are here to tell you about it."

A few moments later they walk in. Two of them. They are old. With beards. Today is Veteran's Day, so they wear their uniforms, blue tunics with blue pants. One has the bars of a lieutenant on his shoulders. They walk slowly and sit down.

I am eager to talk to them. On both my father's and mother's side of the family, I have relatives who fought in the Grand Army of the Republic, the Union Army.

At the first chance I get, I raise my hand. "Sir," I say, "could you tell us about being in the war. What it was like?"

The old man's eyes come alive. "I suppose you want me to tell you about the bloody battles, don't you?" I nod. He shakes his head. "I won't do that. War is hell. Absolute hell. But I will tell you a story about the war," he continues. He leans back in his chair. His eyes get a faraway look.

"The war was over. The bloodiest damn thing you ever saw. My best friend Joshua and I decided we wanted to go to college together. We were lieutenants in the GAR, the Union Army, and we wanted to stick together. So we chose Washington and Lee University."

The old man smiled down at me. His eyes were soft.

"We enrolled in classes there. General Lee—Robert E. Lee, the commanding general of all the Confederate forces—was the president of the university, but we didn't see him much. Occasionally a parade in the mornings. But he marched out of step, on purpose, to make himself ordinary, nothing special. But we admired him nonetheless.

"Almost all the other men there had fought for the South. After all, General Lee had been their commander. They'd've followed him anywhere.

"One day we got a note from the office of the president of the college asking us to stop by. When we arrived, the general was waiting for us. He was a soft-spoken man. A little shy. But powerful. I almost saluted him. He came right to the point.

"'Gentlemen, I suppose it has not escaped your attention that most of the boys at this here school were once under my command in the late war.'

"'Yes, sir,' I said, eager to say something.

"'Well, then, since you are the only two fellows from the Union Army enrolled down here, officers too, I wonder if you might tell me…why? Why did you come here?'

"I looked at my friend, and he looked at me. Finally I spoke up. 'General, sir, my buddy and me, we figured that you were the best general of any of 'em, North or South. Wherever you went, that was the place for us.'

The old soldier stops for a moment. He takes a glass of water and drinks. Finally he goes on.

"The general stood and looked at us, then nodded. There was a faint smile on his face. He shook hands with us both. We left."

The classroom is as quiet as an empty church. The old soldier looks around the room at each one of us. "Think about that, boys."

Notice that in the story, John speaks in the present tense, as if Clymer, 1924, were the present; but when the old soldier recollects the past, he speaks in the past tense. This is because the old soldier's recollection of 1865 is the past from the perspective of someone living in 1924.

John's soldier speaks directly to the reader as well as to him. The result is that the reader experiences the story through John's eyes. It is important for readers or listeners to know through whose eyes they are experiencing events at every turn in the story: It creates belief in the story, and it also increases interest, because the writer and the soldier have a relationship to share in addition to the subject matter of the story itself.

A hundred years ago, readers would not have thought to ask, "From whose point of view are we seeing the story, and is it to be believed?" Until the middle of the nineteenth century, such writers as Edgar Allan Poe, Richard Henry Dana, Walter Scott, William Thackeray, Thomas Hardy, Herman Melville, and many others told their stories from a godlike, omniscient (all-knowing) narrative point of view, and readers accepted this point of view as believable. But in the writings of Stephen Crane, Henry James, and James Joyce, and in the dramas of Luigi Pirandello, readers became more aware of the person through whose eyes the story was being experienced and of the subjectivity of the telling of the story.

For example, if you read a story told from the point of view of one sister who is obviously jealous of another, you know you are getting, in the telling of the story, other biases and other feelings, not the whole truth.

Contemporary readers are less likely than readers from the past to take for granted the truth of a story unless they know something about who is telling it. By recording the relationship of the storyteller (narrator) to the writer of the story, a more authentic and believable view of the family history is told.

Researching the Past

"Who am I?" "Where have I come from?" "Where am I going?" These are the enduring questions for everyone, whether the questions are asked consciously or unconsciously. Advances in modern medicine have enabled people to live a great deal longer than past generations, thereby allowing people to contemplate these questions in the midst of advancing age and good health. Advances in modern technology, specifically the Internet, have allowed unprecedented access to information about the past.

For many years, I thought the dominant influence in my life was my father's highly educated and accomplished German–Jewish ancestry. Fleeing the oppressive Prussian nationalism of the mid–nineteenth century, my father's Jewish forbearers settled along the East Coast (West Virginia) as farmers and then moved to Michigan, becoming in one generation successful merchants and attorneys. In my father's generation, they also became doctors and social scientists. For me, that knowledge always encouraged me to think for myself and to try to see clearly what was happening around me without being pulled into partisan arguments, affiliations, or dead efforts. My mother's family had been sweet, kindly farm folks from Illinois, so far as I knew.

Then came the Internet. Thanks to the Internet, a distant member of my family, Bill, sent a view of his snow-covered home in Virginia to members of the family, myself included.

Bill and I began corresponding about our family: His great grandmother was a sister to my great grandmother. For some time, he had been researching his family, the Clark family tree, thanks to the enormous resources online. (For example, Ancestry.com has compiled and computerized a vast amount of information, enabling anyone to know who their forebearers are without expending a huge amount of effort.) Before long, my former wife, Gail, became interested in this research, along with my first cousin Mary Ellen. With a small army of cousins/researchers hard at work, we found a relative who had been a captain in the Union Army during the American Civil War: Bela Tecumseh Clark. Bela's middle name intrigued us because a general of the Union Army, William Tecumseh Sherman, shared the same middle name. What the link was, we did not know, but some day I'm sure we will. A little more research informed us that Bela's father-in-law was one Colonel Sylvanus Thayer. The U.S. Military Academy's official website acknowledges Sylvanus Thayer as "the father of the U.S. Military Academy." That information surprised and even astonished us—to think that such an illustrious person was an important part of our family history without our knowing about him.

A bit more research told us that Sylvanus Thayer was an unmarried man. Thus we were on the wrong track—or perhaps not. Because they were both of approximately the same age (one born in 1798, the other in 1785) and both born in New England (Vermont and Massachusetts), we suspected they had a common ancestor. Researching that common ancestor we found a half-dozen Thayers who also fought in the Civil War, most from Illinois and Michigan. At long last, we found the grandfather of the two Sylvanus Thayers, as well as Col. William Clark, Bela Clark's great grandfather, who served as an aide to General George Washington during the Revolutionary War.

We found that many other relatives, such as the Grays, the Gowers, and the Culvers from this small area of Momence, Illinois, had also been officers and enlisted men in the Union Army. We found diaries and testimonials to their devotion to the career and politics of Abe Lincoln.

Gradually, I began to realize what impressive, free-thinking, hard-working generations of family lay behind my mother. I began to understand the impact my DNA has had on my behavior more and more fully, which helped me answer the questions "Who am I?" "Where have I come from?" and "Where am I going?"

The reason that I bring this up in a book about writing is that, ultimately, writing is about communication—usually about communication that moves from the writer to the reader, but lately, thanks to blogs, websites, social media, and the like, communication that moves back and forth, with lightning speed.

So, in a project like this, a number of members of the family—Bill, cousin Mary Ellen, former wife Gail, and I—got to know each other a little better. Sister Mary Lee and cousin Tom reappeared too. Starting with a few facts, we have been able to piece together interesting fragments of life during the time when our family moved from the Eastern Seaboard westward through the Ohio Valley and into the Midwest, in Illinois and Michigan. We have shared family photos and memorabilia and analyzed and debated their significance.

In several instances, the possessor of such memorabilia didn't know the significance, but other members of "the team" were able to identify who the subjects were in old photos. In fact, this group—Gail, Bill, and Mary Ellen—have given themselves a name: CHART—Clark Heritage Ancestry Research Team. (Hey, what am I? Chopped liver?)

The ongoing tasks—identifying photos, noting the signatures of guests at weddings, finding links between generations, preserving stories—create a wonderful bond among family members as well as leading to surprising connections with "outsiders." My sons Jeff, an airline pilot, and Will, a Marine, are both fascinated by our link to the father of the U.S. Military Academy.

Through blogging and websites like Ancestry.com, more and more families will find common ancestors, stories, photos, and the like, creating ever-stronger family bonds. The history of every person's family is a miniature history of the larger events that have taken place over the centuries since the founding of our republic. In my case, I discovered that my forebearers counted John and Pricilla Alden—among the first families of the original Plymouth Settlement in Massachusetts—as members of the family tree.

In this regard my family is not unique, as many hundreds of families can easily trace their roots back to such ancestors. Researching these roots is a fascinating task that offers many benefits.

Other Benefits
of Life-Story Writing

Over time I have learned that *Writing from Within* stories—really, sketches from life—can take a writer in many interesting directions. For example, a grasp of storytelling skills makes academic writing in school vastly easier. If you know how to create a teaser at the beginning of a story, understand how backstory helps define what a story (or an essay) may be about, and can use ministories as examples and narratives in larger academic work, you are well ahead of the curve. Likewise, if a student knows how to compose a life story, the academic writing teacher's work of introducing concepts and ideas becomes much easier.

Such skills also make other kinds of creative writing much easier, whether it is inventing personal myths from classic mythic tales or developing an ease in storytelling that enables an academic person with numerous college degrees to write effective stories for children. (A good example of such a story is "Molloko, the California Condor" on page 70, which is from *Creative Stories* by Ines Horowitz, PhD, a mammalogist.)

This story is also is an excellent example of how this writer uses her imagination to come up with a unique perspective from which to tell a story. Many people may have passed through school and done well or poorly without ever using their imaginations. Sometimes it occurs in childhood but becomes redirected toward academic work; sometimes it only occurs in later years or not at all. In future, I want to encourage cultivate your imagination as much as possible. Your relationships will improve, your pleasure in creating will develop dramatically, and your satisfaction in life's pleasures will expand.

chapter 14

How *Writing from Within* Can Help People

Over the past fifteen years, I have explored the many ways in which *Writing from Within* can be used to affect people's lives in a positive way, by bringing to the surface unexpected creativity and previously unexpressed feelings. From the beginning of *Writing from Within* in 1982, I suspected this writing method held untold potential for influencing people's lives; it was up to me to explore this idea further.

At first, I found an home for *Writing from Within* in the senior population with which I dealt. Older adults wanted to write and write well as a means of leaving something for future generations. Many of them, especially the younger oldsters, found an opportunity to review their lives in the stories they wrote about their long and usually fruitful experiences.

I then offered my services to various agencies that work with recovering addicts, such as Kaiser Permanente, and, again, found a welcoming response. The groups that I worked with at Kaiser were filled with men and women who had vast resources of untapped creativity but who, for one reason or another, had strangled the expression of their thoughts and emotions. One young man in particular made an impression on me. He wrote about the moment when his father died: "I had been playing guitar and heard a noise from my father's bedroom. For a moment, I thought about stopping, but I continued playing a while longer. A few minutes later I stopped, went into my father's bedroom, and found him dead. I was horrified, filled with shame that I could be so stupid, so uncaring. I stopped playing the guitar and never went back. That was twenty years ago." I suggested that perhaps it was time to forgive himself and to go back to being creative. He agreed.

Many of the older men in my writing classes had gone through World War II as servicemen. A number of these combat veterans found a great deal of solace in writing about their experiences. One veteran, Chuck Woolf, had been on the destroyer *Morrison*, which went down in the Pacific in 1943. Chuck spent the better part of three years working on his life stories, every few months revisiting the painful moment when the kamikaze attacks caused the *Morrison* to flip over on its back and sink. Chuck described finding himself underwater, going down with the ship, and then suddenly seeing a shaft of light that he followed to the surface, where he and a small number of the ship's crew floated in the oily waters. Fewer than half the crew of 1,500 men survived.

Back on land, Chuck found himself haunted by nightmares of the incident for the remainder of his life. When he finished his book, I asked him how it felt. "I had a good night's sleep for the first time since 1943," he smiled.

As a former USAF officer and believer in the importance of a strong, enlightened military, I have wanted to bring *Writing from Within* to veterans' hospitals. However, that door has never opened. It remains one of the frustrations I have experienced.

In one of my writing classes located in the Fairfax area of Los Angeles, I found that a number of my students were Jewish survivors of the death camps in Poland and Germany during World War II. Most of those survivors found that by writing about what had happened to them, they experienced a sense of release from the pain sharply etched in their memories. One such woman, Joanne B., had been an unsung hero of the Polish resistance. Because she spoke fluent German, her Nazi captors often used her to translate orders from them to their captives. Joanne soon found that brutal orders enunciated by angry, contemptuous, and often ruthless Nazi guards could be softened if she repeated the orders back to the guards "to be sure [she] got it just right." After this process ran its course, the guards usually softened their orders.

Joanne saved hundreds of lives during the time that she was imprisoned in the Warsaw ghetto and in the camps in Poland. Initially she was a secretary for a Nazi sergeant who recorded the names and types of medical equipment rounded up from the Jewish Poles. The resistance asked her to leave the window of the office open one night so they could obtain her boss's rifle, which she did. In a second audacious move, they asked her to suggest to her boss that he should be pedaled around Warsaw in a rickshaw, as happened with others of his rank. A very convincing woman, Joanne persuaded him to do this, and two resistance workers built the rickshaw with a secret compartment in it. Every time Joanne's boss left the ghetto in the rickshaw, the resistance fighters who pulled the rickshaw filled the secret compartment with medical supplies to be dropped off after the Nazi officer had been carried home. In a third monumental act of heroism, Joanne witnessed a group of professional printers being sent off to a death camp against the orders of the German commander in that region. Since the Nazis highly valued skilled printers, Joanne decided to take her chances saving these men by making her way to the commander's quarters, getting his signature on a release form, commandeering a German staff car, stopping the train, and seeing to it that the group of one hundred highly skilled printers was rerouted to the duty of printing.

This fascinating story has never been told publicly, because Joanne wrote it simply to let her son know that her life was not worthless. She did not want her story published except at the hands of her son.

Over the years, my students often said to me, "Mr. Selling, what do I do if there is more information I want to put in my stories about the effects of the trauma I experienced?" After giving the matter some thought, I advised them to write a little P.S. at the end of the story.

•●●●•

When the riots of 1993 occurred in Los Angeles, I asked myself, "What can I do to be of service to my city, so torn apart by anger and frustration?" My answer was to offer a writing class at the Musician's Union of Los Angeles. As a musician myself, I have long known the wonderful bond that exists among musicians of all races and genders. As the class grew, a parade of top-notch musicians passed through the class: jazz great Buddy Collette and his friends Jackie Kelso and Eddie White; Latin jazz great Bobby Rodriquez; virtuoso violist Dave Schwartz; Jerry Velasco, one of the top accompanists for Lena Horne and Quincy Jones; and many others.

Buddy's stories of his drive to integrate the Black Musicians' Union and the White Musicians' Union in the mid-1950s were particularly moving, as were Eddie's stories of growing up in rural Louisiana as a young boy, listening to such legendary singers as Blind Lemon Jefferson.

A man of vision and compassion, Buddy made an effort to bring my work to the attention of a wider audience. At the time, he had been working with a private arts agency connected to the Los Angeles Unified School District. He recommended that it work with me in some capacity. That group, the Learning Tree, submitted a request for a grant to the State of California, and with the funds appropriated, we began a series of workshops in which my seniors, in groups of six or eight, read stories to entire grades—fourth through sixth—in San Fernando Valley schools and would then offer writing workshops to the students, if they desired. In this effort, we were quite successful. Frequently at least 50 percent of the more than one hundred student listeners at a reading would sign up for the workshop. Each senior reader led a table of six to eight students. The school's teachers later reported that after the workshops their students were writing stories more quickly, more fully, and with greater ease than ever before.

In one surprising moment, one of the women in my senior group read a story of experiencing her father's death when she was only five years old. I was a little unnerved by this choice, as I had expected her to read a different story, one that was not so personal. After she read the story, a young girl came up to her with tears in her eyes: Her father had died earlier that week, and she didn't know what to feel or what to say to people. The reading gave her permission to feel what she needed to feel and express what she needed to express. The girl and my senior reader hugged for a long time.

From these many experiences in and out of the classroom, and from looking deep within myself when I wrote my own stories, I know that eventually the educational system will need to recognize storytelling (in an intimate and personal way) as a legitimate skill to be taught. I also know that feelings of rage and pain—feelings that I could see on the faces of the rioters in 1993—need an outlet: People need to be able to look into their own experiences and find paths out of despair and frustration. And so I now look at possible places where *Writing from Within* will lead in the months and years to come.

Chapter 15

Writing from Within and the Human Potential Movement

Storytelling skills can have an abiding impact on relationships. Often, couples having relationship trouble begin and end with accusations and blaming ("you should; you shouldn't"), where a good story might help solve the problem by allowing one person to see the other's point of view more clearly.

Eventually, in writing my own stories, such as "The Jewish Wife," (see page 157 in the "Stories" section) I realized that I had a lot to say about the growth I experienced as a result of the incident that I had chosen to write about. My training in the Stanislavsky Method as taught by Lee Strasberg, Jack Garfein, and Harold Clurman reminded me that virtually all relationships are about character and the actions we take as a result of the character qualities we possess. As I wrote more of my own stories, I began to see my own worthwhile character qualities coming into focus.

Years earlier, a critical point in my life made me face up to some difficulties I had been having in personal and professional relationships. After examining my own behavior, I realized that in everything I had done throughout my life I had exhibited creativity, and that, in not recognizing this trait in myself, I had been limiting my goals and opportunities. Once I accepted this perspective and began to see and promote myself as a creative person, many new opportunities began to surface.

Little by little, I began suggesting to certain students that they look at their stories as mirrors of who they were and how they behaved in life. If they felt they needed to make changes, I counseled, "Write a story about an incident that relates to the change you feel necessary, then look at your story as if it is a mirror in which you can see character reflected, qualities you may not have previously known or appreciated. Once you see your own best qualities, you will see how to make the changes you think necessary." The one thing I did know about human behavior, having taught writing for such a long time, is that most people do not value themselves for the many good qualities they possess. A change in behavior means looking at our best qualities, for those qualities are what we rely upon in times of stress.

Over time, I put these observations together in a sequel to *Writing from Within* entitled *Character Consciousness*, which establishes a path through which everyone can come to recognize their best qualities by observing their behavior in many different life circumstances. The essence of this process is a series of questions that the writer must ask themselves: *Who am I in this story? What are the qualities that get me what I want in this story? Am I the victim of some trauma of the past that has caused me to want to hide certain events of my life? What do I need to do to stop doing so?*

Here is what psychiatrist Douglas Caldwell had to say about this process in the Foreword to *Character Consciousness*:

> Selling's *Character Consciousness* encourages us to see ourselves as capable of growth by changing our perceptions of ourselves. His first profound, heartfelt book, *Writing from Within*, nudged us toward the childlike part of ourselves—the innocence that deserves to be seen and felt, showing us how to find and nurture this part of ourselves. *Character Consciousness* moves the work inward. By exploring early traumas through writing and rewriting them in closer and more intimate detail, we break through and recover heroic aspects of our experience that we have forgotten, ignored, or overlooked. In this way we begin to reframe our experience of trauma.

What this means for the average person is that self-knowledge and self-awareness are important aspects of each person's growth as a human being and that the responsibility for teaching growth need not fall solely in the hands of trained professionals—psychologists, therapists, counselors, and the like. The potential of much of this growth and awareness can be seen in our own experiences if we choose to pay attention, and life stories are an excellent first step toward paying attention.

An example in my own life occurred many years ago, shortly after my first divorce. I had told my wife that I needed to be free of the bonds of marriage. Of course, now she had a lot of power in her hands, such as the power to decide when, if, and how I would see my children. Thus began a five-year, deeply unsettling dispute, not unlike that which many couples with children face: Love is gone, and the struggle for power begins. Here, from the first few pages of *Character Consciousness*, is the brief story of how this struggle for power changed into a life-long friendship.

Writing
from
Within
and the
Human Potential
Movement

111

Defining My Turning Point Behavior and Finding Its Origins

From *Character Consciousness* — Chapter 9

Most of us struggle in our lives with the question, Can I ever really change? Can I turn it around? At the core of existential philosophy and literature in the '40s and '50s was the assurance that, yes, we can change. At the same time, the dominant force in psychology—Behaviorism—suggested it was really quite hopeless for us to try. We were all victims of the forces of something larger—authoritarian political movements, supernatural forces, Big Brother, brainwashing, and the like.

During my darkest moments, I adopted a philosophy of life-as-trickster—that is, just as we are about to get what we want, the universe, the divine trickster, will pull the rug out from under us. I don't know that this point of view served me well—I felt helpless and out of control, Sisyphus-like, condemned to making the same mistakes over and over—many of us have felt this force.

Yet for most of us, there are moments when we have acted well even in the midst of our darkest times. Eventually, after we have rooted out the painful memories and understand how the past has held us captive, we can turn and look at those moments when we have acted well to find the roots of those actions in our early years. Gradually, we can turn things around and see ourselves in the middle of a surprising history of taking positive risks that turn out well. We can trace the origins back to moments of courage, insight, independence.

For example, if I were asked to write my single most important "Turning Point" memory for the past three decades of my life, it would be the following:

Winning

by Bernard Selling

"I'm not going to sit here and listen to you run me down anymore," yells Gail, my ex-wife. She is fuming. "It's just like when we were married." She picks up her purse and marches out of the counselor's office.

The counselor gazes at me for a moment. He is tall, thin, rather serious-looking, and quite young. Maybe thirty. About my age. Gail is twenty-five. We have two kids and have been divorced now for a year.

"Gail's pretty angry at you, Bernard," he says, leaning forward.

"Yeah, she is, huh," I reply.

"Any idea why?" he asks.

"She doesn't like me telling her what to do. She doesn't like me telling her what's good for the kids.... She doesn't like to hear me remind her that the kids are mine as much as hers. I deserve, and I'll get, equal time with them if it kills me," I mutter. My teeth are clenched.

"Bernard. Think about it. You left her, right?" I nod. "So she's getting even. You've been a good father, yes?" Again I nod. "Her only weapon is the kids…and she uses it." Again I nod. He leans back for a moment, then forward. "…and she always will, as long as you keep on this way."

This way? What does he mean by that? I wonder.

He looks at the clock. Time is up. He looks at me again. "If you want to have the kind of relationship with your kids that you say you want, you'll have to stop trying to win."

I start to protest but then decide just to let it sink in. Stop trying to win? Is that what I'm doing?

Over the next few weeks I think about this a lot and decide he may be right.

Several times Gail does things that would normally bother me, but I become more polite, less antagonistic. I begin to compliment her for things she is doing, particularly for the kids.

"You wimp!" hisses Kathy, my wife-to-be. She hates to see me being nice to Gail, giving in to her requests.

"Believe me, I know what I'm doing," I say.

———•••———

After several years, Kathy and I go our separate ways. But Gail and I become better friends. No longer does she try to get even with me. My regard for her grows.

Assessment

Now thirty-five years after our divorce, Gail and I are the best of friends. We have raised the children in a nonpossessive way. We spend holidays together, the four of us. In fact, we celebrate the holidays together even when the kids are not in town. There have been occasions where Gail and the kids and Kathy and her husband and my girlfriend and I all share a pre-Christmas glass of good cheer.

As I look back on that moment in the counselor's office, I am surprised that I was able to act so well and take the good advice that was offered me. I was in the middle of a very hard and lonely time in my life. I was in a great deal of pain and guilt over my failed love relationships and very confused and frustrated about my career as a filmmaker. Yet somehow I was able to calm myself a bit and reduce the level of anger between Gail and me. It

Writing
from
Within
and the
Human Potential
Movement

113

opened the door for what mattered most: our children growing up happy and well-adjusted, feeling their parents cared about them and respected each other and were in their lives, day to day, week to week, year to year, forever.

I befriended my enemy and found her to be a human being like myself. As distant as we were to each other as husband and wife, so we became equally open to each other as parents.

No easy task. I acted well where I could have easily acted in a small, petty, selfish way.

Where did I get that? I ask myself sometimes. Where did it come from?

• • •

As I look back on my youth I see myself as mostly a wimp until I began to grow into my adolescent body in the eighth grade. I recollect one Saturday afternoon that year talking to a girl at a local swimming pool when I glance down and see a toddler sinking to the bottom in eight feet of water. I dive down, pull the baby up, and give it to its mother. The baby is gasping for air but it is okay. So I go on talking to the girl. No big deal. Not bad, Bernard.

Perhaps it is my awareness that my father, despite his illnesses and his rages, never wasted an opportunity to take a trip with me to explore something historical—a railroad, a battlefield, a ship, a museum, a restaurant serving hamburgers on model trains. As far back as I can remember, my father does that, giving me a chance to learn. And I know that I will give those same chances to my two sons, no matter what the obstacles.

These moments in life are very important. They are the moments when we enhance our sense of self-worth, when we touch the nobility that lies within us. Even at our darkest and most confused moments, the seeds of our better selves are at work. Most of us do act well at various times in our lives but do not value ourselves the more for it.

By writing your life story and reflecting back on the person you are, the person you have been, and the person you can be, you set in motion a more positive future for yourself and your family.

• • •

When I wrote this chapter some five to ten years ago, I had not had the pleasure of being a grandfather.

At the age of seventy-two, I can look out on the family I created all those years ago. My sons are productive and engaged in life. They love me, they love their mother, and they love their stepmother, my second former wife, Kathy.

When we divorced, she was saddened at the thought that her relationship with my sons, then ten and eleven, would end. I assured her it wouldn't: "You'll have whatever relationship you want to have." She wasn't sure that would happen, but over the years, Will and Jeff never failed to spend time with Kathy and Ben, her husband. And Isabel and Max, my adorable grandchildren, spend weeks at a time with Kathy, Ben, Gail, and, of course, my daughter-in-law's mother, Dorothy.

Yesterday, my six-year-old grandson spent the day with Grandma Gail as passengers in the turbo prop airplane that my son flies for Skywest Airlines. Gail couldn't wait to relate all the fun that she and Max had riding on "Daddy's airplane."

None of this would have happened had I not listened to the good advice given to me some forty years ago by a young therapist. Writing and reflecting upon my stories has forced me to slow down the way I respond to things. Impulsive, emotional, knee-jerk responses are a thing of the past. Knowing my best character qualities enables me to allow things to happen around me.

Sometimes you just have to get out of your own way, as the saying goes, and allow things to happen.

Conclusion: Bernard's Message

In the introduction to this book, I suggested that you ask yourself as you turn each page, "What is Bernard's message to me, as a writer?" Now is the time for me to share my message with you. To begin with, I will ask you once again, "What do you suppose is the message that lies behind all the advice, techniques, examples, and stories that this book contains?" I suggest you write an answer on a piece of paper:

Bernard's message to me is:_____.

(Use one line only.)

Now I will tell you what my message is:

Keep looking for the larger picture.

Yes, that's it. It is no more complicated than that. Think back to the words of Dale Crum, whose work is quoted extensively in this book:

> Your instruction to get behind the protagonist/antagonist's feelings with their dialogue/actions has helped me the most. My self-centered inner thoughts and feelings [and] narration limited a story's appeal.

Over the thirty years I have been doing this work, I have heard thousands of stories—some wonderful, some self-centered and egotistical, some simple

Writing
from
Within
*and the
Human Potential
Movement*

———

115

and lyrical, some anguished. Those that stand out, the ones remaining in my memory for decades, wed an interesting character to a situation, setting, or circumstance that included a world of fascinating minor characters. These stories weave major characters into an intricate pattern of human relationships and concerns—as intricate as any pattern woven into a Peruvian tapestry from the Pre-Columbian era. Such a storytelling tapestry of relationships tells us about ourselves by means of a story that happened long ago and far away, the sounds, sights, thoughts, and smells from eras that have passed away but remain fresh through the stories we tell. Now start writing.

Stories

Two interesting facts of life become evident for those who write stories using the *Writing from Within* approach. First, the many techniques and approaches of the method do not impede the writer's efforts to create his or her own signature writing style. Whereas many efforts to teach writing to beginners and advanced students often yield efforts that have a certain sameness to the the end product, *Writing from Within* stories emerge with unusual variety as the hallmark of their efforts. Second, most of the stories feature unusual depth in the way that writers looks into themselves, probing for understanding of the situation they find themselves in, able to share the rich inner life that comes with such inner awareness.

We hope you will enjoy this rich assemblage of *Writing from Within* stories written over the past two decades.

— • • • —

Liz Kelly was seventeen when she wrote this story. Shortly after the incident described in this story, which occurred when Liz was sixteen, she dropped out of school, left Wyoming, and came to southern California, where she began working as a live-in housekeeper. On her one morning a week off, she came to one of my life-story writing classes, in which she wrote this story:

Tank Top

by Liz Kelly (age seventeen)

With my limited wardrobe, I don't know how I am ever going to dress cool. It's hard to get noticed being only a sophomore, and I don't want to dress like a geek. I stare into my closet; same old shirts, same old pants, same old skirts. I've worn every combination of clothing possible, and this morning I don't know what I'm going to put on.

I glance out the window. It's a dark gray morning blanketed in soft white snow. It looks so quiet and peaceful. I turn back into my room and cross over to my dresser. I open the middle drawer of the old antique and absentmindedly search through the muss of clothing for a possible outfit. An idea strikes me as my hand passes over a dark gray tank top. I reach back and grab the top from the pile.

"Okay, I'm on a roll now," I think to myself. I slip the top over my head and stride back over to my closet. I take the dark brown cords from their hanger along with the light purple oxford. I'm dressed within seconds, and I open my door and step into the hallway. I can smell the coffee and toast coming from the kitchen.

I hear the showers running, and I know that everyone is up. I look at myself in the full-length mirror that hangs on the rough wood wall. "Not bad. Definitely different, but not ugly," I think. I tuck in my shirt and unbutton the top buttons so that the gray tank shows. I go back in my room to find my old high tops. I want to look casual. I pull my laces tight and then go in search of breakfast.

In the kitchen I run into my older brother, Pat. He's a year older, and we don't get along all that great at times. "A bit revealing, isn't it?" he comments on my shirt.

"No. I'm not showing anything," I shoot back at him.

"Just a little cleavage." He turns back to pouring his milk on his cold cereal. I stand on the other side of the big counter and concentrate on making myself some toast.

"Good morning," says Dad as he comes in and pours himself a cup of coffee.

"Good morning," we respond simultaneously.

Dad looks at me. "Is that what you're wearing to school?"

"Yes," I say.

"She's setting a fashion statement," Pat chimes in.

"I wear it today, everyone else wears it tomorrow," I laugh.

"Go change," Dad says. Pat and I stop laughing. (Pat looks away. If he needs to stand up for himself he does, but otherwise he tries to steer clear of Dad.) I look at Dad's face, searching for a clue to what's going on. I'm not sure if he's really angry. His face is serious, and his brow is furrowed.

I don't wait to hear him yell at me so I take off to my bedroom to change. I hear his heavy footsteps in the hallway. I study the closed door of my room, the planks so carefully put together yet not even touching, the smooth black handle and the solid bar that latches the door shut.

The latch raises sharply, metal clanking on metal. The unforgiving wood creaks at me in warning. "Oh, God," I think. "Why did I have to dress this way? Why didn't I know better?" I watch, unmoving, as my father gives the door one hard push and it sails open, slams into the far wall, and slowly bounces back to its resting place, quivering violently all the while.

In three long strides my father is across the room, and he grabs me by the arms. I'm flung from the window to up against the bunk bed.

My head cracks soundly against the old wood frame of the upper bunk, but I dare not reach my hand up to try to soothe away the pain.

"You are not wearing that to school," he screams. "Don't you have any goddamn decent clothes?"

"No," I want to scream back. "I'm trying to make do with the little that I have," but I don't scream it. I know I have to take his shit. He points his finger at me. His hand is becoming worn with age, but I know how strong that hand still is. He jabs me forcefully in the chest.

"This is my house! I make the rules, and if you are going to live here then you better damn well follow them." His finger is the only thing that keeps his fist from hitting me again and again as if trying to stay in beat with my pounding heart.

"I won't cry," I tell myself. I bite my lip and hold back the tears. "I'll change my clothes, and I'll follow his rules, and I'll take his shit, but he is never ever going to see me cry because of him." I look him in the eye and listen to every word he says. I ignore the shaking of my legs and the tears welling up in the back of my eyes. He gives me one hard shove, and I sit down hard on the bottom bed.

"No daughter of mine is leaving this house dressed like a whore!" he says with finality and storms out of the room. I sit on the bed not daring to move, still shaking like a leaf.

"I am not crying," I say to myself over and over. "It's okay." I take a deep breath. "I'll leave. I'll go live with someone else. I'll run away. I will get out of here somehow, some way." I bring myself to my feet and walk to my closet. "He doesn't care. He never has and never will. Just wait 'til I'm gone."

I grab a different shirt from its hanger and change the shirt I have on. Then I take off my shoes and change my pants for jeans. Off in the distance I hear a door open and then slam shut again. "Good. He's gone to school," I think. I open my door and step into the hallway to check myself in the mirror. Pat comes from the kitchen and watches for a moment as I straighten myself in the mirror.

"The shirt really was revealing," he says.

"It was not that revealing," I argue.

"Liz, if I was Dad, I wouldn't let you dress like that either. You let your boobs hang out, and you'll have every redneck in the school staring at your chest," Pat tells me.

"I am not that big," I say.

"You have big boobs," he says and walks past me into the bedroom.

"Some free country we live in. I can't even dress the way I want to. I was hardly dressed like a whore. Dad can say what he wants and do what he likes, but as soon as I'm gone, I'm never speaking to that bastard again." I talk to myself tough, and I act tough, but my insides feel like spaghetti. I go back to the kitchen, acting as normal as I possibly can.

I eat my toast, trying to keep from choking. My younger brother, Michael, looks at me from across the table with his big brown eyes and just shakes his head. He's three years younger than I am but smart for his age. He believes in keeping his nose clean. He reads his books and does his homework.

I finish getting ready for school and step out the door into the icy cold morning. I slide my feet across the frosty porch and down the slippery wooden steps. Crunch, crunch, crunch. My footsteps are the only sounds in the snow. Thud, thud, thud. In my mind I hear his finger banging into my chest.

"Damn it. I am not going to cry. I have my pride and if I let this little incident get to me then I'm never going to survive the real world." The school isn't too much farther. The gray paved road stretches forever though, right up to the gray sky. When I reach the school door, I take a deep breath, trying to calm my shaken nerves.

"I pray to God I don't run into him," I tell myself. "It really sucks that my dad teaches at the high school, but I don't see him." I dump my stuff in my locker and go to join my friends in the hall hangout. I see my friends, Lori and Joszi.

"Hi, guys," I say.

"Hey Liz, how's it going?" they ask.

"Fine," I reply. Lori gives me a funny look. I'm trying as hard as I possibly can to hold back the tears that seem to be forming in my throat.

"Liz, what's wrong?" Lori asks.

"Nothing," I say as I turn and quickly walk away so they won't see me crying. I only take a few steps, then I dry my eyes and turn and walk back.

"Liz, there's something wrong," Lori says. She puts her arm around me and guides me into the counselor's office. Mr. Cothern, the counselor, gives me a knowing look. I've been here before. Lori sits me in a chair, and I put my face in my hands and cry.

Lori leaves to go to class, and Cothern and I go into discussion.

"I can't live with my father anymore," I tell Cothern. "I can't handle it."

Cothern gives me a serious look. Well, as serious as his looks ever get. Mr. Cothern is a tall man who reminds me of a character out of a cartoon strip. His eyes are always laughing, and I don't think he takes me seriously.

"Cothern, I'm serious," I try to convince him.

"Liz, your dad isn't going to move out, and if you stick around things are going to get better. You can work them out."

"Fine," I say.

I sit and listen a while longer, then I go back to class. I know, only too well, that things are not going to change.

P.S. I began to see that my father wouldn't change so I had to. I dropped out of school and moved to Los Angeles from Wyoming. On my day off, I took Mr. Selling's writing class. I sent my stories back to my family. They began talking about all the things that had happened in the family. My father's rage and the alcoholism that triggered it were part of the discussion. They've been getting help.

• • •

Born in Texas, Sam Glenn moved to Washington, D.C., during World War II, where his father worked for the Army Corps of Engineers. Developing into a fine musician, Sam made a living playing around D.C. while still in high school. Later, he attended the Curtis School of Music, played in a unit of the U.S. Army band, and eventually moved to Los Angeles to pursue his career as a jazz musician. A unique improviser, Sam's solos "swing," yet they retain the complexity of a Bach fugue. In Los Angeles he fell in love with and married a woman with two children and later with his wife had a child, Tammy. Today, at seventy-three, he is a fixture in many fine big bands around the Los Angeles area.

The Board

by Sam Glenn

I'm leaving for college tomorrow. Freshman year. Leaving home. Gotta go through my things.

"Sam, I think I'll set up my sewing machine in your room." Mom's voice sounds like she might start crying as she leaves my room and heads to the kitchen.

What to throw away? What to take with me? What to store?

Oh, there's my work board. Should I throw it away? I've had it since I was nine years old. Wow, what a lot of memories. Look at these cut marks—every direction—hundreds, maybe thousands from X-ACTO blades, razor blades, my Boy Scout knife. Crisscrossing the grain of the wood. And my name burned into the corner. Old English–style letters S A M. Used my woodburning kit. There's a little bit of solder embedded over on this edge. That's from when I built my Heath kit stereo receiver. And all those clamp marks. From the C-clamps I borrowed from my dad's tool box.

How many model planes did I put together on this board? Those really neat ones with wings made of thin balsa strips, covered with colored rice paper, then dampened, stretched, and glued so it was tight like a drum head. Rubber-band powered. Sounds simple, but everything had to be just right. They didn't all fly well, but when one did it was heaven. My favorite was a British biplane from World War I. It was blue. Like the kind that fought against Manfred von Richthoven — the Red Baron.

Oh, there are two holes from my tapered drill bit. From carving roses in clear plastic cubes. Made a bunch of those for Christmas presents. When I got finished, each one had a small rose surrounded by green leaves embedded in the plastic. And all made by drilling up through a single hole in the bottom of the cube.

Even used this as a drawing board. I remember copying a pin-up picture of Anne Francis. I could daydream all day about her or the singer Teresa Brewer. "Put another nickel in, in the nickelodeon."

And how I got this board. Dad didn't get angry or upset with me very often, but his tone of voice was not happy.

"Sam, why did you trade your six-shooter cap pistol and holster for this board?"

At the time I guess it seemed pretty stupid. Brenda, the girl in the building across the street, she was two years older than me, had this board (it was a bread board). She agreed to let me have it if I gave her my cap pistol. It sounds crazy, but we lived in a one-bedroom apartment. We didn't have boards of any kind lying around. This board became my workbench, my companion, my confidant. Most everything I did on this board was quiet so it didn't disturb my mom. In case she was having one of her many migraine attacks.

Well, I guess no kid would appreciate this board now if I gave it to him. It's so worn and used looking and has my name on it. Probably should just throw it in the trash — but, if I tuck it here in the side of the closet, it doesn't take up hardly any room. Never know when a good board will come in handy. Might need it when I come home for spring break.

The Circus

by Sam Glenn

"Hold on, we're here." Dad reaches down and grabs my hand. Mom's right behind us.

It's been a long ride on this Greyhound bus. All the way from Arlington, Virginia, through Washington, D.C., to Maryland. Mom showed me on the map. I'm nine years old, and this is a special birthday present. My first time to see a circus. "Ringling Brothers, Barnum and Bailey," Dad says. "The biggest three-ring circus in the world."

Everybody is off the bus, and we are walking across a dirt field. It rained last night, so the circus people have put straw on the ground, but there is still a lot of gooey mud. I almost lose my shoe when I step in a puddle. Some places where the wagons have gone by make it hard to walk. There's a big pile of poop. The biggest poop I've ever seen. Must be from an elephant. Pee-uuu! Glad I didn't step in that!

"Look, Sam," Dad points, "The side show. Let's go in."

There's a belly dancer. Long black hair hangs down over her blue and gold costume. Her belly button has a diamond in it, and it moves up, down, sideways, and in and out as she dances the hoochy koochy. Dad and I sing, "La la la—la—la—, la la, la la, la la la—." Wow, can she wiggle. Mom doesn't think that's nice. The dancer is picking something up. A big snake—green, brown, and shiny. It looks slimy. She's putting it around her neck. She's still dancing as the snake wraps around her arms and body. Its head is right by her mouth, and it keeps sticking out its tongue. She kisses the snake. Yuuck!

There's a giant and a midget. And a sword swallower. First he swallows a small sword, then a bigger one. Next a zigzag one. Oh gosh! My mom can't look. The lights get dim. He's got a long red thing with a wire attached to it. He's plugging it in. Now he takes off his shirt, puts his head back, looks up, opens his mouth, and sticks the red light in his throat. We can see it through the skin of his neck and then down, down it goes to his stomach, then he turns, and we see it through the skin of his back. Everyone is clapping and saying ooh-ooh. Some kids have their hands covering their eyes. I smell buttered popcorn.

Next we see a bearded lady and a big fat lady.

And the rubber man. He's so funny. He makes weird faces. We all try to put our bottom lip over our noses, but no one can do it except him. I can't even touch my nose with the tip of my tongue. He can twist himself up like knots in a rubber band.

Dad says, "I'm not going to try that! We better go to the big top and get our seats."

On the way we walk past some red and gold circus wagons with bars on them. One has a gorilla in it. There's a cage with a tiger and one with a lion. He has big teeth. He's licking his lips. "Hope they fed him today," Mom says.

The big top is all blue. And so big. Dad looks up. "See that man and woman on the trapeze." I look up. They're waving down at us. The woman is wearing a shiny costume. Mom calls them tights. It looks like silver lizard skin. The trapeze woman swings from one trapeze to one where another man catches her. Here comes the first man, but he misses and falls into the net. Everyone goes, "oooohh!"

The boy in the seat next to us has a little lizard on his shirt. He says it's a chameleon. His mom bought it for him at a stand next to the sideshow tent.

Mom says, "Look at that woman in the long white dress and the man with a black top hat, white gloves, and cane." They bow to the audience. There's a little tiny table. He puts his hands on the table, and then his feet go up in the air. He's standing on his hands. Now he's on one hand. There's a wooden lamp post. On top is a round glass ball. His assistant moves the little table over by the post, flips a switch, and the ball lights up. The man stands on the table, points his finger down, places the tip of his finger on the top of the lighted ball. Then he balances himself with the cane, his feet go up in the air, and he's upside down, standing on one finger. Everyone claps and cheers.

At intermission Dad buys me a pink cotton candy. This is so sticky. The boy next to us is still playing with his chameleon. I sure would like to have one. But Mom doesn't like snakes or even little lizards.

It's time to leave. We stop by the booth where they are selling the chameleons. Dad puts his hand on my shoulder: "Pick one out."

It has a little chain around its neck. I pin it to my brown shirt and watch my little chameleon turn brown. As we ride home on the bus, I pet it on the head with my finger. He's on my shirt the whole way home. He likes to stick out his tongue. I stick out my tongue. He sticks out his tongue. I stick out my tongue. Mom whispers, "That's how they catch bugs. Bugs stick to their tongue." Ugh. I'm not ever going to stick out my tongue. Never, ever again.

Epiphany
by Sam Glenn

Mr. Wigent nods his head. His bald head. I return the nod. Ready. I'm sitting next to the Baptismal. Clarinet in hand. He's next to the altar. Seated at the organ. To think not so many years ago when I was nine, this is where I was baptized, where I became a Methodist. But now I'm sixteen. He seems far away. I look up. Up toward the high vaulted ceiling and to the back of the church. The tall, narrow windows. Stained glass. Rainbows of light stream angle above and across a sea of people. There in the balcony, at the railing she stands. Mary Esther. Like an angel. In her blue robe. White collar. Her black hair held in place with a silver headband, framing her face. Her flawless face. She's home from college for spring break.

Another nod from Mr. Wigent. From the wall of organ pipes, so capable of making thunder and making the floor vibrate beneath my feet, comes a simple melody. I count my measures of rests and now my turn to play the melody. The organ lays down a cushion of notes. Seconds or is it an eternity later, Mary Esther's voice, lyrical, joins us like a triangle. The organ, the clarinet, her voice. The words. "Panis Angelicus." Repeats—"Panis Angelicus."

I glance over at a woman in the front row pew. She dabs her eyes with a white lace handkerchief. Her husband bows his head as if in prayer. A hundred faces, no, hundreds of faces. A tapestry of lives gathered together. I look over at the minister. Soon he will give his sermon. He looks at me over the top of his glasses. Is that a glimmer of approval? That I'm playing okay. The organ, the clarinet, and the soprano. All three weave in and out. Sounds and words. To inspire, console, enrich. To give meaning to all of our lives. Yes. To be a musician. That's what I want to be.

The Ring
by Sam Glenn

"So, Tammy, where did you put your mom's ring?"

"It's still here, Dad. In this little box along with Grandma's. And Aunt Ada's and Aunt Pauline's."

Tammy's my thirty-nine-year-old daughter. It's hard to realize she's moved out. Guess she'll always be my little blonde-haired girl. I'm missing having her here at the house. She is leaving some of her books and things.

"Well, I never would have thought to look there."

"Dad, I hope you're writing stories about these."

Oh, yes. I should. Maybe tomorrow. Maybe next week....

It seems like yesterday.... Just like yesterday—

"Wow, Cathy. I'm glad we made this side trip to see Death Valley and Scottie's castle."

Cathy smiles, her black hair glistens.

"Me, too, Sammy. Good thing it's wintertime, though. Wouldn't want to be here when it's hot."

I know she's older, but we enjoy being together so much and our sex life is—

"Only a few more hours of daylight. Keep that map handy. We'll take this road over the mountains to Lone Pine then head north toward Reno."

Cathy and I have been living together for a couple of months. She's got a great figure. She's forty, I'm twenty-eight—I know, who would have ever thought—but we're on our way to a gig at the Mape's hotel in Reno. Got a few days before we open. My boss is super. Name is Merle Cain. He sure knows how to please an audience. What with his jokes and singing. A Dean Martin type. I'm having more fun than I've ever had. All head arrangements. We never use music. He loves to show off the band. Just four of us. Accordion, bass, drums. And me on tenor and alto sax, flute, and clarinet. I met Cathy one night at the club where we were working. Played a special request on the flute for her, "Green Eyes." In between sets we sat and talked. Went to an all night café for pie and coffee and then asked her out on a date. We've been together ever since.

"Cathy, thanks for letting us take your car. My little '58 Volvo just wouldn't have been comfortable on a trip like this. You say you just got it last May. Brand new. '64 Chevy Bel Aire. I like the white color and this blue and white interior. Drives nice, too."

"Sammy. There's the sign up ahead. Turn left."

"Got it. Thanks. Looks like there's going to be a lot of curves. Next fifteen miles. Use low gears on downgrades. Boy, they've had a bunch of snow but the road looks cleared off. Did a good job."

"I'm going to turn the heater up."

"Okay. I think we'll make pretty good time in spite of these hairpin turns. Oh, now the downgrades start."

"Damn, there's some patches of ice. God, hold on."

Can't hold it. We're skidding. Moving fast. Brakes are useless. Pump, pump. I'm helpless. Car has taken over. The momentum. We're going off the shoulder down an embankment. Branches from bushes thrash, strash, whip both sides and windows of the car. Bump, thump, thud—

We come to an abrupt stop leaning up against a pile of snow. I can't get the driver's side door open.

"Are you okay? Can you get your door open? Damn, this door is heavy. We may have to crawl out the window."

"Good, we're out. Got to get up to the highway. No one will see us down here. White car half buried in the snow."

"We'll have to hitchhike to the nearest filling station and hope they have a tow truck. Hope a car comes along to give us a ride."

After about ten minutes a guy in a pickup truck gives us a ride to a place with a tow truck. It isn't easy getting the car back up on the road, but several hours later we're in Lone Pine. They don't want to take a personal check, but I don't have enough cash. Besides they are asking for almost twice the amount of the original estimate.

"I'm sorry about the dent and scratches on your car, Cathy."

"That's all right. At least we weren't hurt, and the car is drivable."

Another day of driving and we get into Reno. Christmas decorations are everywhere. We find the motel where the rest of the band is staying. El Cheapo. Hey, I'm making $175 a week, and we've been off a week and a half since our last job. No pay when we're not working. Plus got to pay our rent back home, rent here, meals, gasoline. We're due back to L.A. a few days before Christmas. Our first Christmas together. Sorry I don't have a bunch of money, but it's been touch and go since I moved out here a little over a year ago. But Cathy and I are so happy. It's crazy, but I let her quit a good job so we can be together. She's in the process of getting a divorce. Won't be final 'til next June.

"Hi Merle. Yeah, we're okay."

"Good. Get your bags unloaded and come over to my room. The rest of the band will be here in a few minutes."

"Listen, something's come up. The agent that got us this job is trying to book us another two weeks, but it will be in Elko. Are you guys open to that?"

"I guess so. Where's Elko?"

"East of here. It means we won't be back in Los Angeles until after Christmas. I don't have anything else coming up for us until mid-January. Anyway be at the Mape's early tonight. We're in the lounge. There's two other acts. We do three shows a night. I need each of you guys to come up with something I can feature you on."

Opening night is smooth. Well except for the bitchy girl singer in the first act. She's pissed 'cause she didn't get first billing. And our drummer and bass player who are supposed to be friends. Hell, Billy the bass player brought Chuck on the band. During our last show for the night, I thought they were going to get into a fight backstage. But Cathy is there for every show. Sitting at the bar cheering us on. One more thing for the girl singer to be upset about. She only had a couple guys listening to her first set. And they were drunk and talking real loud through every one of her songs. Kept asking her when she was going to take her clothes off.

I'm doing "Stranger on the Shore" on my clarinet as my feature song. But not like the recording. I hate Acker Bilk's sound. I do it soft, and low, and slow, and with just a slight vibrato. Subtone up close to the mike. The last half Bud does block chords on his accordion with me in the upper register like the Glenn Miller sound full out and then a chromatic run down to finish the tune just like we started. Soft and low and slow. The audience loves it.

Billy Ates sings "Those Ol' Cotton Fields Back Home." He can sure do that country-western stuff. Course his uncle is Roscoe Ates on *Grand Ol' Opry*, so Billy should be good at it.

The days and nights roll by. Saturday afternoon Cathy and I take a walk down the main street of Reno. I spot a jewelry/pawn shop with some musical instruments in the window. We go in. There's a bunch of rings in the glass counter. Diamond engagement rings. One tray has gold rings. I have Cathy try one on. It's just a plain gold ring. I ask how much. The salesman says it's discounted down. We can have it for $14.95. So I buy it. He puts it in a little box nestled in cotton padding and then in a small bag with the receipt.

"Thanks a lot. Happy Holidays!"

I put the bag in my overcoat pocket. The next day, Sunday, I'm off.

"Cathy, let's drive over to Virginia City. I'd love to see it. I hear Mark Twain worked for the newspaper there when he was just starting out."

We get directions and head out. It's up in the mountains. Lots of curves. We stop at a lookout point. It's a cold, crisp day. Clear so we see the valley below. I pull the ring out of my pocket.

"Cathy, I don't know where this is going. I know this is not an expensive ring, but I love you, Cathy."

"I love you, too, Sammy."

We enjoy seeing Virginia City and head back. We stop at Trader Vic's for some Polynesian food and coconut and rum drinks in Tiki mugs. With the little umbrellas on each one. We get to keep the mugs. They look like those statues on Easter Island.

Merle's girlfriend is in town. We're in the room right next to them. This week she and Cathy have been making homemade tree decorations. Merle found a couple of tree branches that look kind of like tiny Christmas trees. Well, you have to use a lot of imagination. Doesn't look like we'll be home for Christmas. We'll take the trees with us to Elko. Along with cardboard stars covered with aluminum foil for the tops. Someone must have been drinking when they cut out those stars. Strings of popcorn and curlicues of strips of paper cut out of magazine ads.

Back to work, second week. Friday night. Break time.

"Cathy, where did you get the corsage? It's beautiful. I've never seen one like that?"

"I know, Sammy. I don't know if you noticed, but when you played 'Stranger on the Shore,' the casino got very quiet. People stopped for a few minutes and didn't pull the handles on the slot machines. The bartenders didn't make any noise mixing drinks. This elderly woman came over and asked me who is that playing. I told her it was my boyfriend. She said, "Well, hon, you should be wearing this." And she took this corsage off and pinned it on me."

"So, who in the world is she?"

"Mrs. Mapes. She and her husband own this hotel and casino."

Just got the word from Merle. We're not going to Elko. So it's back to L.A. We're going to head over to San Francisco. See my army buddy, Bob. He's a drummer. Then we'll take the coast route down by Hearst Castle. We'll be home for Christmas. That little tree's coming with us. Merle's working on a possible New Year's Eve gig for us. Hope it comes through. Don't have much money for gifts, but it will be good to be home.

"Dad, Dad. What are you thinking about?"

"Oh, nothing, Tammy."

"Dad, does this ring have something engraved on it?"

"No, I never had anything put on it. Maybe something was already on it. I don't remember. That was over forty years ago."

"I think it does. Let me get in some better light. It's kind of worn from Mom wearing it all those years. I can make it out."

"So, what does it say?"

"True Love."

Karl Grey grew up in Texas, the son of a bandleader of the 1920s and 1930s (and later a booking agent for Jelly Roll Morton and others). His mother was the singer in his father's band. Karl's father barely knew Karl and died when Karl was very young. His mother later remarried but maintained dreams of celebrity, style, and status. Karl was a hindrance to her, and she never let him forget it.

The Garage

by Karl Grey

If I hold my breath just like I do when I shoot and brace my arm against my leg just right, I can paint the chrome strip on my model car so good that nobody will be able to tell it's painted by hand. I love building model cars. I love painting all the detail on them that I can, because nobody else I know can do it as good as I can, and that's what has won me trophies for the last two summers at Mrs. Sherman's Lakewood Hobby Shop.

The sweat on my leg—with my arm braced against it—is starting to make me slip, but if I can hold on long enough I can finish this strip down the side panel of my '55 Chevy convertible. Man, is it ever hot. It'd sure be a lot better if she held these contests in the wintertime, then I wouldn't have to sweat so much when I'm painting. I guess I could wait until it's a cooler time, but right now all I want to do is paint my '55. Besides, a summer night in Texas is about as cool as it's going to be for a while anyway.

In the background I can hear the sound of the air conditioner in the window in the den and the TV turned up too loud so that my mother and stepfather can hear it while they are washing the supper dishes. The door from the den to the kitchen is shut so the den will stay cool, but they want to hear *The Ed Sullivan Show* until the dishes are done. My mother washes, and my stepdad dries, and they have their drinks, scotch and water over ice, until they're done. My stepdad tells her all about what went on during the day at work, and she says, "Uh-huh."

I have all my windows open, but I keep the curtains shut so that nobody can see me in my room at night. The only way I can stay cool enough is to sit in my underwear. I wouldn't mind if somebody saw me in my underwear if I wasn't so fat. In fact, if I wasn't so fat, I would probably walk around in my underwear in front of people. If I wasn't so fat, the sweat would roll straight down my body and make me look better, like the guys in *Strength and Health* magazine. My sweat just gets caught in the creases between the rolls of my fat, and then it mixes with whatever dirt is on my body to make "fat mud," which isn't too bad until I stand up. When I stand up, I look like I have stripes on my body. My belly button really gets the worst of it, but nobody can see that. I just have to make sure I dig it out when I shower, otherwise it smells bad.

The model contest is a week away, and because I'm such a good painter I think I can win a first-place trophy this time. The other kids use model putty to make some pretty neat-looking custom cars, but none of them can paint as good as I can. Crap! The paint's running. What caused that? Now I have to take all the paint off and start over, and that can make the plastic look bad if I don't get it off right. There it is, a little piece of molding overrun on the chrome strip. Why didn't I see that when I was shaving it with my X-ACTO blade? Too late now, all I can do is take it off and start over.

I can hear the sound of the locusts outside, the whir of the air conditioner in the den, and the faint sound of conversation in the kitchen. I have to go to the garage to get my trimming blades. I wish I hadn't left them there, but Billy Pike wanted me to carve notches into his six-shooter, and my mother won't allow him into the house.

"Billy Pike is not the right kind of person to be in my house. He'll mess things up, and then you won't clean it up. You never do."

So I had to take my blade kit outside. At least I'll get to cool off when I go through the den. As I stand up, the sweat in the folds of my fat rolls down my body and catches in the waistband of my underwear. As I open the door to the den, the blast of cool air hits my wet skin. Ahh, that's more like it.

"And now, tonight, on this stage—"

I pause to see who is going to be on *Ed Sullivan* and to get as cool as I can. Buddy Hackett. I keep walking, through the other door from the den to the kitchen. There they are, my mother and my stepfather. Their backs to me, facing the window over the sink. She is washing with her drink off to her left, and he is drying with his drink off to his right. I bet they don't even hear me. My mother removes her hand from the suds, picks up her drink with the sudsy Playtex Living glove.

They hear me. She says, "Close the door! Do you think we're trying to air condition the whole house? Where do you think you're going like that?"

"I'm just going to get something in the garage," and I open the door. Shit! The outside garage door to the street is open, and I already shut the kitchen door. I don't want to go all the way back to my room to get something else on…I'll just turn off the light. I know just where the X-ACTO kit is. I can just run out and grab it and run back in and nobody will see me.

I hit the light switch, run into the dark, and grab the X-ACTO kit. Slam! Click! All of a sudden, the lights are on, and I am exposed to the neighborhood, standing in the garage in my underwear.

Panic seizes me. I feel ashamed and embarrassed. Through the door I can hear my mother laughing. I drop the kit and start to pound on the door. I'm pulling at the handle and hitting the door.

"Please let me in! Please unlock the door." I can hear my mother on the other side laughing at me. I'm pounding on the door, and I'm sure the whole neighborhood can see me in my underwear. They have all come out of their houses and are standing in the dark street watching me like I'm on the screen at a drive-in movie. I can hear them laughing at me and my mother laughing at me and I can't stand the way I feel. I am so filled with panic.

I pound and pound on the door, but all I hear is the echo of laughing from both sides colliding on me. It's like this dream that I have over and over. I am walking on a sidewalk when all of a sudden I'm naked. I want to hide so that the other people on the sidewalk don't see me, so I duck around behind the row of trees that is between the street and the sidewalk, but the street is full of cars and all of the drivers can see me, so I go back around the trees, but then the sidewalk people can see me and pretty soon they have all stopped and all of the cars have stopped and they are all laughing and blowing the horns and saying, "Look at the naked fat kid. Does he even have a dick?" The sound gets louder and louder and I can't get away.

CRASH!

The kitchen door flies off the hinges and wood splinters as it hits the stove on the other side of the kitchen. I am in the house before the door hits the ground. My mother screams, and the scotch and water breaks on the floor. My stepfather has his belt undone by now and is pulling it through the loops of his pants.

I am running, into the den, into the cool…and my back stings, again and again, as I drop to the floor and roll myself into a ball and take it on my back. I'm safe now. I'm inside myself, and nobody can see me while he continues to hit me with the doubled-up belt.

"Thank you ladies and gentlemen, it's been a really big shooooow tonight. Next week on this stage, Elvis Presley"…and the crowd screams and my back stings, but it's cool in here and nobody can see me.

• • •

Dale Crum grew up on a farm during the Depression, hard times in Arkansas. His father and mother were solid, God-fearing people, although his teacher/father was a big fan of F.D.R. Tired of his small-town roots, Dale joined the navy just before World War II. After the navy, he followed his parents to Seattle, where they had moved during the war. Dale got an education through the G.I. Bill and went to work for Boeing in Seattle. Later he met the woman of his dreams, and they settled in southern California.

Smoke Rings
by Dale Crum

My cigarette smoke drifts towards Mama's open bathroom window. I smoke two packs of Camels a day and crave nicotine early. Sunshine splashes on the pink shower curtain. Multicolored gold fish fluoresce among its folds.

Reminds me of tame Calicos, orange Orandas, and Bubble Eyes in the Marshall Islands. They swam close to my navy face mask in the coral reefs only three years ago. Wish I were there, now. These rainy Seattle streets depress me.

I stand up and look in the mirror. Out-of-focus wallpaper surrounds bloodshot eyes and scruffy whiskers. Eeeyoo, my breath smells rotten. My tongue feels like sandpaper. I hate these cigarettes! Or, rather, I hate myself for liking them.

"Stunt your growth," my dad used to say.

But he said that about playing with myself, too.

Someone rattles the doorknob. Mama calls, "Dale, you in there?"

I yell, "Won't be long" and reach for the Listerine. Oh, didn't think she would get up before seven o'clock. Too cold to go outside and smoke. I pick up the towel stuffed in the crack at the bottom of the door, spray air freshener all around, and unlock the door.

Mama rushes in. She comes out with a sniff. "Thought you quit."

"Yeah, going to college."

"Not what I meant. You got a good job at Boeing."

"Just made up my mind. Talked to Elsie about it."

She frowns, "Oh, her? You like her?"

"She's a college sophomore in California. She'll show me around."

My B-50 flight control rigger's job only pays one dollar and ten cents an hour. That's union swing-shift wages, too. Boeing hired me a year ago for seventy-five cents an hour. Maybe Harry Truman here in the beginning of his first full term can kickstart the peacetime economy.

I sold my 1941 Buick sedan for eleven hundred dollars. Bought a cream puff '37 Chevy sedan for only four hundred. The G.I. Bill will pay for my college tuition. With a part-time job I can have fun in the sun and learn something, too.

But, when the sun shines, how can I leave Seattle? All shades of green mixed with azaleas, rhododendrons, lilies, peonies, roses, black-eyed Susans, tall fir trees, deep blue sky, pure oxygenated air, and seventy-degree temperature. Can I leave my parents again and their extended family of loving church people?

I cough and spit out nicotine phlegm. Hush up, my brain throbs. It rains all the time here. I sit still in Mama's rocking chair and rethink what I just thought. I can't leave my good friend, Vera, a divorcée who works in the blue-print room. Yeah, I can. She has two little kids that her rich mom takes care of in Portland.

I stopped there once when they were all together. Her mom called me gauche because I refused a pair of her late husband's pajamas and slept in my underwear. Mama doesn't know about Vera.

Nor Joanne, the Catholic girl I sometimes go out with. Joanne's parents don't like Protestants.

I really like Betty and Rosemary from our church. Mama does, too. But Betty's father, Walter, doesn't like me. We went out for breakfast once. I put ketchup on my sunny-side-up eggs. Most everyone does that in the navy. Walter snickered, called me a hick, and used the word gauche, too.

Can I leave my playground basketball team or fast-pitch softball team? I'm the pitcher, and we're in first place in the "A" league. Man, I gotta have another cigarette and run to my car.

Elsie double parks her mother's car beside me. I stub out my cigarette and jump in the seat beside her.

She beams, "Mom says I can ride down to L.A. with you."

Whoa! Her mother is a straight-laced woman from a straight-laced church. Takes two days to get to L.A. Unless you want to switch drivers and speed non-stop on that narrow, winding Highway 99.

Elsie stops in her driveway. Her mom, Mary, rushes to the car. "Oh, Dale, I'm so glad you decided to go. I trust you with Elsie. I know you will have an enjoyable trip."

Mary, a former Alaska school teacher, holds my interest more than Elsie. I could talk to her all day. I think most mothers want to marry off their daughters by the time they're twenty years old. Wait a minute. Something's going on here.

Elsie drives to a soda fountain. The jukebox plays, "Cigarettes and whiskey, and wild, wild women. They'll drive you crazy, they'll drive you insane."

Elsie smiles, "I like chocolate."

I pinch off her straw sleeve. "How about Willie?" I think he's still her hot-headed Cajun boyfriend.

"Willie? I don't know."

"Crazy about you, I recall."

"Finishing up summer school, I think."

"Uh-huh," I grunt. "Pretty possessive?"

She frowns, "Mom doesn't like him."

"Uh-oh," this time I say under my breath. Takes only a second for the picture to develop in my mind. Mary wants me to take her daughter alone to California. She knows Willie will find out. Poof! There goes Willie.

I leer like Groucho Marx, "Long drive with me."

Elsie stares at me for a long time, then takes a cigarette from my package. I hold my Zippo lighter up, and she moves to the flame like a moth to a backyard barbecue. She inhales a little bit, coughs, and waves the smoke away from her face.

"This your first?"

"Yes, first time I inhaled."

For a whole week Mama walks around with a quizzical look after I tell her, "It's to save money. Share expenses."

I keep moving, too. I don't sit still long enough for her to quote the Bible or other proprieties to me.

We get on the road and run out of things to talk about after about two hours. Elsie takes over and drives to Eugene, Oregon, with me still awake. When I take over, she empties the ashtray on the parking lot. The word "gauche" comes to mind again. I hope I don't need those butts if I run out of cigarettes. She falls asleep with a hip pressed into mine.

That old Marine at my teenage filling station hangout pops up. He cautions, "Millions more babies would be born every year if men didn't exercise what little restraint they have." He says that while he watches the backsides of pretty women wiggle by.

Elsie's body pushes harder into mine. She stirs me. I can't drive anymore and pull into a rustic motel with a "Vacancy" sign. A light mist falls.

I shake Elsie half-awake. "Got any money?"

She hands me a twenty-dollar bill. Narrow rows of flat bricks line each side of a muddy walkway. I teeter back and forth on the bricks and run straight into the lobby with dry feet.

"How much for a room?"

The bored clerk looks up from her *True Romances* magazine. She spits out of the side of her mouth, "Six dollars."

"Give me two adjoining rooms."

Her eyes flicker. She looks out the door before she hands me the keys. She makes me feel weird. Why spend the extra six dollars?

I carry the bags and balance on the bricks while Elsie splashes down the middle of the muddy walkway. After I plop down her bag, I move to the door.

She gives me the same quizzical look I saw on the clerk's face.

She mumbles, "Wait, where are we?"

"Grant's Pass, Oregon. Good night."

She raps on the thin wall between us. "When do we get up?"

"Early," I holler and run water in the sink.

We reach Los Angeles late the next day. I park in back of the women's dorm, shake out the kinks, and open the trunk. I turn with Elsie's bag and bump into a guy. He hugs Elsie and asks her, "Drive nonstop from Seattle?"

"Nope, Willie, this is Dale," she replies. "Stopped in southern Oregon."

He persists, "Side of the road?"

"Nope. Motel."

She swivels her body away. Willie's face turns color. He slobbers into his red bandana handkerchief. I steel myself for his next question. In the same room?

He makes choking noises. No words come out. They stand nose to nose. I set her bag down, back out of the lot, and light up a cigarette before he clobbers me.

I've seen riled up Cajuns in the navy. They hold both hands together in a giant fist and slam down on someone's head. Pole-axed, they call it.

Four days later I sit near Elsie in the cafeteria. She waves her left hand at me. A large rock sparkles on her ring finger.

She giggles, "Me and Willie."

I give her a big epiphany smile of admiration. "Congratulations."

She outsmarted both her mother and me. Made Willie jealous enough to pop the question. I feel relieved. For once I don't need another cigarette. Any more may drive me crazy, may drive me insane.

My Sister's Shadow

by Dale Crum

A slight squeak or scratch at Dad's back door flutters my eyelids. Prickles tickle my neck. I rise up from the sofa. Shake the cobwebs out. A burglar? The wind? A dream?

When did I fall asleep? When *Fibber McGee and Molly* went off the air, I guess.

In the dim light a ghostly shadow floats along a wall. Mama's grandfather clock strikes three. Rustles follow the shadow into the hall. Sounds that a woman's dress might make. A whiff of perfume tickles my nose.

Uh-huh, either my oldest sister, Cleo, or older sister, Marguerite. Gotta be Cleo. Marguerite, the valedictorian of her high-school senior class, doesn't go out much. She's going off to college on a full scholarship in a few days.

But Cleo, a twenty-year-old kindred spirit, underachieves like me. She came in late many times but never this late. And, to my knowledge, not sneaking in the back door. Who, what, kept her out so late?

I think about her latest boyfriend that I know about. A man in his twenties standing about six feet three nicknamed "Tinesy" for his height. Real name's Clarence, I think. I don't know whether he ever played basketball. My high-school team has only one boy over six feet tall.

Tinesy has some kind of county job but spends a lot of time in the local pool hall. An expert pool player who plays for money with about a dozen other pool sharks.

From time to time I watch him from across the room while he wins or loses quite a bit of money. The sheriff doesn't run me or my teenage friends out of the pool room as long as the proprietor says we are behaving.

Tinesy never looks me in the eye or acts like he wants to make friends with a sixteen-year-old. He strikes me as a man who's out for only one thing with my sister. Sex.

I decide to seek advice tomorrow from my good friend Milt. He has older sisters, too.

Morning comes. Cleo doesn't come to the breakfast table. Bright-eyed Marguerite sits across from me. My resentful eyes rove from Mama to Dad. I feel that my sisters get away with lots more than I.

What if I stayed out 'til three in the morning? These devout Christians would heap fire and brimstone on my head. Maybe they didn't hear Cleo come in last night. But they do know about her late dates.

Milt guffaws when I express my worry about my sister being with Tinesy.

"Dale, your nose hangs out of joint a mile. None of your business what your sister does. You don't trust Cleo, and your parents do? How funny."

"But Milt, my parents seem out of touch. You and I raise hell all over this town. They never hear about it. They don't know about Tinesy. My sister needs protection."

"From fast guys like Tinesy? Buy her a box of condoms. What protection do other guys' sisters have from you?"

I blink, "That's different. Can I stand by and watch my own sister...?"

"Become a fast woman?" He hoots, "Excuse me, did I say that? She might become an old maid. They call every single girl an old maid if she's over twenty-one."

I shrug, "So what?"

"Girls have to circulate. Find somebody. Parents know that. Geez, you stupid ass."

"Um, Milt, how much do you know about Tinesy?"

"Like most single men in this town, drinks beer, shoots pool, fortunate to have a job, chases girls. What would you hope to hear? That he goes to church two or three times a week? Let me tell you about some churchgoing, whore-hopping guys I know."

"Cleo doesn't go with church guys. Claims they're too sissified."

He sneers, "Sounds like what my sisters might say about you, Dale. Have you had your ashes hauled lately?"

"I don't kiss and tell, Milt. I don't feel sissified. Better watch out for your sisters."

"Oh, ho, Casanova. You don't worry me."

He cackles like the Shadow. Only the Shadow knows what evil lies in the hearts of men.

Hmmm, Marguerite will leave for college soon. Cleo may find a husband. I will become the oldest in the family, with my younger sister and two brothers looking up to me.

I won't have to share a birthday cake with Cleo, who has her birthday two days before mine. Also, if I find some fast girl, I won't have two tattle-tale sisters to rat me out. I will inherit a better room in the house, too.

In the evening everyone except Cleo gathers around the radio for the *Jack Benny* program. Near the end a tall shadow silhouettes itself on the screen door. Cleo and Tinesy come in holding hands. Gee! First time, I believe, that he has set foot inside our house. He seems taller than he does at the pool hall. Looks me in the eye for the first time.

Cleo wraps her arms around him and gushes, "Daddy, Mama, we have some-thing—"

Dad waves his arms. "Shhh, later, later. I want to hear Dennis and Rochester."

I make room on the sofa. Only after the last Jell-O commercial and the orchestra plays "Hooray for Hollywood" does Dad turn off the radio and swivel back to Cleo.

Tinesy clears his throat. He and Cleo blurt out, "We got married last night."

Dead silence compresses our living room. Time and space seem to disappear, as predicted by Einstein.

Mama dabs her eyes. "Cleo and Clarence. What a nice sound! That's wonderful. Congratulations!"

She jumps up and gives them both a big hug. She may never use his nick-name, "Tinesy."

Dad extends his hand to Clarence. "You got a mighty fine woman for a wife. Where do you plan to live?"

"With my folks for awhile. Had to work today. Tonight we're going twenty miles away to Mammoth Spring for a couple days."

He bends down and whispers in my ear. "I'll teach you how to stroke, not hit, a cue ball someday soon. Put some English on it."

I steal a glance at Cleo's radiant face. Oh, no, she may cause Clarence to hang up his cue stick for good.

● ● ●

Paula Diggs grew up in Illinois and attended the University of Michigan in Ann Arbor for a year before she and her English professor husband moved on to Michigan State University. At Michigan, she took the same English courses and hated the same professors as author Bernard Selling. In later years, she became a counselor, artist, and writer.

The Turkish Ambassador

by Paula Moore Diggs

"You know what a Turkish ambassador is, don't you?" Tom Rankin's deep-set blue eyes hold mine as he leans against the wall between the living room and kitchen at the Winders' home. Another English Department party. Our corporate benefactor, Dupont, gave the U of Del a huge endowment to bring big names on campus for a lecture series. The English Department got a chunk to bring famous authors here in hopes of putting Delaware on the cultural map. Sam, our department chair, explained to me that because I'm the youngest at twenty-six and best looking (which isn't saying a lot), I'd be one of the few wives included in the festivities. He didn't mention my cum laude degree… oh well. That invite didn't include lectures, just the parties where old guys run their hands up under my skirt at dinner.

"No, I don't know what a Turkish ambassador is," I tell him. Tom gives me a sly look. He was at the lecture that an author, James Dickey, gave. Dickey's book *Deliverance* was just made into a film. He even played a part in it and strummed his banjo. A very big name. "Dickey told us a Turkish ambassador is sent in when the director thinks he may be losing the audience's interest," Tom tells me. "A guy walks across the scene, everyone says, 'Who's that?' Someone answers, 'the Turkish ambassador,' music swells, and the audience is hooked, waiting to see what will happen. Dickey talked a lot about filmmaking, then he played his banjo." Tom smiles at me and leans further against the wall. Next to him on a bookcase rests the Winders' son's fish tank. Fish are at the top gasping for air. The water needs to be changed. One fish floats slowly to the bottom. Gills pumping. Tom's mouth keeps moving faster, but no words come out. He slides noiselessly down the wall and sits, feet splayed out. Finally topples over on his side, mouth still moving. Cigarette smoke and the reek of alcohol rush into my face as this movement of his large six-foot frame disturbs the air. Sloshed.

His wife, Kay, and I exchange a look. We're friends. Kay is a voluptuous cutie in her prim gray dress, at thirty-one a Playboy bunny of a faculty wife. Maybe a little overweight, but fun. We're a pair with my five feet seven inches and 110 pounds, which makes me "model thin," as the hubby says. Kay and I are both artists. We share hubby stories. I can see my dear guy on the couch. His eyes glisten in the murky air, and the bottle of Jack Daniels next to him is almost empty. A graduate student on her knees on the floor in front of him says her confession.

"Forgive me, professor, but it has been three days since I cracked a book."

"Go, my child, and read no more," he answers.

Kay and I ease our way into the kitchen to help the host's wife, Martha, who's scrambling eggs for a snack for the fifteen or so guests who are hanging on at 1 AM. First lecture, then dinner, then this party. The guest of honor left two hours ago. His party goes on. The '60s, what a lively time.

Kay and I are put to work chopping mushrooms and onions because we are sober and can be trusted with sharp tools.

"Let's go to N.Y. on Friday," Kay says to me. "I want to see John." Kay told me her story about John. Former boss at J. Walter Thompson, a big PR firm. A handsome art director. They almost had an affair. Never consummated but tried under a bridge one summer night. He couldn't get her girdle off, and she laughed so hard he gave up. He was married anyway. "We'll take the train and go to MOMA. There's a new show of dead chickens splattered on walls," she says.

"Yeah, that sounds fascinating," I answer. A couple of artists out on the town. She knows I'm sick of painting portraits of people's children for a pittance, and with two young children I'm a little restless. Hubby is very demanding. A day in the city would be good. I think I can get away.

Watching himself standing and swaying in the other room, I think he owes me one. "Yes, I'll go on Friday," I tell her.

"I'm going to leave when I finish with the mushrooms. Conversations with drunks are boring. I'll call you."

"I'm sure I can get away. Beverly next door will watch the kids. She has a crush on my hubby."

"Who doesn't?" Kay says.

"I'll tell him we going to look at the new abstract expressionist exhibit. He knows you are opening a show soon in Wilmington," I say. "I hope it stops snowing. Slushy underfoot. Too much snow for December."

Martha finishes the scrambled eggs. Kay and I add our choppings. I step over Tom still lying across the doorway. A fish in the tank floats belly up. I slip up the stairs for my coat. Quick as a wink, Leroy, Martha's husband, is behind me. Trying for one last feel of my thigh.

"That's very annoying," I say. Small and sleek, he turns and scurries back to help his wife pass plates. Digging my coat out from under the couple on the bed, I hurry downstairs. I shake my car keys at hubby as I open the door to leave. He smiles blissfully through his alcoholic haze.

"See you," I say. I step out into clean, clear, dark air. A mixture of stars and snowflakes. My breath catches on intake. I scrape the windshield to remove some ice. A solemn figure crosses the street and stands by the lamp post. He is wearing a tweed jacket with elbow patches, smoke from his pipe blows out in front of him. I catch a scent of it. Hmm, Balkan Sobranie, a Turkish blend, I'd guess. The music swells. I start the car and drive away.

New Shooter
A novel by Paula Diggs

Chapter One: Just Listen to Me

A huge slobbering Doberman Pincher clamps his jaws on the little dog's throat. Blood shoots out and splatters all over me. A swarm of bats flies at my eyes. I can't see. Run and climb a tree to get away. Climb higher and higher, foot slips and start to fall. Falling and falling down, down, down.... Below me a large bug stands on home plate, his bat in position to swing as I fall in front of him. A hand touches my shoulder and grabs me. "Help," I cry, "help, help me, please!"

"Calm down, Suzanne. It's all over. No one's going to hurt you. You're dreaming." Daddy Don and Mother stand by my bed.

"No," I tell them. "Out there on the street. I can hear them."

"It's only crickets, Go back to sleep. You're seven years old, a big girl, stop imagining things. Nothing's going to hurt you now."

Those bad dreams keep bothering me. Things without heads follow me around. They try to make me eat stuff that smells bad. Spam. Poison. It makes me gag. Sometimes I throw up in my bed. Last night was the worst ever.

So when I come down for breakfast the next morning, Mother tells me I look like something the cat dragged in. What does that mean? I couldn't get back to sleep at all. Ideas of dark things jumped around in my head. All night. A claw grabbed me. It held on. I had to stay awake or they would get me. I was alone. Really alone. All by myself. No one would help me.

"I cried in my sleep all night, Mother. I thought they were coming to get me. I could hear their feet." Mother takes things in and out of the drawer. Over and over. Everything nice and tidy.

"You should've gone back to sleep. That's all over," was all Mother said to me. She didn't say, "Oh, you darling girl, I wish you'd sleep with us." That's what I really needed her to say. I don't think they understand I need to be in their bed where it's safe. It's scary to be alone sometimes.

Do you ever have trouble sleeping because of the noises? I know I heard something moving around outside. Maybe because of those terrible murders I just solved and things that happened to my friend Judy's family. Mother says it's only my imagination that makes me have bad dreams. If Mother and Daddy

Don don't let me sleep with them, all night I have to tell myself new stories where I find out the answers and solve terrible mysteries and everyone loves me and wants to be my friend. That calms me down so I don't start screaming and wake up everyone. Sometimes it isn't real. A big imagination is part of being me. My name's Suzanne, Suzanne Collier. Grown-ups always say, "What's your name? How old are you?" Mother says you can't ever ask them how old they are. That's rude. Bad manners—grown-ups know all about manners. It's not bad manners if they ask me, "How old are you, little girl?" I get in trouble if I'm rude and then I have to go to my room. Then I just scream and cry until Mother or Daddy Don feels really sorry and lets me out so they can have some peace and quiet. For once. I'm seven going on eight. I know how old Mother is, she's twenty-nine, and she takes an empty Coke bottle and rolls it on her behind so she won't get fat since she had my baby sister, Kathleen. I know lots of things. Daddy Don is thirty-one years old. He's something called a psychologist and always wants to know what I think about something or how I feel. Once he asked me what I want to be when I grow up. I know I'm a detective now because I try to figure out why things happen. Detectives find out why. That's what they do and what I want to become. A detective. Sometimes it's horrible. I just watch what happens carefully and think about it. Bad things are out there. I like arithmetic. Numbers always add up. You can figure them out. That's my best subject. It isn't easy to be me. I ask too many questions.

My teacher always makes me work in the hardest arithmetic book she can find so that I stay busy and don't bother others by asking questions. I'm the best reader in my class, but the girls don't like me. I don't think the boys do either. No one really likes me or chooses me to play with at recess. Kids are lots harder than numbers. Those girls call me nosey because I ask so many questions. Or maybe because I like to smell things. Everyone's head smells different. Baby Kathleen's smells like sunshine and cookies. One time the university president, Mr. Katell, came to our house for dinner. Mother made fried chicken and cheesy party potatoes. I got to help bring the rolls around to people. Daddy Don had a serious face. When I went behind Mr. Katell, I noticed his nice bushy hair, so I took a good smell of his head. It had a strong smell of tobacco smoke and oil. I said to him, "You smell just like a bear." That's a nice friendly thing to say. Winnie-the-Pooh is a bear. All those grown-ups got red faces, and Daddy Don started humming. Mother said, "Upstairs!" to me. That hurt my feelings. I sat in my room by myself and sang, "The bear went over the mountain, the bear went over the mountain, the bear went over the mountain, to see what he could see." No one came to tell me to put my PJs on when it got dark. No one brought me supper even though fried chicken is my favorite. I could smell the food downstairs through the heating grate in my floor. After the guests left, Mother came upstairs and stood at my door. She didn't say anything. She just stared at me. Later I heard Daddy Don say, "She's only a child." Mother told him, "I have to teach her a lesson." I study my lessons all the time. It's better if they yell at you. Sometimes I feel like no one likes me. Not ever Mother, and she's supposed to, I'm her child.

I bite my fingernails when the girls make faces at me. Mary Beth is their leader. She has blonde curls and bows in her hair. She kicked me in the shin once when I told her I could teach her the times tables. She couldn't learn them. Prime numbers are more fun than times tables anyway. Prime numbers are perfect just by themselves. School isn't very much fun for me at recess.

Daddy Don says it will be easier when I go to university. When will that be? Daddy Don teaches at the University of Illinois. He is a professor of psychology. That is a hard thing to be, because you study people all the time. His assistant, Philo, is my very best friend. Grown-ups usually don't make faces but they never listen; Philo listens to me. He's twenty-three. My best kid friend is Judy. She's eleven. She's a sad, quiet girl, because her parents are dead. When you are dead, it's like you are asleep but you don't wake up. Ever. Mother doesn't want me to think about dying all the time or ask so many questions about the dead robin I found because it gives her a headache and she has to lie down. Mother says we should be happy. She likes to smile. Even when Baby Kathleen does number two in her diaper and smells to high heaven. Mother hates to be disturbed when she goes into her room to read. She always shuts her door. Sometimes I sit outside and sing my little lonely song to her. It goes like this, "Mother went into her roooom, Mother went into her roooom, I'm here all alone, Mother, and I want to talk to you." I sing it over and over until she comes out. Then she doesn't seem happy. Mother doesn't like to listen to all the ideas I have to tell her. "Please stop talking Suzanne, don't talk, please, please, please." That's what she says to me. "Go get something to read, honey."

I'm learning to be a detective, so I guess I should read everything. I'm not supposed to look at newspapers. I get too excited and talk about all the stories that I don't understand. Mother and Daddy hide the newspapers under the kitchen sink. I found this one today and took it out behind the garage at the end of our lot. It's musty and dark back here, and no one can see me. I read every word. Even the want ads. I might want a job as a detective. I know how much everything costs. I like this newspaper. It's the *Champaign-Urbana Free Press* — today, June 8, 1944. Seven-year-olds like me shouldn't read so much. That's what our fat neighbor, Mrs. Collins, told Mother. Mother doesn't want me to read about bad things like that terrible man, Hitler. It's nice and cool here under the leaves. Grown-ups want you to think everything is nice and if it isn't, it's your fault. Mother doesn't like it when I pretend I'm a witch and scare Baby Kathleen a little so she screams. I can't say "mean," because that's rude. "Real or make believe?" is what Mother said to me when I told her the mean man walking by our house was going to hurt somebody. I could see it in his mean, bumpy face and bugged-out eyes. I knew something bad was going to happen. Teachers always think it's my fault. When Butch pulled my pigtails and made me cry, my teacher wanted to know what I did to Butch. Butch used to be the marble champ at my school.

I got a new agate shooter for practicing my flute for a recital. It was hard to practice that flute. I hated scales. "Do, Re, Mi, Fa, Sol, La, Ti, Do." Does that make any sense? I had to watch out my window when I did them and tried to learn a new song for the recital, because that's what my hero, Nancy Drew, the detective, would do. Watch. You have to keep your eyes open all the time. What happened isn't pretend. I could tell you all about it, but I don't want you to be scared. I'm hardly ever scared, but sometimes I get the jimmers all up and down my back and just gasp for breath. I saw something that was once part of a man's head. That scared me and made my stomach hurt. Here comes my kitten, Mr. Sir Kit Cat. He likes to sit with me and purr. He can see lots of things with his cat eyes just like me. So I'll tell how the mystery started just a few days ago not long after I got my kitty, if the bad parts won't scare you and keep you awake at night. There were five dead people. Murdered. Five is a prime. Prime numbers are so beautiful. Just like beautiful birds flying in the sky. Just perfect all by themselves.

•••

Marilyn Wirth was born near the city of Richmond, California, not far from Oakland. She grew up a free spirit and attended art school as a young woman. She became an art teacher and, following her father's lead, a successful business woman.

The Story of Little Rickey
by Marilyn Wirth

The melting snow trickles down my boot tops, wetting my woolen socks. The wind howls through the pine trees, creating an eerie sound. Strong gusts blow over the branches, causing large chunks of snow to cascade in clumps to the lower branches. The blowing powder hits my face and back.

The pathway back to the parking lot is quickly covered in areas of gathering snow. I reach my hands into my pockets, thinking the deeper I can shove my hands into my pockets, the warmer I'll be. That is not the case this time. I could kick myself for not staying in the warm cabin, feet up on an ottoman, sipping hot chocolate. I have to be stupid to be out in this element. Mother Nature has unleashed a storm that was not even predicted by the local deejay, and I am out in it by myself, alone. I chide myself for loving the inclement weather and my desire to take a hike.

I zip up my down jacket right to the ends of the collar and turn it up, cover-ing my chin. My woolen hat is no match for the wind. The cold air penetrates each knit hole. I read once that you can save yourself from freezing by stuffing newspapers next to your skin. I could use a small piece of newspaper now, wrapping it around my head, then pulling down the cap—no such luck, rather no such preparation. "I am so stupid to do this" filters through my controlled bravado.... I turn and head down the trail. Large pines line the trail on each side like a misplaced fence.

As long as I stay between the trees I can make it back to the parking lot... stay focused. I feel the cold hit my shoulders as I shake off the snow.... I didn't plan on this.... After an hour of freezing and wandering on lost trails, I see the parking lot in the distance. The remaining car is mine, covered in a soft blanket of white.

Mom runs to the door. "Where have you been?" her voice screeching over worry and annoyance at my ill-planned hike in the woods.

"I'm so sorry," I say, stomping my heavy boots on the entry snow screen. My lips are numb, the sorry is lost. I look at her face. She's angry.

"Get in here and get warmed up." Mom grabs my arm to pull me into the house before another gust of wind rattles the door. I note her absence of hugs. Who would want to hug a snowman just in from the cold, I say to myself.

"Yeah," I answer, my teeth chattering. I shed my near-frozen coat, tossing it on the couch. My two little dogs jump around, greeting me with their happy dance. It's so good to be here. How could I have been so possessed to take a hike in this storm. I sigh. I'm safe. I plop down on the couch, unlash my snow boots, and stick my soaking-wet socks near the roaring flames of the fireplace. Rickey and Kelly jump on my lap, licking me with a welcoming glad-you're-home-Mom greeting. I love my doggies, petting each one on the top of their heads as they bounce around my knees.

Mom hands me a cup of hot chocolate. "I almost lost Rickey today," she says in a low voice. Mom turns away and settles herself in the easy chair.

"What? Huh?" I say, focusing my attention on the chocolate. I wrap my cold hands around the steaming cup.

"Lost Rickey?" I blow on the chocolate to cool it.... "Yeah, what happened?"

Mom adjusts her lap blanket, making herself comfortable on the couch. I prepare myself for a long story.

"Well, I let the two dogs out to do their business...just for a minute...no more than five...and when I opened the door to let them back in...Kelly came in and Rickey did not." Mom looks at Rickey, shaking her head.

"And...?" I say, impatient for the bottom line.

"I called and called and nothing absolutely nothing...no Rickey.... He was gone."

"You're kidding."

"No…Mimi…." She raises her hand to protest my interruptions. "Fortunately, what happened has a happy ending," she says. She raises her hand to stop my questions and to wait for her to finish the story.

I snuggle Rickey to my face. He licks my cold nose. Rickey is a silky terrier, adorable, incredibly feisty, clearly the alpha dog. His small size is no match for even a German shepherd. Once the neighbors' dog, Misty, came to visit. Misty just poked his nose up to the screen, just checking out the house, and Rickey nearly blasted through the screen getting to Misty. I can't have Rickey around other dogs, it's always the same. He may be small in stature but not small in attitude.

"So Rickey just disappeared?" I say.

"Oh, Mimi, I was so worried…. I had to put on my winter garb, boots and all, walked all around in this weather…calling and calling his name…no Rickey." Mom pulls her blanket up to her chest.

"And…then what happened?" I say.

"Well, just as I was coming back up the driveway, a group of renters from across the street came walking by. I yelled, 'Have you seen my little dog?'

"'No,' they answered, 'ain't seen him….' One guy shrugged his shoulders. 'Nope. Ain't no dog out in this weather.'"

"Oh, Mom, how awful for you…" I set Rickey down on the floor and lift Kelly to snuggle him to my face.

"Well, at least a good hour goes by, and I then I see this same group coming back from the lake." Her blanket falls to her lap. "I grab my coat to go out, thinking maybe they saw Rickey at the lake on their walk." She pauses to take a deep breath.

"'Nope, ain't seen your dog no place, lady, not on the path and not by the lake.' By now I was absolutely panicked thinking how upset you would be if Rickey was lost." Mom's face tells it all—concern, panic, frustration. "It would have been my fault." Her voice trails off.

I turn my head to listen. "Mom, things happen," I say, but I am seething that Rickey was out in the cold. Lost.

"Well the rest this group of folks just continues walking by, they don't even look at me…they don't even look up. I just stand there shaking from the cold and for what I was going to tell you…no Rickey…lost…gone."

"Oh…then what happened?" I ask, looking at Rickey, who is now sprawled out as close as possible to the fire without singeing his fur.

Mom gets up to pour us more hot chocolate. "Well the group continues by, and along comes this little kid…a straggler. I say 'Hi,' and he comes over…. 'Cold, isn't it?'

"'Yeah it sure is...my hands is cold,' he says. He isn't wearing any gloves. Well, I lean down and say, 'Hey, little one, have you seen my little doggie on your walk? A cute little gray dog—' Before I could finish describing Rickey, the little kid blurts out, 'Yeah, we gots him in our house...he's locked in the closet...we's gonna keep him. My daddy say he's 'pensive...doggie...I wants to keep him...but Daddy say no...we's gonna sell him.'

"Oh, Mimi, I could barely keep from yelling...those bastards stole Rickey, lied, didn't have him and—"

"And," I interrupt, "we would never have known had that little kid not spoken up." I hear my own voice raising a few notches. I am furious. "Then what happened? Mom?"

"I was just about to go in the house and call the police, but then I thought better of it. My heart was racing, I was so angry. I just said. 'Well, honey, you need to bring my doggie back to the house, he isn't yours' in the sweetest voice I could find.

"I stood by the front door window waiting...and waiting...no little kid... at least twenty to thirty minutes." Mom waves her arms around. "The doorbell rings...it's the little kid. I could tell he had been crying...looked as though someone slapped his face."

"Oh," I say, getting toasty under my throw blanket.

"He tosses Rickey to me, doesn't even say a word, he turns in a moment and runs down the driveway, through the storm. I watch him all the way back to their house," her voice high pitched. I can hear a sense of relief as she recounts the story.

"How awful!" I say. "What terrible people...to steal my dog."

Mom walks over to me and in a scolding manner points her finger in my face. "We really are lucky to have Rickey back, and you...this has been nothing but a worrisome day for me." Mom's eyes squint, she shakes her finger. "And from now on, Mimi dear, I will not babysit your dogs." Her face frowns. "Never again, and you, dear one, you will not go out in weather like this again...hiking...you're nuts. Enough said. End of story."

"Sorry, for the trouble, Mom," I say. "How about stiffening up our hot chocolate with a little brandy toddy?" I open the cabinet and reach for the bottle.

"I forgive you, but no more dog sitting," she says. "So much for resting and enjoying this storm...and I was going to enjoy my book today." I can see she is still reeling from her eventful day.

The wind howls through the nearby trees, blowing and shifting the snow piled on the deck. It's getting dark. I have to take the dogs out to do their business.

● ● ●

Gail Field was a junior at Colorado College when she met her first husband, an instructor at the U.S. Air Force Academy in Colorado Springs, in September 1964. By June 1965 they married and headed for California, where her new husband (me, Bernard Selling) intended to get a degree in film and work in the industry. Gail finished her degree in Spanish, got a master's degree, and had two children during that time. She began her teaching career in the fall of 1968. Within a year, they divorced. Gail met and married her second husband not long after, had another child, divorced, and began a career in business, all by age thirty. She retired in 2008 after twenty years at WellPoint (Blue Cross) as its beloved and highly respected director of Human Resources.

Information I Don't Want to Know

by Gail Field

The clock on our kitchen wall says 7:30 PM. The last rays of sun are disappearing over the Pacific and the air is still warm. Marty hangs up the phone in our kitchen, a somber look on his face. "I am worried most about my mother," Marty says as he hangs up the phone. "With my father gone, she will be a handful." He has just confirmed his flight to Colorado for the funeral of his father who died, leaving his wife, Maxine, Marty's mother, a widow—a woman who never balanced her own checkbook but spent her time throwing dinner parties and pestering her children.

"I'm so sorry, honey," I say. "Sorry for you and for your mom, too."

Marty rubs his beard pensively, and I go to him and touch his arm. He stiffens and looks away at nothing in particular. "I had better start packing," he says and retreats to our home office. There he can find privacy and shelter from his thoughts of his mother and of the funeral just two days away.

As I watch him go, I think of the past several weeks in which I have sensed a shift in our relationship. We have been married now just two months, and already there is a lessening of intimacy between us, a shutting off, as if the newness of it all is too much to bear. Is it the stress of a new beginning? Has he been worrying about his parents all this time and not told me? Or is it something about work that is on his mind? Something else he is not sharing with me? I want to comfort him now but don't really know if he needs comforting, or if so, about what? If I had more clues, I could help him more, be a better wife to him.

In the beginning our thrice-weekly lovemaking seemed just right, at least for me. But quickly our intimate times diminished in frequency and fervor. Marty seldom is ready to make love. It puzzles me, as I have always heard that a man's urge is stronger than a woman's.

Tonight we fall into bed and I reach over to Marty and caress his back, which he has turned to me. He does not respond. "You won't be back till Wednesday,"

I tell him, still stroking his back and fearing to put into words what is on my mind.

"I know. I've got to get some sleep."

Marty turns farther away from me in the bed, clearly on the way to sleep.

In the morning he leaves for Colorado, gives me a wan smile, and I watch him go, shoulders sagging as he slips into the car heading for the airport.

It's Friday night; the boys are at Bernard's, and I am alone. I have decided to clear a small place in our home office where I can put my teaching resources while leaving most of the space for Marty's research papers and psychiatry books.

I pick up a sheaf of old papers that have been sitting in a pile on the window seat since we moved in. There are psychiatric articles, old letters, receipts, and handwritten notes. There is a paper-clipped bunch of pages in a rushed version of Marty's handwriting. Looks like it has been written in a rush or in a stream-of-consciousness style.

I read the scrawl.

Fear of being thought gay blocks men from sharing emotions with each other, from talking more deeply than work and the weekend. It's hard enough to work out how to relate to women, but men also miss out on forming solid and emotional bonds with other men. It's scary enough to form emotional bonds with and trust people, let alone to worry that you'll be ostracized for being gay.

It's easier for me to write this while smoking pot. Easier to put my thoughts on paper....

For a moment I stop breathing and clutch the pages without moving. Is this Marty writing about himself? When did he write this? Is he writing it for research? Was he smoking pot when he wrote this? What does this mean for me? For us?

I look around the room at the shelves of books on psychiatry and sex in general. I pick up book after heavy book, mostly textbooks, searching the sections on sex. I look at the indexes of the books under sex: loss of libido, impotence, homosexuality, physical disorders, psychological disorders.

Myriad descriptions of sexual variety fill the pages. One article tells of a study of men and their mothers: "A majority of homosexuals describe their mothers as having been dominant at home." Another quote: "Homosexual men experienced their mothers more negatively...."

I grow weary of the search and anxious about what is written.

I will ask Marty about it when he comes home from Colorado.

Wednesday comes and Marty returns, seemingly more at ease but silent about his experience with the funeral and with his mother. He is reticent to talk about this and many other things, including his feelings. Did I not notice this before? If I did notice, his silence did not bother me. Now more than ever I wish he would open up to me to tell me what pains him, what frightens him, what moves him.

When he seems relaxed and at ease, we sit down at the dining table together. I begin tentatively. "Marty, I have been reading some of your textbooks about sex. I have been puzzled as to why you don't seem to want to make love very much anymore."

Marty moves slightly in his chair but makes no reply.

"Much of what I read seems to suggest homosexuality." I wait for a response. He shakes his head. "No."

"But you don't seem responsive, and don't seem to enjoy sex with me. What I've read seems to indicate — "

"No, no," he says, pursing his lips as if stopping the flow of speech.

"But why, then? Why are you not interested? Please tell me the reason. Something?"

"No, nothing." And he turns away. I know he feels cornered, and he shrinks back into his chair.

I am left alone with no answers. I will not tell him I read his handwritten note. I want him to tell me out of his own desire to be truthful, to open up to me. I want to know his inner thoughts. I want to connect with this man who is my husband — not just on paper, but to really know him. To love him and to know that he loves me, and trusts me enough to tell me the truth.

I glance at the clock glowing on my bedside table. It is only 9:00 PM. Still early. I will try again in a few days, a week. I'll see how it goes. Maybe he is right. Maybe he has had to deal too much with his mother. I will wait.

A Normal Life?

by Gail Field

A bluish shaft of light from the hospital ceiling illuminates the side of my husband's face — setting off his sparse beard and the almost undetectable quiver in his strong, square jaw. My husband stands over me holding my hand while I lie waiting on the gurney just outside the delivery room. "It's a boy," I say. "We'll name him Martin and call him Marty, just like you."

Marty grips my hand even tighter, his long fingers circling my hand. He swallows hard, blinking, not saying anything. For the first time ever, I see tears moisten his face. He swallows again. "Good job." His voice cracks and he looks away. I have never felt his hand so tight in mine.

The roses that Marty sent me grace the windowsill in my private room overlooking the entrance to the UCLA Hospital maternity wing. Outside on the narrow patch of green along the driveway entrance, a bed of asters swoon and sway, bending their heads in the slight August breeze, inviting me to take a long look. I, too, was born in the fall, and asters have always been my favorite flower. They bloom just when the weather is changing, just when the cool air comes to surprise us with its announcement of fall. The roses in my room are lovely, romantic, beautiful. But the asters signal a change. Something mysterious and yet inviting. I smile as I think of the change that is coming for our family. This moment, this day, this outcome is what my husband has wanted ever since we met, and I would guess for long before that.

It was my mother who convinced me that having a baby with Marty was the right thing to do. "He hopes it would be a boy," I began. "I am not sure I am ready, since Jeff and Willy are still in preschool."

My mother leaned forward, her soft eyes settling on the neat and clean kitchen counter, the flowers in the window, the pictures of family in silver frames on the cabinet tops. She must have been surprised at this orderliness compared with the way I kept my room as a girl, clothes piled high on the rocking chair, dolls scattered about the house. She smiled and lowered her voice.

"You know," she said, her tone soft yet strong, "a good wife does what she can to please her husband. And I know how much Jeffrey and Willy mean to you."

I didn't want to hear this. I preferred to make these decisions myself, without input from my mother. She didn't know the whole truth, and there was no way I was going to tell her. Instead, I nodded as if in agreement and said I understood. I felt like a teenager again, half listening to her, not objecting, then making my own decisions in secret silence.

If she knew Marty spent every Friday night out with his gay friends, doing God only knows what, then she would certainly have an opinion. Then I would have to grapple with that, too, as if I were a child trying to please, caught between the desires of Marty, my parent's wishes, and my own sense.

Outside my hospital window, the sun is setting now, and I fall into the bed, tired from the labor and from the months of waiting for this day. Now, at age twenty-six, I am a new mother for the third time.

I am wondering what my mother would say now, thinking of what I would tell her if I were willing. I'd tell her that I am not really sure whether my decision to give up the birth control pills and have this baby was out of wanting to please my husband or whether I thought I could change him, whether I could make him love us more. Whether I wanted to rescue him from a lifestyle I thought would lead to misery for him and for me. Whether I feel I know what's best for him and for me. Feeling that I could make it all right, like it says in the psychiatry books in Marty's office. I wish I could tell her everything and have her understand without judging.

I would tell her that so many times I have taken just one step, without resisting, and things have turned out all right. Like the time I didn't push Marty when he told me he wanted to go out every Friday night to be with his gay friends. Perhaps my reluctance to resist has brought my husband closer to me as I helped him see the value of family and of a traditional lifestyle. So different from what he thought he wanted be, and maybe, just maybe, what the deepest part of him wanted all along.

When it's time to leave the hospital, we wrap up tiny Baby Martin and set out to pick up the boys, Jeff and Willy, before heading home. I hold this baby tight, this baby with the big nose, brown hair, and soft, smooth skin scrunched in a ball. Smooth, scrunched in a ball. So tiny. So much hope.

I put the baby on the backseat so that I can greet each of the boys with a big hug before they see the baby. The boys, Jeff, five, and Willy, four, run out of their father, Bernard's, house and rush to the car. Willy gives me a hug then opens the back car door and jumps inside, not seeing the baby and barely missing landing right on top of him!

"Willy! Watch out! That's your new brother!"

Willy looks at the small bundle of blanket and baby. "Oh, oh!" he says and slides to the far side of the car. Now warned, Jeff gets in more carefully, and we take off for our home.

Once we settle into a routine, husband Marty is cheerful and helpful. "Let's go to the movies and take the baby," he suggests. So we bundle him up and take him to see *A Clockwork Orange*. "Won't they complain if we take a baby in?" I ask.

"Nope," says Marty with a sly smile. "We'll wrap him up like a present with a peephole in the blanket. They'll never know!" We laugh about our private joke, and I am happy to have my husband back on Friday nights with the family.

I see that he is more attentive, more engaged with me and the boys. We go to Magic Mountain, to Acapulco, to pony rides, and to the park. We pack the baby in the car and go on Sunday drives. We are family, and it feels good.

"We should move to a bigger house," says Marty. "One with room for Baby Martin and more room for Jeff and Willy, too."

We settle on a house in the upscale neighborhood of Brentwood with bedrooms for the boys, a room for a live-in maid, and even an office in front with two exits where the previous owner, also a psychiatrist, saw his patients.

The widow who is selling us the house must love asters, too. The front yard is abloom with them, in yellow, sunny orange, and golden brown, vibrant with new life. I breathe the crisp air blowing through the tall trees in the front yard. Fall is here. Winter will soon follow.

"Marty," I say, pulling in my arms against the fall breeze. "I'll be signing the boys up for their new schools. We'll find the post office and the grocery store and the good restaurants. So much to do to adjust to our new life. It's exciting and a little intimidating."

"Uh-huh," he says slowly as he bends down to pluck a flower. The petals of the golden brown aster are beginning to fade. Marty squeezes the flower and lets it drop to the ground. He turns to me slowly and puts his hand on mine. He looks at me with the same look he had on the day Baby Martin was born. It is a look I'll remember always. "Yes," he says. "A new life."

Mother would be happy for me, for us. "I'm happy, too," I say silently to her. "I know things change, and if they do, I'll be ready. Thanks for listening."

Appearances

by Gail Field

"There are ghosts in this house," I say to myself. I take a look in the bathroom mirror. I recognize my face, but something is different. Twenty-eight is too young to start with the droopy eyes. And that smile. The smile doesn't seem as full as it once was. One of those apparitions is me. I wonder who else knows about it. I look at the young woman in the mirror. Hmmm. Is she hiding something?

My husband, Marty, comes into the bathroom, getting ready for work. "It's Friday. I'll be home late."

I look at his face in the mirror, searching for a sign of some emotion. Some hint of what he is thinking. His face is pleasant but impassive. His eyes widen as he looks in the mirror. Does he see that his wife has changed? Does he see the person that she once was? Or the ghost that she is now?

Marty shrugs slightly and turns without waiting for a reply, slipping out the door and off to work.

After three years of marriage, I thought we had built a warm and solid family that includes my two sons from my first marriage and our son, Marty III, all of whom we have doted on and enjoyed so much. But just this week my husband and I had a conversation that started this feeling of ghostliness in me.

It was Saturday, and Jeffrey and Willy were at their dad's, and baby Marty was taking his noontime nap.

I had entered the living room, putting Halloween pumpkins and scented candles on the mantle. Marty looked up from reading his newspaper, lips pursed, looked at me, and let out a sigh as if he had been holding his breath. "I'll be going out this Friday night."

I looked at him, puzzled, as he had been going out every Friday night with his friends since he told me he needed some time to spend with friends. His gay friends. He had told me he had led a gay lifestyle, and even though this was no longer part of his life, he just wanted to spend time with them as with any friends. Going out on Friday was not something new.

I sit down across from him, putting the candles in my lap. Marty sets the paper aside, looking at the floor and then across at me.

"You always go out on Friday night," I say, not moving.

He looks down at the paper. "Well, I should tell you."

Marty slides his fingers along his cheek, pressing down the hairs of his beard. He looks at me then, "I want to…start seeing people. I mean gay people. Gay men."

I hold my mouth shut hard against my teeth. I stop breathing.

Marty continues, his voice low. "I mean not just as friends."

I have to look away. I have to swallow hard. I had told myself that this moment would never come. But here it was.

I don't want to know details. I want to be in some denial. I want to pretend this isn't happening. But some kind of self-preservation kicks in by way of evening the score.

"I need my space," Marty says.

"Then I need mine," I say. "I will go out, too. I have read all the books on open marriage. We have a maid. Olivia will take care of the kids on Friday nights."

Revenge. The feeling flows over me like hot lava. It kills the present pain with even greater pain. Already I am not who I was.

Friday night comes, and I am pacing the carpet in my bedroom. What will I do? Go to a church gathering? A movie? Out with a friend? Nothing appeals.

I wonder what Marty is doing right now. Oh, no. I don't want to think about it. I push the thought away.

I look in the closet and pull out a simple but festive dress with a white, ruffled collar and slide it on. Okay, I'll go to the Young Adult group function at the Unitarian church.

The community room is festooned with Halloween decorations, and the tables are set with orange punch and pumpkin cookies. I find a seat at a long table, and a young man comes to introduce himself. "Hi, I'm Jim, the chairman of this group. Welcome. Haven't I seen you here before?" He is soft spoken and a little fidgety as his hands clasp and unclasp over the marker he is holding.

"Well, I do attend church here sometimes," I say.

"Good. Here's a name tag. You can use this marker."

"Thanks," I say, as he starts away, then turns back to me.

"Nice to see you again," he says, smiling.

The event of the evening is a talk on relationships by a woman who is a Reiki therapist and marriage counselor. "A relationship is all about energy," she proclaims. "That's what chemistry, puppy love, and love at first sight are all about. Energy."

I am not sure I am ready for all this relationship talk. When the program is over, I head for the door.

Jim rushes toward me. "Leaving so soon?"

"Oh, yes. I have to get up early tomorrow," I say, my first lie of the evening.

"Well, I hope you will come again. I like your energy," he says with a wink.

Driving back home, I think of the evening and how I can feel myself already changing. I know I cannot expect things to be as they seem. I feel I have been turned inside out and upside down. Energy, hah! I feel I have been drained of it all.

I go into the house, and it looks the same. But one cannot judge by appearances.

I get ready for bed, slip between the covers, and browse through a magazine, distracted.

I can hear Marty coming home through the front door. He comes quietly into the room. He steps close to the bed, still wearing his jacket and tie. "How was your day?"

"Okay," I say, "and yours?"

"All right. Do you want the light on or off?" His voice is soft and smooth.

"Off is fine. I am finished reading for now."

Marty takes off his glasses and his clothes, turns out the light, and slips into bed next to me. "Sleep well," he says.

"You, too."

The room is dark and I hear the furnace kick on. The breeze blows by the bedroom window. It is October. Winter is coming.

Goodbye to All That (Summer 1975)

by Gail Field

"I just can't go around pretending to be something I am not."

My husband, Marty, stands under the chandelier in the living room of the condo we have been renting for the last few months as an economy measure, having put our house in Brentwood up for sale. The light falls on his face, and he squints as he speaks, his voice coming out in low squeaks.

"What do you mean?"

"I don't want to live the heterosexual lifestyle anymore. In fact, I can't do it."

He is speaking plainly, but the words don't fall together as they should. Didn't we have an agreement? Friday nights out on his own haven't been enough? Except for the very private life of our bedroom, he seemed to fill the bill of husband and stepfather as well as a doting father of our four-year-old son, Marty III.

And now this. Yes, I was seeing people on the side. An old friend from church. Phillip, my hairdresser. A friend of a friend. How did I think this could go on forever? How much in denial have I been? It is the age of open marriage, and I have read all the books, seen the movie *Shampoo*, and talked in whispers to other women wanting to explore. But I have not thought it would have consequences. Not if I was careful — if I played it safe. The goal was to do whatever I could do to keep my marriage intact. To keep my balance, I needed a way to find personal satisfaction.

We have behaved to the world as a close-knit family, going places and sharing experiences. We have taken the kids to the Grand Canyon, to Acapulco, and to local parks and playgrounds. We've welcomed our newborn and shown him off to the relatives. We have had dinner parties and discussion groups in our home. And all the while, we had an agreement. Each of us could go our own way without being questioned, but we would always come back home to each other.

Marty turns as if to leave the room, to escape my questioning. I have seen this from him so often. Sometimes I have been relieved not to be confronted.

I couldn't comprehend what Marty was saying. What did this mean? Once again was I going to have to live the life of a single mom with kids? Only this time with three instead of two?

"You have to tell me more than that," I implore. "I have to know how to look at this."

Marty's square jaw sets itself, the muscles beneath his beard tightening, his breath shallow. He looks away, his eyes glazing over.

"Who is this person? Where did you meet him?"

"At a gay bar."

Oh, God.

Outside, the waves slap on the sandy beach, just a few yards from our front door. It is nearing sundown now. The shadows will be lengthening and the fish will be feeding, the birds rushing along the beach to find their evening meal.

I catch a glimpse of myself of a few years ago, a young divorcée, having struggled to find a path through the maze of disappointment, anger, and regret at the ending of my first marriage.

I had not expected such pain as when Bernard and I divorced. We fought for four years. Money, visitation rights. Squabbles in court. Money down the drain. My friends had been urging me to get all I could. "Take him to the cleaners," advised my friend Connie. She seemed older and wiser than I, so I jumped on the bandwagon. But she was wrong. All the fighting in court came to naught. A waste of time, money, and energy.

Out of the blue, after one of our court sessions, Bernard called me up and in a pleasant voice listened to my ranting about the court proceedings and about his intransigence.

"You're not being reasonable!" I fairly screamed into the phone. "You have no idea what I am going through or what the kids really need!"

In that phone call, Bernard just listened and for once didn't interrupt me. Finally, I ran out of steam.

"I know what you mean. I have thought this over, and I have decided to stop trying to win. I just want to stop fighting about it all."

I didn't know what to say. That wasn't the track I had been on. I was ready to fight, as usual. I was stunned and had to hang up the phone and get a grip. Then I called him back, and he was still calm, still willing to listen.

"I'm through fighting," he said. "I have been wanting to win, and I realized that was getting in the way. What I really want is a good environment for the boys. One where you and I aren't fighting all the time."

Bernard's calm assurance came through again. And in my heart of hearts, this is what I wanted, too.

"Okay," I said, hardly wanting to speak for fear of disturbing the mood and Bernard's intention. "Sounds good to me."

I hung up the phone, hoping this was all for real. Hoping that the relief I felt would grow into appreciation. That we could actually coexist without bickering. That the boys would be saved from having their parents argue. That there would be peace for us all.

I wonder now if Marty and I are in for bouts of arguing and court fights. Whether the pain will be as great as it was with Bernard or, finally, the resolution as welcome. A swirl of questions floods my mind.

I give Bernard credit for making the first move so that we could coexist in relative harmony for the sake of the boys and each other.

Now I am not sure how this is going with Marty. Here in our rented condo, the trappings of family life mock me, even now. The heat rises in my body, threatening to take me to a dark place. I have given in to anger more than once.

"So who is this person?" I ask again. I no longer know the man standing in front of me and wonder about him, too.

"His name is David, and I want to start seeing him more. I don't want to have to lie to you about what I am doing or where I am going."

Marty looks at me expectantly, and I remain silent. Afraid to say anything. Afraid to be in this conversation.

"So we need to separate," he says. "Our lease here is almost up, so I'll talk to the landlord. You'll want to look for another place, too." This house that has betrayed me and my dream of family closes in on me as the shadows lengthen. I must go outside to breathe in the salt air. I step out onto the sandy lot that is our front yard. The warm sand seeps into my sandals as I walk the few yards to the water's edge. There are two young boys playing on the beach, tossing a ball. One boy slaps the other and runs away with the ball, then falls into the sand, laughing.

I want to call out to them—to tell them to keep playing until they drop or until dinner. "Play on!" I want to say. The other boy picks up a stick and throws it high in the air and catches it just before it hits the ground. The other boy, fresh faced and quick on his feet, rushes to grab the stick. The boys fall together, laughing again. I want to laugh, too, at the turn of fate in my own life. "Play on," I say to myself. "Play on!"

I turn now to head back to the house. The great ball of sun sinks into the ocean horizon, leaving a pink dusting on the clouds, as gentle and sweet as a baby's ear.

—•••—

Bernard Selling was born in Michigan, the son of a psychiatrist and a teacher. He attended the University of Michigan, where he joined the band, majored in literature and art history, and played in every musical possible. After graduation, he joined the USAF and went partway through flight school, doing well until his mother died. Possessing a graduate degree, he was assigned to the USAF Academy, where he taught humanities courses. Following his years in the USAF, he married, attended UCLA's film school, and made short fiction films for many years. After attending the workshops of Joseph Campbell in the late 1970s, he discovered his niche in life: teaching people to write their life stories.

The Jewish Wife

by Bernard Selling

"It's a nice piece of work," Gene says as we look at the first print of my documentary film, *Henry, Boy of the Barrio*. Gene, a buddy of mine, has been an occasional character in the film, as I followed Henry around for a number of years, filming and befriending him. "But, you know," he says, "I really think you want to do fiction films…and if you do, then you need to learn how to work with actors."

Could he be right? I ask myself. I digest his words for quite a while as I begin, then finish, a series of documentary films on young Chicanos in East Los Angeles. The year is 1969, and the civil rights movement is thick with fervor here in Los Angeles, and I'm in the middle of it, with my films on life in the barrios. But something is gnawing at me, and Gene's words have really struck a chord.

Hmm...

My stomach is tied in knots as I ascend the stairs of the Strasberg Institute on Hollywood Boulevard. Actors are weird, I think to myself. I remember how strange they seemed, romping through the rehearsals and performances of *Finian's Rainbow*, *My Sister Eileen*, *Kismet*, and the countless musicals I played as a member of the pit orchestras throughout college and at the National Music Camp in Interlochen, Michigan. Yeah, but they were amateurs, I tell myself.

In the USAF, I directed *Tea House of the August Moon* and had more fun doing it than I could imagine. I knew nothing about directing. But the casting had come out well, and I just sort of moved people around on stage a little here, a little there. It was a howling, sold-out-both-nights success, and I loved every moment of it. In fact, that taste of directing on stage prompted me to come out to Los Angeles and get into films. Now I'm about to get my first taste of real actors—professionals, serous workers like Paul Newman, Brando, and the other Actors Studio people.

I get to the top of the staircase and look around.

"Hello dahling," purrs a tall, skinny woman with dark hair and deep shadows under her eyes.

Ahhh! I jump back. She is everything I can't stand about actors. Weird. Really weird, like Yvonne De Carlo in *The Munsters*. Oh, God. I cringe. C'mon, Bernard, don't stop now. "Where...where's the office?" I croak.

The fee to enroll in the director's course paid, I plop down in a chair in the auditorium. Dan Petrie, the director of Lorraine Hansberry's *A Raisin in the Sun*, is now in the third week of the six-week course. He grins, welcomes me to the class, and hands me a scene to direct. "I'm afraid there's only one left," he smiles.

I read it. Okay, I can do this, I think to myself, and I agree to have it ready the following week. I get some actors together, rehearse, and put it on.

At scene's end, I'm pleased. I think it went pretty well, though both actors seemed a little wooden. It was quite dramatic, or at least the lighting was. I'm the only director who actually lit his scene. The others just depended on the actors.

Dan asks for comments. Each of the twenty guys in the unit shakes his head sympathetically. Ah, shit! I'm devastated at the way they've dismissed my work without a word, and I'm pissed off, too. Feels awful, like the way I felt when Coach Jones yanked me off the floor during the basketball team's practice in the tenth grade—when I guarded my man the wrong way. I gaze at the empty stage. What did I do wrong this time? I wonder.

During a break, Dan eases over to me. "It was a little unfair to you, asking you to do a scene when you hadn't been in the unit before. I commend you for jumping in and doing it." I nod in appreciation. "Trust your actors," he says with a little smile, then turns away.

Three weeks later, another director, Lonnie Chapman, comes in to work with the class. A gravelly voiced ex-Marine, he is a long-time member of the Actors Studio. I recognize him from a number of really good movies done in the 1950s and '60s.

He tells us all kinds of stories about working with well-known "Method" actors.

"Jimmy Dean…he…well, to give you an idea, one day he was rehearsing. The scene demanded that he dislike the other character intensely, so Jimmy just imagined that the guy had shit all over his shoes and focused on getting away from the smell." Lonnie chuckles to himself. We laugh, envious of being in the Studio in the fifties.

Lonnie gives us a list of things to look for in working with actors—vocabulary like the magic If, private moments, sensory work, prior circumstances, circumstances surrounding an object, subtext, intentions, and adjustments. I scratch my head. What's this all about? I wonder.

Each week several actors come in with a scene memorized, and Lonnie demonstrates how he and the actors improvise some of the moments that could have happened before the scene opened, in order to make it all more real for the actors. Looks interesting, but huh! Way beyond me.

He hands out scenes for us to do then explains what each is about. "Brecht's one-act, *The Jewish Wife*, is about a Jewish woman, a doctor, who is forced to leave her country," he says, "because she is Jewish, although her Christian husband, also a doctor, is allowed to stay. She is hurt and enraged." Hmmm. Not long ago I asked my adopted brother, Fred, a German Jewish refugee and relative on Dad's side of the family, "Did your father die of a heart attack as I was told as a child?" "No," he replied. "He died in a concentration camp." *The Jewish Wife* looks like my kind of material. I reach for the play.

Lonnie arranges a cattle call of actors willing to participate in our scenes. As they mill around on stage, I spot an intense, serious, very attractive woman in her early thirties. I introduce myself then ask her if she would be interested in doing *The Jewish Wife*.

"Every actor's dream," she replies. "But a little scary." Dark-haired and dark-eyed, Jean is black Irish, like my wife, Kathy, but could be believable as Jewish. A tall, solid, amiable, blond-haired actor in his late thirties named Kurt is my choice to play her husband. A perfect foil.

"Oh, God," says one of the other actors. "Jean B—? Fine actress. But moody. Jeez. Tremendously ambitious but really frustrated and frustrating." An alarm bell goes off in my mind but—oh, well, the show must go on. We begin to rehearse.

"Okay, walk over here and deliver your lines," I say to Jean. She does as she is told. Nothing happens. It's dead. "More forcefully," I tell her. "With passion." She is silent, then complies. Over and over, week by week, we work. It's boring and dead. God, what is wrong? I ask myself. Kurt seems completely uninspired and Jean is more and more frustrated with him...and me.

Jean starts to come to rehearsals late. I, as a conscientious director, have to reprimand her. "Jean, we just can't have you coming in late like this. We have a scene to put on." She stares at the ceiling. The next rehearsal she misses altogether. That's it, I think. She's out. I can't do this. Actors! Temperament! Moods! They're all weird.

The following Saturday, Lonnie assembles us at the institute and we watch a fine actor, John Ragin (of *Quincy* fame) do a scene from Pirandello's *Man with a Flower in His Mouth*. I notice how deeply he reaches into each moment in the scene. Every line comes out of some past hurt and experience. I see that the lines say one thing but the scene is about something else. Jesus, I think. Now I understand what subtext means.

I begin to think about my scene. These actors have been trained to understand a scene and bring it to life without a director. You, Bernard, have given Jean no chance at all to do that. You have been directing her every move—just like what happened in that scene you did in Dan Petrie's class. Oh my God. That's it.

I'm driving through Hollywood on the way to a film lab. Call Jean now, I urge myself. I stop and pick up the phone outside a liquor store on Cahauenga Boulevard.

"Hello?" Jean's voice is tired and heavy.

"Jean, it's me, Bernard." I practically sing into the phone.

"I was afraid it might be you," she replies. "Listen, I want to tell you—"

"Jean," I interrupt, hardly able to contain my excitement. "I'd like to set up a rehearsal for Friday if you can make it. We still have a week before we bring it to Lonnie."

"What I was going to say is: I can't work with you, Bernard. It's too—hard."

Yeah, what she's saying is I'm too stupid and insensitive a director for her to waste her time on. She's right on that count. "Jean, listen. Something has happened. I understand what's been going on."

"No, I can't. Don't try to talk me out of it. I've thought about it long and hard. It would be too embarrassing to get up in front of the Actors Studio people—"

"Jean, please." God, I am almost begging. "One rehearsal. That's all I ask. If it doesn't work, then we'll just—let it go."

"I don't know…," she wavers.

"Believe me," I add. "You'll see. Friday. 1:00 PM. Forty-five minutes. That's all."

There is a long pause, then her voice comes over the receiver, resigned. "Okay, Friday."

Friday morning all three of us assemble in one of the rehearsal rooms.

"Thanks for coming," I tell the two of them. "I realize it's tough working with a new director who doesn't know the Method. It's been frustrating for both of you. Thank you for being patient." They nod, knowing the truth of what I am saying.

"In a minute, I want you to walk out the door," I say to Jean, pointing toward the door, "and turn down the hallway to the right. I'll signal you when to start."

I walk out the door and down the hall to the rehearsal room where ten actors are waiting—mostly big men, heavy, solid, even kind of scary, and one or two women.

"Thanks for helping me with this improvisation," I say. "I want you to stand on either side of the hall and when the woman comes out I want you to—." I pause, thinking. "Make her feel how unworthy she is, being Jewish, unworthy of living here in your community." They nod and I lead them into the hallway outside the rehearsal room where Jean is waiting. They take their places.

I step to the doorway and signal Jean, then move out of the way.

A moment later, Jean comes out the door. On her face is a look of boredom. Suddenly, the look is replaced by surprise at all the people there.

"Where the hell are you going, filthy Jew!" yells one guy. "Get out of here!" Jean looks shocked.

"Scum of the Earth, go back where you came from," says another, spitting at her.

"They should've killed all of you. Not Christ, our Savior," screams another.

A woman pushes the Jewish wife, whose eyes become dark pools of terror. She looks haunted and bewildered.

"We'll take care of you," hisses a short, fat man. "Wait and see."

Jean passes down the line—pushed, prodded, insulted. The veins stand out on her forehead. She is no longer the confident, black Irish beauty whom I had cast. She is pale, frightened, nervous, and frail. At the end of the line, she runs back into the room. She heads straight for her husband and begins the scene.

"You…you…all the people like you…because of you I must leave my country, just as much my country as yours. Why must I be the one to leave?" On and on she rages.

I've never seen anything like this in my life. This isn't acting. This is being. I watch and listen and wonder at the power of this actress.

When the scene is over, Jean slumps down into a chair. Exhausted. I say nothing. Finally, she opens her eyes. She is neither happy nor satisfied. She wipes the sweat from her forehead. "We have a lot of work to do between now and next Saturday." The words escape her mouth with difficulty. "Let's work tomorrow."

That night, at home, I am pleased. "It was something to see," I tell Kathy, who is happy that I am happy. She knows how tense and difficult I have been the past three weeks.

We rehearse two or three times after that. I give Jean and Kurt very few instructions. Mostly I try to make more visible the imaginary circumstances that the two of them have had to endure in the weeks before the wife's departure—and we work on the relationship between the two, whether they like each other, love each other, trust each other, improvising these moments to make them real, letting the two of them draw their own conclusions.

At the end of the last rehearsal, I take Jean aside. "Jean," I say, "when you perform the scene tomorrow—at the climax, when you are really feeling what it's like to have to leave, wherever that is for you, turn to the audience and make them feel as if they are all the ones responsible for your leaving. You can even come down from the stage and walk among them if you like." She looks at me quizzically, then shrugs.

Saturday, at the Institute, hundreds of people mill around waiting for the scenes to begin. Agents, friends, and family of all the directors and actors are there to see the work. No Jean. Jesus, I fret.

I stand at the stairs watching and waiting, the same stairs I had climbed four months before. Still no Jean. A small, bent woman with her gray hair fixed in a bun walks past me, but no Jean. Damn. I glance inside the auditorium. The lights are dimmed, and the scenes have begun. I walk inside, one eye glued to the stairs. After the third scene ends, Lonnie announces, "And now *The Jewish Wife*, by Bertholt Brecht." I start to raise my hand to tell him that—

The small, gray-haired woman appears on stage. My God in heaven, it must be Jean. The transformation is astonishing. Her voice is small but penetrating. A sense of utter conviction and belief envelope every word. The relationship between the two, their strained affection, his guilt, her rage, becomes painfully evident. Little by little we in the audience are transported to a time and place thirty years past when omnipresent evil ruled, while more human impulses mean little or nothing. At the climax of the scene, she turns to the audience:

"Why must I leave my country, with everything that I love and cherish left behind, my husband, my work, my children? Why must it be I who has to leave?"

The audience gasps. Their sense of horror is palpable as she looks into the soul of each one. The scene ends and the applause is virtually endless. The little gray-haired woman appears and straightens up. The applause continues.

Moments later I seek out the actors. Each is surrounded by family, friends, and industry people. I catch Jean's eye for a moment. She hardly says a thing. I understand. She is still the Jewish wife. Still caught up in the moment. But a little nod escapes her. It is all I need.

I know now the joy of working with an actor on the deepest level of imagination. I have learned a lot more about myself in these last few weeks, especially about my imagination and how it can touch that of another person.

Gene was right. My future has become a little clearer.

Appendixes

The Appendixes that follow contain and amplify two important elements of the *Writing from Within* process.

Appendix A: Writing Vivid Life Stories: The Basic Steps of Writing from Within

For those who are familiar with my work *Writing from Within* and would like to reacquaint themselves with the process, I have included a reminder in this section. This summary will also serve to introduce the process to those who are not familiar with the *Writing from Within* process, possibly readers who are mostly interested in the book for the kinds of things that make fiction interesting but who at the same time would like to understand the roots of this new material, no matter whether it is applied to fiction or nonfiction projects.

Appendix B: Creating a Supportive, Nonjudgmental, yet Insightful Writing Group

For those who would like to participate in writing groups formed around this process or who would like to improve the feedback process in groups already functioning, I have provided a step-by-step outline for achieving both safety and effectiveness in such groups. The foremost consideration in the creation of such a group or group process is for each writer to feel both safe from unnecessary or injurious (no matter how well-intentioned) criticism while at the same time getting a very real sense of how the members of the group have received the writer's work—not in the head but in the heart and the gut. For each person who is providing feedback to be able to articulate this experience takes time and energy. Consequently, those in groups that seek to provide this kind of feedback must be constantly vigilant to ensure that each listener's feedback comes "from the gut"; that is, the feedback must always come from the listener's *feelings*, not from his or her *thoughts*.

Success in this effort will generally result in the writer's increased willingness to take risks, try new things, and make changes.

Writing Vivid Life Stories:
The Basic Steps of *Writing from Within*

The basic steps of the *Writing from Within* process allow a writer to acquire the skills necessary to write a very readable story while also developing the feedback skills (see Appendix B for more on feedback) that will help the writer look at their work objectively. Each rewrite leads the writer into a comfortable sense of where to go next to allow the story to unfold in the best way possible. (The *Writing from Within Workbook* takes the writer through each step of the rewriting process.)

Writer's block and the frustrations that occur when the writer's path becomes too steep are also discussed in *Writing from Within*. A story often develops its own momentum, and the writer must get out of its way. Blocks frequently occur when the story wants to go one way, but the writer wants to impose their will on the story. If the writer has given a story's characters viable character traits, those qualities will seek to exercise themselves on some situation or other. The wise storyteller creates those situations and then steps back, allowing the characters to go to work. This is as true for the writer of life stories as it is for the writer of fiction.

If a storyteller follows this path, transforming the narrative of the story (through action, dialogue, and inner thoughts and feelings) becomes a natural and comfortable process. However, if the storyteller does not provide the central character with adequately defined qualities, then they will find it difficult to write action, dialogue, and inner thoughts and feelings. The solution to writer's block and inertia can usually be found in the degree to which we, as writers, give our characters the qualities they need. Yes, it's all about character: what the character wants, how they go about getting what they want, and the qualities of the minor characters that flood the main character with a light that demands self-examination and action. (For more about these issues see "Your Writing Process" on page 3 of the Introduction)

First Steps: Writing in the Present Tense, Simplifying Language, Feelings

The first steps in the *Writing from Within* process enable the writer to experience the power of the present tense and to find the expressiveness that lies in the English language when the writer takes out anything intellectual. Likewise, when feelings—physical sensations or emotional responses—are added to a story, the audience becomes glued to what the writer has to say. These are among the most powerful early steps of *Writing from Within*.

WRITING IN THE PRESENT TENSE

In the beginning of *Writing from Within*, I include a number of steps designed to allow the writer to experience the maximum recall of the experiences about which they have chosen to write.

The first step asks the writer to create the first draft of the story in the past tense and then to rewrite the same story again, this time in the present tense. The goal is for much more of the story to become available to the writer—that is, the writer's ability to recall the past now works better and better.

One hazard may pop up at this point: In some cases, your subconscious protects you from things that are painful to recollect. If this is the case, you may need to be satisfied with a story draft that is a little more distant and written in the past tense. You can always begin the present-tense rewriting process anytime and with any story.

EXERCISE 1: MY FIRST MEMORY (FIRST DRAFT)
Go ahead and write a first draft of your first memory. The story of your first memory may be short—a paragraph, for example. That's fine. There's nothing wrong with writing a short story.

Topics That May Trigger Your Earliest, Most Vivid Memories
1. Your first experience with a birth in the family
2. Your first experience with a death in the family
3. Your first experience being all alone without Mommy or Daddy
4. Your first experience in the hospital—tonsils out/other illness
5. Your first experience riding on a train, boat, bus, or airplane
6. Your most vivid memories of Mom and Dad
7. Your first day in school
8. Your most embarrassing moment in school

9. Your first time being really afraid

10. Your most vivid recollection of Grandpa/Grandma

11. Your first time getting into trouble

12. Your best friend in school

EXERCISE 2: MY FIRST MEMORY (REWRITE)

Have you written entirely in the present tense? If not, go ahead and make any needed changes. Remember that the present tense really helps the reader be *in* the experience.

Write in the first person singular (use *I*, not *we*).

Note: In years gone by, many of us who are of some age were told in school, "never use *I* in anything you write. It is too self-centered." In those days, the goal of academic teaching was to be objective, in an effort to be truthful. Likewise, most novels and short stories were written in the third person "he…" However, in the last twenty-five years, a great deal more interest has developed in the uniqueness of the person doing the writing. Therefore, *I* has become quite acceptable in autobiographies, short stories, and novels, and even in academic writing.

Here's a story about someone's first memory:

First Memory

by Steve Dix

I am four years old, and I am learning to tie my shoe. I keep trying. I have finally done it. Now I can go tell my mom I've learned to tie my shoe.

SIMPLIFYING LANGUAGE

Many people who try to write find it difficult because they fear the judgments that other people will make about their work. They will feel good about their work if the thoughts that others have about it or the comments that others make about it are not in any way hurtful or critical in a negative way, as I outline in the feedback section in Appendix B (see page 189).

Everyone has an inner voice that can be very critical. This voice may sound a lot like a parent's voice or that of one of your teachers. You need to learn to soften the voice of your critic so you can be creative. You will need to learn where and when to rely on that critic, because it often wants you to listen to it at the wrong time. In other words, it interferes with your creative voice.

Getting and giving feedback that is not judgmental or critical—that is, not full of *shoulds* and *shouldn'ts* that may make you feel like you want to stop writing—also helps. In this manner, feedback helps the creative part of you go ahead and be creative.

(For more about giving feedback, please see "Feedback" in Appendix B.)

IF TELLING A STORY FROM A CHILD'S PERSPECTIVE, USE AGE-APPROPRIATE LANGUAGE

Many of us have within ourselves a ferocious self-critic that often stops us from trying anything new and different. "You'll probably fail, so don't try it," the critic says. This is particularly true of our efforts to be creative, especially when we try to write. One way to circumvent this self-critic is to write in a way that is not "us." That is to say, when we write from a perspective other than our normal self, the critic is often willing to stay silent.

I have found that an effective way to silence your inner critic is to see if you can write in a way that sounds believable as the child you once were. In other words, if you write about being in school for the first time at six years old, it helps if you do not sound as though you are sixteen or seventeen but as if you are six or seven.

If your story is written without adult-sounding words and phrases, your readers may find themselves believing the story more because they are in the story more fully: "I really believed I was listening to a child of six telling her story. I was right there with you the whole time." On the other hand, if the story contains many adult-sounding phrases, a reader may say something like, "The adult-sounding words took me out of the story. I was in it, but then I was bounced out, as if I were suddenly watching from a distance."

What can you do to sound less grown up? Mostly, take out certain things from your writing.

Let's suppose you are sixteen and looking back on a time when you were about six years old. If you were a reader, would you believe the following extract is supposed to be coming from the perspective of a six-year-old?

> There were times, I suppose, when it seemed as if one would never be permitted to mature at a pace that was reasonable for my age. No, I was forced, albeit in a kindly fashion, to repeat ad nauseam the chores and duties attendant upon childhood: taking out the garbage, playing sports, minding my manners, and obeying the strictures of my parents.

No one reading this passage would suppose for a moment that a child had written it. Why? *Children don't talk or write that way.* Let's look at parts of this passage to see what is not childlike about it.

Vocabulary and Phrasing
"permitted to mature"
"reasonable for my age"
"ad nauseam"
"attendant upon"

These are all phrases no child, other than one attending college at a remarkably early age, would ever use.

Qualifications
Children virtually never qualify or modify their statements. "I suppose" is a qualification, as is "albeit in a nice way."

The Objective Voice
Children virtually never employ "One," the objective voice.

Lists
Cataloging chores and other adult tasks in an orderly manner is an adult way of organizing. Children are usually less orderly and logical.

Now let's look at the passage after rewriting it in a way that may not be childlike but at least is not obviously adult.

> From the time I was six or seven until I was eleven, my dad insisted that I take out the garbage every Thursday. What a chore that was! It seemed as if he'd never give me any real responsibility, just chores. But I remember one time when he…

Here we have a voice that could be adult or child. The passage is simple, straightforward, and gives the reader a clear mental picture of the situation being described. The narrator's voice and point of view do not intrude on the action or the progress of the story.

Let's take a final look at the garbage incident rewritten in the present tense:

> I am twelve years old. Dad makes me take out garbage every day. Yuck. Every day for six years. "When do I get a chance to do something important?" I wonder.

Suddenly, the story is more intimate, more vivid, and more personal—all traits that make for good stories and that you should seek to bring out in your writing.

EXERCISE 1: SPOTTING ADULT LANGUAGE — "WILLEM"
Now test your ability to spot adult language in this story by a young girl. Circle any such language and make any changes you feel will help the story sound more believable as the work of a child.

Willem (First Draft)

by Jade

I have no recollection of the first years of my life. Looking way back into my early childhood, I come up with this little picture, a picture that has surfaced every once in a while whenever I am thinking of the old days.

I must have been three or four. There was a big sprawling backyard. A tall hedge concealed the main house, some distance away. The house was quiet; my mother must be resting. It was siesta time, the time after lunch when the shimmering tropical heat made people drowsy. It was also Sunday, but the drone of my father's machines was not there. My father must also be resting. My father had a house industry at that time. He bought up spices, such as pepper, nutmeg, cloves, cinnamon, etc., from the farmers overseas on the other island, then he ground and bottled them in a special building on the grounds. To assist him, he asked Willem to come over from his hometown on a far island to work as his foreman. Willem also lived with us in an outhouse.

I liked Willem, because he always spent time with us, whenever there was a chance. That afternoon was no exception. He showed my brother and me some magic tricks, and then he said, "Kids, I am going to show you how strong I am!" He asked Joni, another workman, to go fetch the bicycle. Then he lay down on the grass, and Joni was told to drive over his chest. I was greatly impressed when Willem stood up unhurt. Then he said, "And now the van will drive over me."

Again he lay down on the thick grass, and supposedly the car drove over him. I was in awe that nothing happened to Willem. This was where I got befuddled. I am sure I had not told my mother then and there, because she would have taken some action regarding Willem's way of entertaining us, and she would have remembered the incident. As it was, when years later I talked about it, Mother said, "Nonsense, he must have tricked you." But I still wonder, did it really happen, or was it just my imagination?

Compare your rewritten version of the story to the way the author rewrote it:

Willem (Rewrite)

I am sitting in the grass. The grass is cool and green and very thick and soft; I sink in it. I like to sit there. The sun is very bright, but the hedge behind me makes a shade.

My brother is here, too. He is bigger than I. Papa and Mama are not there. I know they are in the house a little far away behind the hedge. But

Willem is there. He is very big, almost as big as Papa. I like him. He always has something nice for me and my brother.

What will he do today? He is lying in the grass. There is also Joni. I do not know him too well, but he does not matter. Willem is there!

Willem is saying, "*Anak mau lihat Willem digiling sepeda?*" ("Kids, want to see the bike run over me?") Joni already goes to fetch the bicycle.

Here he comes straight at Willem lying in the grass. Then the bicycle is already on the other side of Willem and Willem is standing up and laughing. He laughs at us kids. And then, with a laugh in his eye, he tells us that Papa's big truck will now run over his chest. Again he lies down in the thick grass, the car comes and it is over him; only his head sticks out, and he is laughing at us. I hide my head. I am afraid, and I grab my brother's hand. But I still look. Willem is already up again. Willem can do anything!

Years later when I talked about it, Mother said, "Nonsense, he must have tricked you." But I still wonder, did it really happen?

This rewrite of Willem is a much simpler story than the first version. We as readers are in the event rather than watching it from a distance. We feel as though the event is happening to us, as if we are the child watching the truck go over Willem, wondering how such an awesome thing can happen.

EXERCISE 2: MY MOST VIVID MEMORY (FIRST DRAFT)
Write a story about your most vivid memory when you were any age from birth to twelve years old. You can write the story in the past tense or the present tense. If you initially write it in the past tense, do your best to rewrite it in the present tense.

EXERCISE 3: MY MOST VIVID MEMORY (REWRITE)
When you have done that, look over the story to locate any words or phrases that sound as if you are older than the age you are in the story. If you find such words, take them out and rewrite the story so it sounds believable and uses the words a child of that age would use.

Use what you have learned here to give yourself and others story feedback.

ADDING FEELINGS

Now it is time to write another story and to add a new ingredient to your "writing stew" by adding *feelings*. Here is an example of a simple story that includes feelings.

A New School

by Lupe Acosta

I am eight years old. I'm walking into my brand-new school. As I walk into my homeroom, I feel as though everyone is staring at me. I think to myself, "What if my friends get lost and don't meet me at the lockers, then who am I going to hang around with?"

I hope I don't arrive late to any of my classes, cuz I'm afraid that the teacher might tell me something in front of the class.

The day goes by pretty fast, and I have no problems. I finally go home.

Lupe writes about a very common early vivid memory—a first day in a new school. Other common vivid memories are a birth in the family, a death in the family, a separation or divorce, or a special family event, such as a birthday, a holiday, a trip, or a religious celebration.

If you have trouble remembering something vivid, try thinking about the first time something happened, such as the first time you went with your father or mother on an adventure or the first time a teacher told you to behave in school.

Some Vivid Memories

1. You remember the birth of your sister or brother.

2. An accident happened to a family member or to a friend, and you saw it.

3. You made a mistake and were teased by other kids.

4. You were in the hospital getting your tonsils out or recovering from some other sickness.

5. You rode on a train, bus, boat, or airplane for the first time.

6. You remember some moment about Mom or Dad, happy or sad.

7. You went to school for the first time.

8. Something happened that made you really afraid for the first time in your life.

9. You remember something vivid about Grandpa or Grandma.

10. You had a good friend in school, but something happened between you.

11. You remember a wonderful celebration—birthday, Christmas, etc.

EXERCISE 1: MY EARLIEST VIVID MEMORY (FIRST DRAFT AND FIRST REWRITE)

Write the first draft of your earliest vivid memory. Once you have written your story, apply step one (write in the present tense) and step two (simplify words and sentences).

The next step is to add *feelings* to your story. The following exercise will help you to identify some feelings you experienced in the past.

EXERCISE 2: IDENTIFYING AND DESCRIBING FEELINGS

Now, let's name some of the feelings you experienced as a child. (Circle one or two—there are no right or wrong answers here.)

1. When I woke up in the morning, I was (happy / sad / anxious / worried / excited) about going to school.

2. When a teacher or my mother or father told me I did a good job, I felt (happy / good / surprised / pleased).

3. When I was younger, my little (brother / sister) used to hit me. When that happened, I felt (angry / stupid / ashamed).

4. I remember a time when a friend of mine was hiding and jumped out and said, "Boo!" That (scared / surprised / annoyed / angered / bored) me.

5. I wanted to go to college and get a good job. Of course, I knew it would take a lot of money to go to college. When I thought about it, I felt (worried / depressed / angry / excited / confident / sad).

6. When I went to the movies with my (girlfriend / Mom / Dad / boyfriend) and they put their arm around me, I felt (happy / warm / loved / annoyed / hopeful / afraid).

A story is often about something happening. In the story, people do things to or with other people. They have thoughts, and they express them. They also have and express feelings. In a good story, the audience cares about what the characters are feeling.

So if you give feelings to the character who represents you in the story, the audience will enjoy the story more.

EXERCISE 3: ARE MY FEELINGS IN MY STORY? (SECOND REWRITE)

Ask yourself whether your feelings are in the story. If not, add them. ("I feel sad," "I feel happy," etc.) As before, begin your story with "I am…" and provide your age when the memory happened.

Here is the previous story with feelings added:

A New School

by Lupe Acosta

I am eight years old. I'm walking into my brand-new school. It seems so big and scary. I can feel the butterflies in my stomach as I walk into my homeroom. I feel as though everyone is staring at me. I think to myself, "What if my friends get lost and don't meet me at the lockers, then who am I going to hang around with?"

I hope I don't arrive late to any of my classes, because I'm afraid that the teacher might tell me something in front of the whole class. How embarrassing. The day goes by pretty fast, and I have no problems. I feel relieved to finally go home.

Do you see how much more interesting the story is when feelings are included? The story sort of pulls you into it, right? This happens when you include your feelings. Every time an action takes place, it's good to bring your feelings into the picture, so keep in mind that it's okay to put feelings in places other than just at the beginning and at the end of your story. Remember, the audience sees the story through your eyes.

For the audience to believe what the people in a movie are feeling, the audience has to read the expressions on their faces or figure out what they are feeling from the way they act. But the audience of a written story will believe anything you tell them about how *you* are feeling, because they are seeing the event through your eyes. It is therefore okay—and even a good idea—to tell the audience what those feelings are.

Eventually, you will start bringing your feelings into the story as you write your first draft, but for now, adding them in one of the rewrites is fine.

Second Step: Brainstorming, Adding Dialogue, Adding Thumbnail Sketches

We have explored three of the *Writing from Within* steps to writing an effective story:

1. writing your earliest memory in the past tense and converting it to present tense
2. simplifying the words and phrases in your first memory as you rewrite so the story sounds like it is being told in an authentic child's voice
3. adding feelings to the story so the reader can more easily connect to the characters

Brainstorming, the next step of the *Writing from Within* writing process, is designed to help you find an endless wellspring of possible stories in your own life experiences. Next, adding dialogue makes the story much more complex by emphasizing that the story is about more than one person's concerns. After that, you'll learn how to create a quick look at a new character through the thumbnail sketch.

This is a good exercise for collecting ideas to write about. Many writers of life stories will say, "I don't know what to write about. I can't think of anything." Brainstorming can help.

Let's look at the word BRAINSTORMING and break down the word into its parts:

BRAIN: That's right, the thing inside your skull where all your *thinking* happens. It is to your body what city hall is to a city. *All orders start there.*

STORM: This word means, "to whirl around with great gusts of wind."

BRAINSTORMING: It's a whirlwind inside your brain. It also means letting your thoughts wander around and explore, and letting the pictures in your mind go wherever they wish to go.

Brainstorming about your life memories means to search out and allow your life memories to appear in your mind.

Before starting a brainstorming session, fold a piece of paper into six parts and tear it so you have six small pieces of paper. Do this three more times so you have a small stack of blank pieces of paper. You may also cut 3 × 5-inch index cards in half. As long as you have a stack of twenty to thirty cards, you will reap the benefits of this exercise in brainstorming. Here, in bold type, is what I wrote when I was doing this for myself.

Brainstorming

by Bernard Selling

1. **Train burgers**—Dad takes me to a restaurant to see a model train serve hamburgers.
2. **Fighter plane/eyes**—A WWII fighter plane flies overhead—I can see the pilot's eyes.
3. **Lone Ranger/kick me**—Boy next door pins a "kick me" sign on my back after he asks if I want to be the Lone Ranger.
4. **Kowala**—My teddy bear when I was three.
5. **Lionel train**—My first train set at Christmas. I was four.
6. **Handlebars**—My tongue sticks to the handlebar of my tricycle. I'm three…scared.

I then did twenty more of these.

EXERCISE 1: BRAINSTORMING VIVID MEMORIES
Now let your mind go back over your memories, over the events and people

that are vivid. For each new memory that comes up, write down a word or two on a piece of paper.

Once you have written down these moments, you can begin to figure out which ones are the most "vivid" memories. Have fun with them. Let the sad ones be sad and the funny ones be funny. When you begin recalling these moments, they come faster and faster, like a racer going downhill. You pick up speed. That is the whirlwind part of the brainstorming process.

Also, if you remember one kind of memory, such as my memory of my dad taking me different places, you may remember more memories that fall into that category. For example, here are the results of a quick brainstorm I did specifically about my dad taking me places:

Dad Taking Me Places (Brainstorming)

1. To Bablo on boat (Detroit River) when I was five.
2. To the Smithsonian Museum, in Washington, at twelve. Saw Eohippis, size of a hand, first horse.
3. To Railroad Fair, in Chicago, at twelve. Got sick.
4. Inside big train engine cab, at nine. Very hot.
5. His office in Detroit, I was five.
6. To a zoo in Detroit, I was four.
7. Captured German sub, in Detroit, I was six.

For the purposes of writing your next story, you may wish to brainstorm about how you got to your current city and state. Did you come from another country, another city, or another place in the city? Was the trip vivid for you? If yes, find and write about those vivid moments.

In your life, you may have done many things, been many places, and seen many things. If you have come from another city, another state, or another country to the city and state in which you are living, you have lots of things to write about. Other topics to write about include some of the moments between you and members of your family. These often yield good stories.

EXERCISE 2: ANOTHER VIVID MEMORY (FIRST DRAFT)
Think of another vivid early memory that happened to you. How do you feel when you write about it? Make a picture in your mind and then write about it. Keep in mind the things you are going to do when you write. If you feel sad and happy at different times in the story, write those feelings down on paper.

Once you have explored this vivid memory, go ahead and write a new story from this memory.

EXERCISE 3: ANOTHER VIVID MEMORY (REWRITE)

Do you remember the steps for rewriting? Good. Now rewrite your story.

Add any feelings you wish and change any verbs into the present tense. Ask yourself, "Are there any adult-sounding words or phrases that I need to take out or change to words and phrases that sound believable as the words of a child?"

Notice that I ask you to add new things in the rewrite, not in the first draft. That is because the goal of the first draft is to get the basic story finished, not to make it perfect.

You are now ready to go on to the next step: adding dialogue.

ADDING DIALOGUE (TALK BETWEEN PEOPLE) TO A STORY

In the story you have just written and rewritten, think back to the memory that inspired it. Did the people involved say things to each other? If they did, put that dialogue in your story. You may remember the exact words that were used, but if you don't, *write more or less what was said.*

The story is now more interesting, yes?

Dialogue makes writing interesting to read, because it brings characters to life.

EXERCISE 1: HOW DIALOG SAYS A LOT ABOUT CHARACTERS

In the following exercise, circle the type of person who is speaking:

1. "Gol' darn' you, varmint, draw that six-shooter if you got the guts," says the old (cowboy / bus driver / school teacher / garbage collector / rock guitarist).

2. "Hey, man, what's happening in the 'hood?" says the (school teacher / lawyer / congressional representative / African-American jazz musician).

3. "You must not linger any longer on this assignment, boys and girls. Time is up," says the (cowboy / bus driver / school teacher / pet-store owner / congressional representative).

4. "Four score and seven years ago, our fathers brought forth upon this continent a new nation, conceived in liberty and dedicated to the proposition that all men are created equal...," says the (drunk / talk-show host / cowboy / former president).

These lines of dialogue can tell you who is speaking and maybe even give you an idea of what the speaker looks like. The great thing about dialogue in a story is that it's okay to make it up, although you should try to keep to the truth as much as you remember it.

Often you can create dialogue from what you have already written on your paper. Here is an example:

"Mom told me to go to the store" can easily be turned into "'Go to the store,' Mom told me."

Note that writers insert *quotation marks* ("...") around the words in dialogue that are to be spoken by a character.

Now, let's learn how to separate different speakers. Notice the marks of punctuation inside the quotation marks, after the "he says," or "she says," and notice how this phrase can come after the first phrase in a sentence or at the end of the sentence if it is short.

(")Go get my mirror(,") laughs Cinderella's wicked stepmother. (")I must see if I have grown more beautiful since I last gazed upon myself(.")

EXERCISE 2: USING QUOTATION MARKS AND PUNCTUATION

Here are some exercises to help you learn how to use quotation marks and punctuation. Put the proper quotation and punctuation marks in place. You may write more than one mark inside each ( ).

1. ( ) Go home right now ( ) I tell my sister.

2. ( ) Where do I get off the bus ( ) I ask the bus driver.

3. ( ) There must be fifty girls here waiting to try out for the team ( ) I say to my friend ( ) Maybe we should just go home ( )

EXERCISE 3: CONVERTING TEXT TO DIALOGUE AND USING THE CORRECT PUNCTUATION

Rewrite the next three sentences, turning them into dialogue and using the correct punctuation marks and quotation marks as shown in the following model:

Mom told me to go to the store becomes "Go to the store," Mom told me.

1. Mom tells me to go to sleep.

2. I whisper to my sister that I don't understand why she always teases me.

3. I yell at her to stop hitting me.

Quotation marks and *proper punctuation* help identify who is speaking.

Start a new paragraph every time a new person enters the scene or speaks. In fact, start a new paragraph every time the speaker changes in a scene.

Here is an example of what would happen without marks of quotation and punctuation:

How do you know if I am speaking or you are speaking when writing looks like this I ask my students. It sure is confusing one girl, Janet, answers back. So Mr. Selling, tell us, huh? huh? another student says.

Here is an example of what happens when the necessary marks of quotation and punctuation are included:

"When a person is speaking, use quotation marks so readers will know he/she is speaking," I tell students.

"How do I know if you are speaking or I am speaking?" Janet, one of my students, asks.

"Each new speaker gets a new paragraph," I tell her. "And put quotation marks around the actual words a person says."

EXERCISE 4: USING THE CORRECT PUNCTUATION AND CORRECT PARAGRAPH FORM

Rewrite the following sentences using the correct paragraph form as well as quotation marks and proper punctuation to help the reader identify who is speaking. Remember to start a new paragraph *each time a new person speaks*.

1. There are three girls standing on the corner. I walk up to them. ( ) Which one of you is Nancy ( ) I ask them.

2. ( ) I'm Nancy ( ) says the biggest one. ( ) Wha'cha' want ( )

3. The two cowboys sat down on the bench outside the marshall's office. Each of them began rolling a cigarette. ( ) You seen the marshall ( ) asks one of them. ( ) Nope ( ) says the other cowboy ( ) a small mean fella with a scar down his cheek. ( ) I think the marshall is a chicken ( ) says the first cowboy. ( ) Mebbe he is and mebbe he ain't ( ) says the third cowboy, nodding toward the stranger walking toward them.

EXERCISE 5: ANOTHER VIVID EARLY MEMORY (FIRST REWRITE)

Try adding some dialogue in this draft. You may not remember exactly what was said, but that's okay: You can invent what was said, as long as it feels like the truth. When you have finished writing, ask yourself whether your story has been improved by including dialogue.

EXERCISE 6: ANOTHER VIVID MEMORY (SECOND REWRITE)

Make a picture in your mind of the memory you just wrote. Did you write it in the *present* tense? If not, rewrite it in the present tense. Did you add your *feelings*? If not, add them now.

Did you add dialogue? If not, go ahead and do it if you can. Don't worry about using perfect spelling or grammar when you are writing something new. After you have finished your story, you can check your spelling. However, the one important thing to include in the first draft is the proper punctuation (including quotation marks) for dialogue. Yes, that's right—even in the first draft.

Make it a habit so that you don't even think about it, you just do it. Proper use of beginning and end quotes allows you and your readers to grasp very easily who is speaking.

ADDING THUMBNAIL SKETCHES

An effective storyteller, whether journalist, biographer, or novelist, usually provides the reader with a brief portrait of a character as they enter a scene. This picture may include some sense of the person's physical nature ("a tall, thin man with a pronounced Adam's apple") as well as a sense of his psychological nature that can be discerned from his actions ("despite his gangly appearance, he had a robust, outgoing nature, rare in such a spindly man"). You help yourself as a writer when you include such portraits, especially if something contradictory about the image makes the portrait memorable.

This type of quick sketch is called a "thumbnail sketch." THUMBNAIL SKETCH = *sketching/drawing + plus something the size of a thumbnail*

In a good story, clear, vivid pictures of the characters are important so the reader can visualize what is happening.

Here are some examples:

1. The tall stranger comes toward me. He has a mean smile on his face.

2. Melissa is chubby, her fat cheeks always stuffed with food.

3. My dad has bushy eyebrows. They go up in the corners. It makes him look a little crazy. He is always laughing.

What people do also helps the audience get a picture of them. Here are some examples:

1. She sat in the corner, kicking the chair in front of her. (bored or angry)

2. She looked out the window, rubbing her hands together. (cold, worried)

EXERCISE 1: DEVELOPING THUMBNAILS OF
FAMILY MEMBERS AND FRIENDS

Now develop some thumbnail sketches of your family members and friends, using their looks, expressions, size, actions.

1. My brother (or sister), _____, _____

   _____

2. My father (mother), _____, _____

   _____

3. My friend, _____, _____

   _____

Appendix A:
Writing Vivid
Life Stories:
The Basic
Steps of
Writing
from Within

181

EXERCISE 2: BRAINSTORMING YOUR FUNNIEST MEMORIES
Think back to the funniest things you remember in your life. Do some brainstorming, using the pieces of paper to choose the funniest moment. Who is in the picture with you? Write their names down here. (If you can remember, include hair color, eye color, height, weight, etc.) _____

_____

Final Steps: Inner Thoughts/Feelings, Climax, Finding the Opening, Adding a P.S.

The six steps explored so far have given you content for your stories (brainstorming), techniques for making your stories come alive (narrative, dialogue, and thumbnail sketches), and opportunities for your readers to grasp the content of your stories more effectively (sentence simplification).

Now we will look at ways to shape your stories to make them more accessible to the reader—that is, find ways to take what is in your mind and shape that material into objects the reader can almost see, touch, smell, and taste, as if you were a sculptor modeling your ideas in words instead of clay while deepening your sense of the central character's inner thoughts and feelings.

ADDING INNER THOUGHTS AND FEELINGS

Every writer has three things to work with: narrative, dialogue, and inner thoughts and feelings. Your first draft of a story may be all narrative, but as you progress through several rewrites, you include more dialogue. Now you can begin to add expressions of inner thoughts and feelings to your story.

Inner thoughts and feelings are the thoughts people normally keep to themselves, thoughts that no one else hears. They are so private, people sometimes don't even realize they have them. Often they are expressed as a question, and sometimes they are followed by an answer that seems self-critical.

For example, let's suppose I get on a bicycle for the first time, begin to go faster and faster, lose control, and bump into a tree. My inner thoughts might be:

> You disobeyed Dad, who told you to wait for him, and look what happened.

or

> Why did you do that? You dummy. If you had waited for Dad, this wouldn't have happened.

or

Uh-oh, Dad's gonna be mad. I ripped my pants. Oh, me. Oh, my. What am I gonna do? Better invent a story: The bike took off by itself.

Here is another example:

"Go to the store now," Momma says. "I mean now!"

"Oh boy," I say to myself. "I think I'll call up Martin and he can meet me there and we'll buy some candy." I pick up the quarter on the kitchen counter. "Yes, Momma," I say. "If I really have to, I will." "Oh boy, yum, yum."

These thoughts and feelings from the deepest part of the character make a story interesting because they allow the reader to see into the character's deepest self.

EXERCISE 1: ADDING THOUGHTS AND FEELINGS – "MY HAPPIEST MEMORY" (FIRST DRAFT)

Write the story of your happiest memory. Based on the previous steps, what questions should you ask yourself to make the story better?

1. Have I...?
2. Did I remember to...?
3. Did I remember to...?

The answers are (1) *written in the present tense*, (2) *add feelings*, and (3) *add dialogue*. Now it is time to add *inner thoughts and feelings*.

Now let's explore another step in the process.

EXPANDING THE CLIMAX OF THE STORY

CLIMAX: The high point of feeling or conflict just before the release

One of the techniques you can use to make a story interesting is to find the climax of the story (where the feelings inside the reader are strongest) and expand it, making it fuller, deeper, richer. The climax is usually where conflict, struggle, or effort gets more and more intense until it reaches a transformation point, like water boiling in a pot. When the water gets hot, it turns to steam and expands, and soon it boils over, reaching a climax.

Here is an example:

One day my brother comes home. He is in a bad mood. He sits down in front of the TV. I am doing my homework. He tells me to go to the store and buy him some cigarettes. I tell him I have to do my homework.

At this point, the story has conflict: One person wants one thing and another person wants something else. As the two people dig in, neither willing to yield, the story builds toward a climax:

I tell him I have to do my homework. I ignore him. He yells at me some more. I keep ignoring him, hoping he'll get tired.

When you get the sense that someone is about to win or lose, to fail or succeed, you have reached the climax of the story.

The climax is what you want to expand in the story, making sure the reader can see the conflict fully and completely.

Let's examine the conflict:

He tells me to go to the store. I tell him I have to do my homework.

This is the part you can expand. What techniques could you use?

1) _____ 2) _____ 3) _____
4) _____

Here is the same conflict expanded at the climax of the story, using dialogue, feelings, actions, and inner thoughts and feelings.

My Brother, James

"Go to the store," my brother, James, tells me. "I want some cigarettes." He is sitting in front of the television set at my mom's house with a beer in his hand. I don't look at him. I just keep doing my homework. "I said, 'Go to the store. I want some cigarettes.'"

"I can't," I say. "I have to do my homework. Momma told me to stay here and just do my homework. No matter what." I still don't look at him.

"Huh! You do what Momma wants, but you won't do what I want. Is that right?" I turn to look at him. His face is all red, and his eyes are crazy looking. "Maybe I should just leave. That would serve you right. I'll just leave. That would serve you right," he laughs, sort of crazy.

What would Momma and me do if he left? We don't got a father, and Mom doesn't make enough to support us. It scares me to think about that. I keep trying to do my homework. Maybe I should do what he wants.

He gets up and goes into the kitchen.

The story is getting interesting, right? The brother wants one thing, which is _____. The child wants another thing, which is _____. The brother is trying to get what he wants by _____.
The child tries to get what he wants by first _____ the brother and then by _____.

The story can now go in one of two directions. If the brother isn't very understanding, the conflict could get worse:

He gets up and goes into the kitchen. I am kind of scared. He comes back with another beer. "Look, kid, you do what I say in this house, you understand?" I nod my head. He pushes the back of my head kind of hard. "You go outside and stay out 'til you decide to do what I tell you." I sit in my chair, afraid.

"Go on, out!" I get up and take my jacket. It is cold outside. "You leave that jacket here. You have a lesson to learn," he says. His eyes are hot and mean looking. I go outside and sit on the stairs. I am getting colder, but I won't get him his cigarettes. He is not going to get the better of me.

If the brother is basically a good person who is just a little tired, the story might sound like this:

He gets up and goes into the kitchen. I am kind of scared. He comes back in a moment with a smile on his face.

"I'm sorry, kid. I'm just in a bad mood. I had a bad day." He gives me a punch in the arm and smiles. "Go do your homework."

That would be a happy ending: While he is at the refrigerator, the brother realizes he is being very hard on his younger brother and apologizes for being so self-centered.

These examples show two different ways the climax of the story could go. They each use dialogue, feelings, inner thoughts, and actions to expand the climax of the story. Can you see more of the picture this way? Do you get more of the child's feelings?

The following is another example of a story in which the climax of the story has been expanded:

Tank Top (Excerpt)

by Liz Kelly

"Liz, there's something wrong," Lori says. She puts her arm around me and guides me into the counselor's office. Mr. Cothern, the counselor, gives me a knowing look. I've been here before. Lori sits me down in a chair, and I put my face in my hands and cry.

This is where the first draft originally ended. The following paragraph continues the story, expanding its climax:

Lori leaves to go to class, and Cothern and I go into discussion.

"I can't live with my father anymore," I tell Cothern. "I can't handle it."

Cothern gives me a serious look. Well, as serious as his looks ever get. Mr. Cothern is a tall man who reminds me of a character out of a cartoon strip. His eyes are always laughing, and I don't think he takes me seriously.

Appendix A:
Writing Vivid
Life Stories:
The Basic
Steps of
Writing
from Within

185

"Cothern, I'm serious," I try to convince him.

"Liz, your dad isn't going to move out, and if you stick around things are going to get better. You can work them out."

"Fine," I say.

I sit and listen a while longer, then I go back to class. I know, only too well, that things are not going to change.

P.S. I began to see that my father wouldn't change, so I had to. I dropped out of school and moved to Los Angeles from Wyoming. On my day off, I took Mr. Selling's writing class.

I sent my stories back to my family. They began talking about all the things that had happened in the family. My father's rage and the alcoholism that triggered it were part of the discussion. They've been getting help.

(Please see page 117 for the entire story)

The most effective way to build the climax of the story is first to identify it and then to use all the techniques at your disposal to give a complete picture of what is happening at that moment: narrative, description, action, dialogue, inner thoughts and feelings, thumbnail sketches, and the like. In fact, it will seem as if the scene is taking place in slow motion.

A different type of climactic moment occurs in a movie from 1966, *A Man and a Woman*. In this climax to this firm, the central character (Jean-Louis Trintignant) gets off a train and falls into the arms of the woman he loves (Anouk Aimée). A then-new type of lightweight, handheld camera allowed the cinematographer and director to circle the couple in slow motion, as if a web of love were weaving its way around them, giving the viewer the impression of two lovers who are so overcome with love for one another that when they see each other they are able to tune out all of the noise and activity at this busy train station and think of nothing but one another.

EXERCISE 1: THE MOST VIVID MEMORY I HAVE SHARED WITH SOMEONE MY AGE (FIRST DRAFT)

Write a story about the most vivid experience you remember sharing with someone your own age. It may be an argument, an intense discussion, or something you did together. Use all the techniques we have discussed so far, but *do not try to create a good beginning in this first draft; leave that to the second draft.*

EXERCISE 2: THE MOST VIVID MEMORY I HAVE SHARED WITH SOMEONE MY AGE (FIRST REWRITE)

Check your work to make sure you have written in the present tense, added feelings, and included some dialogue. If not, go ahead and add these elements now.

EXERCISE 3: THE MOST VIVID MEMORY I HAVE SHARED WITH SOMEONE MY AGE (SECOND REWRITE)

Once you have written and rewritten your story, identify and expand upon the climax of the story.

Now let's look at another step in the process.

FINDING THE BEGINNING OF THE STORY

Often, writers don't know how to begin their stories. They think that they need a great beginning, and if they don't have one, they can't write the rest of the story. Is that the way you feel? You shouldn't! Don't worry about the beginning until you have finished your first draft or two.

When you have done all the other things to make your story easy to read and interesting that we have already discussed, such as adding dialogue, adding feelings, and adding inner thoughts and feelings, then you can work on your beginning.

Step 1. A good way to begin a story is with *dialogue* or *action*.

Look for the first instance of dialogue or action in your previous story. Can you move it up to the beginning of the story? If you can, it will make an effective beginning.

Here is an example:

First Draft

I am about four years old. My family is going to a friend's house, and they have a dog. "I want to pet the dog," I tell my mom.

"Sure, I'll go with you," she says.

"Now, be careful," she warns when we get there. I pet him a couple of times with Mom nearby. She sits down again.

"Can I pet him alone?" I ask.

"Sure," my mom says.

When I approach the dog, he bites me on the lip.

Now let's see what happens when the writer puts the first two lines of action or dialogue (in this case, dialogue) in front of the opening narrative ("I am four years old."):

Rewrite

"I want to pet the dog," I tell my mom.

"Sure, I'll go with you," she says.

I am about four years old. My family is going to a friend's house, and they have a dog.

"Now, be careful," she warns when we get there. I pet him a couple of times with Mom nearby. She sits down again.

"Can I pet him alone?" I ask.

"Sure," my mom says.

This change gives the story a better, more-interesting beginning, doesn't it?

Step 2. After beginning your story with some *action* or *dialogue*, you may want to bring some factual information into the story later in the first paragraph or even in the second paragraph.

ADDING A POSTSCRIPT

Sometimes a moment in your life will have a great impact on your life. Not only will you remember it vividly, but you will feel its effects for a long time to come. Sometimes you will not fully understand that impact until you have written about it.

It is often a good idea to add a P.S. (postscript) to the end of your story that makes it clear what impact that moment had on your life. Notice in Liz Kelly's story on page 120 that she adds a P.S. at the end of her story. It clarifies the what and why of the path she has followed and allows for some retrospection.

EXERCISE: ADDING A P.S.

Write a story or use one of the stories you have already written and add a P.S. at the end if you have any other information you want to add.

When you have finished your rewrite, you can begin to *edit* your story. That means checking your *spelling*, your *grammar*, and your *punctuation*. You can use any kind of language that you want in your dialogue, but make sure to spell and to punctuate it correctly.

Creating a Supportive, Noncritical, yet Insightful Writing Group

At this point, I want to step back from our work on technique to talk about the process of giving and getting criticism. A key aspect of succeeding as a writer is knowing when and where to get guidance, support, and assistance. Most writers need feedback from members of a writers' group, an editor, or some other trusted source. I want to suggest ways of getting positive support and feedback and tell you how to get the most out of it in order to continue to grow in your work.

Everyone has encountered criticism from different people during their lives. You probably remember how stung you felt when teachers, parents, and even friends criticized you when you were doing the best you could. Such criticism felt particularly harsh when you were doing something artistic—writing, painting, drawing, or playing a musical instrument. Often, you simply stopped doing these artistic things. Gradually, you internalized this criticism and developed your own inner critic.

Now that you are going to do some writing, you need to retrain this inner critic. Otherwise, you may not go on writing after the first bit of harsh criticism you receive when you share your work with others—and you do need feedback.

Retraining your inner critic is no small or easy task. It can be accomplished, however, by patience, discipline, and a positive outlook. The same process can also be used to retrain the critic within members of your support structure. First, consider the kind of feedback you as a writer would like to experience. Then I will outline a process by which the wild, undisciplined, even destructive critic within you can be converted to a purposeful, disciplined, insightful one.

What Is Supportive Feedback?

A group, or even one like-minded person, can help you get the kind of feedback you need. This person or group to whom you are going to turn for support needs to develop a disciplined response to your writing to protect you and make you feel safe while guiding you in the direction of better work.

That discipline involves adhering strictly to the following agreement, which each participant will make with other participants: Feedback to each writer after they share a story will be Nonjudgmental, Noninvasive, Corrective, and Affirming (NJNICA, for short). Each person giving feedback agrees to avoid any statement that sounds judgmental or invasive, no matter how innocently they intend it. During the early sessions of any group, one person may be appointed to be on the lookout for such judgmental and invasive statements.

A. Typical judgmental statements are:
   You should have.... You could have.... You ought to have....
   If I were you, I would....
   That (story, thought, paragraph, etc.) was too (sentimental, clever, abrupt, silly, slow, confusing, boring, etc.).

B. Typical invasive questions and statements are:
   Why did (or didn't) you...?
   Why were you...?
   You sound like you were trying....
   You often...or always....

Any one of these statements can discourage a writer. Instead, ask members of your group to try

A. Nonjudgmental corrective statements, such as:
   I would like to (see, feel, know, be able to follow, etc.)....
   I had trouble seeing the picture.
   I had difficulty following the action.
   I needed to feel the character's feelings.
   I found my attention wandering.
   I needed to hear the characters talk to each other more.
   I had difficulty finding (or following) the spine.
   I didn't know what the central question of the story was.
   The key question was answered before I had a chance to get involved or get excited about it.

B. Nonjudgmental affirming statements, such as:
   I saw the picture clearly.
   I was right there with you the whole time.

I knew what each character (or the narrator) was feeling from one moment to the next.

The dialogue drew me in and helped me know each character.

The balance of narrative, dialogue, and inner thoughts and feelings held my interest.

These are important considerations. A potential writer can listen all day to nonjudgmental, noninvasive, corrective, and affirming (NJNICA) comments. This writer can listen for only a few moments to invasive or judgmental statements. Then they will begin to defend themself, their creativity will turn off, and they will stop writing.

You may find that your support system is only one person, or perhaps you and a friend decide to write your life stories and share them. One person is enough if their feedback is nonjudgmental, noninvasive, corrective, and affirming.

The great advantage of working in a group or with a friend is that the writer can stop being the critic and simply create. Each person can then be a responsible critic for the other writers when they read their stories. So keep looking for one or two people with whom you can share this special journey of self-exploration.

However, if the person you select to review your work simply says, "I like it," or "I don't like it" and shows no inclination to go beyond this level of criticism, get a new partner. Likewise, if they make judgmental or invasive comments, find someone who is willing to provide NJNICA feedback. If you find yourself alone and unable to develop a writer–reviewer relationship with anyone, then try to develop these NJNICA qualities in yourself.

If you are a teacher and you wish to encourage your students to write their life stories, it is important to develop habits of NJNICA feedback in them.

The exercises below will help you develop NJNICA feedback and may be tried alone or in a group.

1. Review "Willem," starting on page 171.

2. Give yourself and your friend or group at least one session per story.

Appoint one person to roleplay the "writer" of the story. If you are that writer, you may defend what has been written any time you feel the feedback is hostile, judgmental, invasive, or superficial. When the critique of "your" work is over, tell the others what it felt like. Also, point out who was providing NJNICA feedback and who was not.

3. If you are giving feedback, describe your responses to the story aloud. If you are doing this alone, talk into a tape recorder, speak aloud, or, as a last resort, write it down.

Focus your attention on how you responded to the story rather than on how the story is written (that is, "I needed more detail," "I found my attention wandering," and so forth, rather than "It's too long, too confusing," and so forth).

If the person roleplaying the writer begins to defend himself, it is a clue that you or others in the group are being judgmental, invasive, or superficial. Find a NJNICA comment that will make the point.

Remember, by giving NJNICA feedback that focuses on your reactions to the story, you leave the writer room to make choices about what to change and what not to change.

Have each person in the group defend or absorb feedback for five minutes. Continue until each person in the group has had a chance to roleplay the writer. The comments may be repetitive, but the purpose of the task is to experience (1) being a writer under the gun and (2) changing your mode of giving feedback from judgmental or superficial to NJNICA.

4. Address the following issues:
   - Is the point of view a child's or an adult's?
   - Is the story written in the present or as a recollection?
   - Is the level of language a child's or an adult's?
   - Is the situation believable?
   - Are the writer's feelings clearly expressed?

5. When the initial critique of each story is complete, read the final version of the story aloud, again appointing a writer to defend or explain the work. Remember, there are no right answers to the issues. You are attending to the task of creating feedback and promoting lively discussions.

6. After the third session, you will be ready for feedback on your own stories. If you have not written your earliest memories yet, read the first two main sections in Appendix A and then follow the steps below if you have one or more persons giving feedback.

   A. Tell your earliest memory aloud into a tape recorder or to your friend or group. Get a few NJNICA comments and then retell the story in the present tense: "I am five years old and I am…" rather than "I was…."

   B. Write your story just as you have told it aloud. If the group is large or time is running short, do the writing at home, but try to do the writing immediately.

   C. Repeat NJNICA feedback for each story.

D. Each writer in the group should repeat the storytelling/writing process until they are comfortable writing and receiving feedback. At this point, the writing can be done at home.

Remember that each new person added to the group or class needs to be taken through this storytelling/writing process. New group members need to be encouraged to listen for NJNICA feedback and given a little time to develop NJNICA feedback. With practice and time, the whole group's feedback—and unity—will be all the better for it.

Other Books by Bernard Selling

Character Consciousness: From Self-Awareness to Creativity. This book moves the experience of personal writing from the technical arena of "how to write well" into "how can we see ourselves in our writing" in a way that not only produces self-awareness but opens the door to greater creativity.

The Art of Seeing: Appreciating Motion Pictures as an Art Form and as a Business. Hollywood has created a mass audience that appreciates film in a certain way—by appealing to emotions. But contemporary audiences wonder whether there might be other, more interesting ways to appreciate films. This book outlines that other way of experiencing films—by *seeing* into what's on screen in the same way that painters of the past nurtured their viewers' ability to "see" what was around them.

The Duke's Musician: A Spy at a Renaissance Court. The first in a series of docu-novels that take place during the Italian Renaissance. Told through the eyes of an ambitious, young English musician and featuring the beautiful Cecilia Gallerani (whose portrait was painted by Leonardo da Vinci), the novel follows the rise to power of the visionary Ludovico Sforza, who schemes to displace his hated brother, Galeazzo Sforza, duke of Milan, and his brother's powerful allies.

Predators: The Enemies of Milan. The second in the series of novels about the rise of Ludovico Sforza, visionary duke of Milan, and those who would cause him to fail: the pope in Rome; his sinister, rapacious nephews; and the doge in Venice.

The da Vinci Intrusion. Leonardo da Vinci's arrival in Milan causes intense discomfort for William Castle who must rethink his importance to the court of

Milan, even as he continues his efforts to bring peace to Milan in the wake of a military victory over the Venetians.

The Hidden Treasures of Renaissance Milan: The Castles of Ludovico Sforza and Those of his Friends and Enemies. This coffee-table book (including 350 color/b&w photos) is the product of four decades of research on Sforza's life and of the trips I have taken to Italy.

Writing from Within, 3rd edition. This book provides an abundance of techniques and solutions to the problems of writing life stories. A wide variety of sample stories and illustrations are included. A semi-bestseller, over 65,000 copies sold. "A seminal work in the field of autobiographical writing." — Leapfrog Press

Writing from Within: The Next Generation. This book integrates the present e-book, *Writing from Deeper Within*, and the best material from *Writing from Within*, 3rd edition, into a fully rewritten book.

Life-Story Writing Workbooks:

Writing from Within Workbook — Hunter House Publishers. The *Writing from Within Workbook* provides step-by-step instruction in the various beginning steps that were highlighted in the third edition of *Writing from Within* while also presenting the new steps presented in *Writing from Deeper Within*.

First Steps to Creative and Academic Writing — *Workbook I.* This workbook provides the step-by-step instruction in the beginning steps as highlighted in *Writing from Within* while providing more advanced ideas and content for academic writing in grades 6 through 12.

Self-Awareness/Relationship — *Workbook II.* This workbook focuses on helping each of us discover the best character qualities that exist within us, as described in my book *Character Consciousness*, through additional exercises in expanding the concept of the P.S. mentioned in *Writing from Deeper Within* into a full-blown Self-Assessment as described and amplified in *Character Consciousness*.

Please go to BernardSelling.com for more information about these books.

Printed in the USA
CPSIA information can be obtained
at www.ICGtesting.com
JSHW052017140824
68134JS00027B/2512

9 780897 936477